BILL SANSING · JAMES CARROLL "T" JONES · TOM STOLHAN

JACK COLLINS · MIKE COTTEN · BOBBY MOSES · JAMES SAXTON

ADLEY · CHRIS GILBERT · BOB MCKAY · JAMES S

ITTIER · JAY ARNOLD · PAT KELLY · DOUG ROOSEVELT

RANDY MCEACHERN · GLENN BLACKWOOD · DWIGHT JEFFE

KENNETH SIMS · WILLIAM GRAHAM · MIKE HATCHETT · BRYA

JOHN HAGY · ERIC METCALF · OSCAR GILES · CHRIS SAMUELS

ON · DEREK LEWIS · RICKY WILLIAMS · MAJOR APPLEWHITE · COR

HOWARD TERRY · NOBLE DOSS · ROOSTER ANDREWS · KEIFE

E · DELANO WOMACK · WALTER FONDREN · BOBBY LACKEY ·

DON TALBERT · DUKE CARLISLE · DAVID MCWILLIAMS · TOMMY

TREET · TED KOY · HAPPY FELLER · EDDIE PHILLIPS · JERRY SISEM

LEAKS · KEITH MORELAND · EARL CAMPBELL · ALFRED JACKSON

ON · JOHNNIE JOHNSON · JOHNNY "LAM" JONES · MIKE BAAB ·

N MILLARD · ROBERT BREWER · JERRY GRAY · TONY DEGRATE ·

TE GARDERE · STONIE CLARK · TONY BRACKENS · JAMES BROWN

REDDING · CHRIS SIMMS · MICHAEL HUFF · DAVID THOMAS ·

MARSHALL · BILL SANSING · JAMES CARROLL "T" JONES · TOM

Y GURWITZ · JACK COLLINS · MIKE COTTEN · BOBBY MOSES · JA

WHAT IT MEANS
TO BE A LONGHORN

DARRELL ROYAL ★ MACK BROWN
AND MANY OF TEXAS' GREATEST PLAYERS

BILL LITTLE AND JENNA HAYS McEACHERN

TRIUMPH
BOOKS

Copyright © 2007 by Bill Little and Jenna McEachern

No part of this publication may be reproduced, stored in a retrieval system, or transmitted in any form by any means, electronic, mechanical, photocopying, or otherwise, without the prior written permission of the publisher, Triumph Books, 542 S. Dearborn St., Suite 750, Chicago, Illinois 60605.

Library of Congress Cataloging-in-Publication Data

What it means to be a longhorn / edited by Bill Little and Jenna McEachern; foreword by Darrell Royal, Mack Brown.
    p. cm.
ISBN-13: 978-1-57243-951-1
ISBN-10: 1-57243-951-3
    1. Texas Longhorns (Football team)—History. 2. University of Texas at Austin—Football—History. 3. Football players—United States—Anecdotes. I. Little, Bill, 1942– II. McEachern, Jenna.

GV958.T4W53 2007
796.332'630976431—dc22

2007019525

This book is available in quantity at special discounts for your group or organization. For further information, contact:

Triumph Books
542 South Dearborn Street
Suite 750
Chicago, Illinois 60605
(312) 939-3330
Fax (312) 663-3557

Printed in U.S.A.
ISBN: 978-1-57243-951-1
Design by Nick Panos.
Editorial production and layout by Prologue Publishing Services, LLC.
All photos courtesy of UT Sports Photography.

CONTENTS

FOREWORD

What It Means to Be a Longhorn

IT WAS A LONG LIST, and I wasn't on it.

The University of Texas was looking for a new head football coach in December of 1956. We were in our first year at the University of Washington, and I had never been mentioned as a candidate for the Texas job. I remember once that Edith and I were driving through Austin, and we drove around the campus. I thought at the time, *This sure would be a nice place to coach.*

Ed Price had resigned after the 1956 season after Texas had finished 1–9. They had interviewed some high-profile coaches, including Bobby Dodd from Georgia Tech and Duffy Daugherty from Michigan State, but both had turned the job down.

After a few more unsuccessful inquiries, the athletics council and the regents wanted so much to change that they came around to the thinking of, *Who's the young coach out there who's on the rise? It's not working to go for the old, established coach, so let's find some young coach.*

So they called Duffy, and he gave them my name; and they called Bobby Dodd, and he gave them my name. They placed the calls so that the coaches wouldn't have time to consult with one another and decide on a pick. They got individual opinions, and both of them recommended me. Prior to their calling those two coaches, I wasn't on the list. I was nowhere to be found. My name had never come up, and I just wasn't a candidate.

But Coach Dodd knew me when I was at Mississippi State; and Duffy had always been a good friend of Coach Bud Wilkinson's at Oklahoma, and I had met him at the national conventions. It just so happened that both of them thought of me.

Edith and I were in bed in Seattle, Washington. I'd been talking about the Texas job and that it sure would be nice if we could land down here. Seattle was so far away. Coaches didn't make the money then that they make today. We couldn't afford to pay for a trip to take the kids on an airplane to visit their grandparents in Oklahoma, and it was too far to drive because the vacation would be half over by the time we drove down there. So I was hoping Texas would call, but I wasn't full of myself enough to throw my name out there.

We were just going to sleep when the phone rang. The voice said, "Hello, Darrell, this is D.X. Bible from The University of Texas calling." I covered up the end of the phone and said, "Edith, this is it, this is The University of Texas." Just the fact that he was calling made me think maybe they were thinking of me, and of course, he invited me to come in for an interview.

Just as I supposed, The University of Texas was a great place to come to. But we had a lot of work to do. The guy who walks into a 1–9 record does not inherit a warm bed. Mr. Bible was on his last days as athletics director, and a lot of things needed to change. The dressing rooms hadn't had anything done to them in a long time. The facilities were subpar for The University of

A young Darrell Royal was only 32 when he became the Texas Longhorns' head football coach in 1957.

In perhaps the most famous picture of the Darrell Royal era, Royal gives James Street the play that led to the Longhorns' 21–17 victory over Notre Dame in the 1970 Cotton Bowl game. The scoreboard tells the story.

Texas, or at least for what I had in mind. They had all of the assistant coaches in one room, and each had a phone on his desk. They had to try to carry on recruiting conversations with all of them talking at the same time, in the same room. I didn't have a secretary, we had just one for all the football coaches.

But the changes we needed were obvious. I knew that any time I made a correction in the dormitory, or the facilities, or the working conditions, I was on the correct side. I wasn't overbearing…we just couldn't tolerate it the way it was.

I understood that. I kind of welcomed those things I saw that were run-down and not up-to-date, because it was a change that could be made to better The University of Texas athletics program. It was discouraging in a way, but it was encouraging in another.

I started asking questions. I remember going to the stadium and seeing it surrounded by barbed wire and a chain-link fence with grass growing up it. I asked what purpose it served, and they told me that it was where they took up tickets. I asked if we couldn't move the gates back to the stadium and make it look nicer. They said they didn't know, that it had just always been there. We had to find new ways to do things, on the field, in the dorm, and with the program. The important thing was, they wanted it to be different, and so did I.

The University of Texas has never been satisfied with second or third place. The people who have gone to school here demand better than that. A lot of them have had great success after they got out of here, and they couldn't understand why The University of Texas wasn't winning consistently, why they couldn't occasionally win the conference. The conference was the thing when I got here. The national championship was way out of sight. We were fighting for lone victories, which would lead us into the conference championship. And then when we got the conference championship, the goal was to win it all.

To go through undefeated, you have to escape from a very, very tight trap where you are going to be beaten if something doesn't happen. It's the same way with winning close. You have to be careful that those adverse things don't happen to you. And you are just lucky if you go through the season undefeated, because later you can look back and see where you could have lost a couple of games.

That really is what happened to us. In the 1960s we had a tremendous run. From 1961 through 1970, we finished in the top five seven times, won seven Southwest Conference championships, and had three national championships. We had great coaches and great players, and, as I've said, the ball bounced right for us a whole lot of times.

When I think of what it means to be a Longhorn, I would define it in three words: "It's a chance."

It's an honor to be a Longhorn, but to me, it has always stood for a chance. If we make the right moves, we've got a chance to be with the people at the top. That same thing isn't true of every school. Some of them just have no chance to go to the top. The University of Texas certainly provides that chance. It's a good recruiting tool to talk about the history of The University,

Darrell Royal addresses Mack Brown's team during practice; Brown had welcomed the legendary Darrell Royal back to his program.

and to explain that to young prospects. It's about being the state university, and it's about pride, but it is always about opportunity. Mr. Bible set a standard for coaches that has been lived up to several times. You have a chance to do it here, and that chance is what makes it a great coaching job.

And it is always important to maintain your integrity. I grew up in a time where we were sometimes dirt poor, and the only thing you really had was your character and your integrity. The University of Texas has always stressed that. I tried to do the right thing in recruiting by the rules and in graduating kids, and I had it explained to me when I was hired that anything shy of that would not be tolerated at The University of Texas. But they didn't have to tell me; that's what I was going to do, anyway.

I was 52 years old when I stepped away from coaching, and I have now spent 50 years of my life in association with The University of Texas. It's a great reunion when I run across the old players, and the memories are strong.

People have often asked me how I would like to be remembered, and my answer is pretty simple. I tell them that, on my tombstone, I don't want it to say that I never made a mistake.

I'd like for it to say, "He meant well."

—Darrell Royal

FOREWORD

What It Means to Be a Longhorn

I GREW UP IN THE 1960s in Cookeville, Tennessee, surrounded by male role models who played football and were football coaches and high school administrators. At that time, Texas was one of the more popular teams on TV, and in our home we all took coaches like Wally Butts at Georgia, Bear Bryant at Alabama, and Darrell Royal at Texas as examples of what college football coaches should be and what we wanted to be like.

I was a running back, so I liked watching Steve Worster and Chris Gilbert and Jim Bertelsen and James Street. The Longhorns were the best team in the country at running the ball. After I decided to be a coach, it was natural for me to go back and look at the people I wanted to be like, and I wanted to be like Coach Royal.

When I became the head football coach and athletics director at Tulane University, our president brought in a consulting team to look at our athletics program. The group included Don Canham, the athletics director at Michigan; Gene Corrigan, who was with the Atlantic Coast Conference at the time; Chuck Neinas, who was head of the College Football Association; and Coach Royal.

Several of those guys would become my close friends later, but at the time, I spent most of my time enjoying Coach Royal and asking him about what he saw that he liked, why he was successful as a coach, where were the things we needed to improve, and where he saw us going. We continued that friendship at gatherings like the College Football Hall of Fame dinner in New York. The Hall of Fame is something that all coaches dream about being in, and Coach Royal is a prominent member of that group. I even

Mack Brown's teams have the best record in college football in the 21st century.

talked to him a couple of times by phone when we were at the University of North Carolina.

During the season of 1997, things were going really well for us there. My wife, Sally, was the most successful land developer in the Chapel Hill area, and our football team was ranked in the nation's top five. That was our home, and we were happy there. In 1994 we had played Texas in the Sun Bowl in El Paso, and I remember Sally being so impressed with Bevo, the band, and the spirit Texas showed.

Still, when DeLoss Dodds called me about an interview after John Mackovic was reassigned, Texas was a long way from our minds. I agreed to talk to the committee when I learned that Coach Royal would be there because one of my first thoughts was, *What a life's dream to coach where Darrell Royal coached*. It wasn't only about Texas at the time, it was about him and what he had built here. Also, I knew that I would not take the job without talking to him and having his endorsement. It was important to me that he came because it showed that he was interested in me, and he was the one person who could make some sense out of why Texas hadn't been a consistent winner for more than 20 years.

I did not want to come to Texas and fail, and I had to know what we needed to do to move forward and get it fixed. I asked him for his help, and he told me, "I'm too old for a regular job, but I'll help you where I can."

He's done that. He introduced me to people who cared about the program. Soon, not only was he a role model, he had become one of the great friends of my life. He has that ability to take complicated things and make them simple, and so many of the things that he told me that day in Atlanta have come true. He said The University of Texas was like a bunch of BBs that had been dropped from a box and scattered all over the floor. He said my job was to get the BBs back in the box. "The University," he said, "is a powerful place, but it has to be the power of one. It can't be scattered and disjointed. There are so many allegiances; it has to come back to being Texas."

When Sally and I came to Texas, we had many great friends and memories in North Carolina. But the way we looked at it, we weren't "leaving" North Carolina, we were "going to" Texas.

The one thing that Sally and I saw then and have come to appreciate even more in our 10 years here is that we've never seen more passionate people. They are very proud. They are the most hospitable people you could ever imagine being around, and they do an amazing job of raising their families.

Mack Brown and his Texas Longhorns won the 2005 BCS National Championship.

Another thing that we liked about The University of Texas is that it stands for integrity. Academics here are hard, and a young man must be a student in order to be an athlete, so when he gets out of here, he can be successful. As a player, you can win all the games because everything is first class, but when you graduate, you know you've paid your dues and can reap benefits from all you've learned here.

We've come to understand some basic things about Texans. What some people think is arrogance is really pride, and it's a pride that goes deep to the roots of where the state itself came from. A lot of people have talked about the pressure that is put on the head coach at Texas. I see that as passion, rather than pressure. Texas people are passionate about their football. Whether you like The University of Texas or not, being a Longhorn means that everybody in this state has an opinion of what happens in Texas football, every single day. Coach Royal told me that, and I didn't realize it. But being a Longhorn means that there's a tremendous amount of scrutiny. There's a standard that is set higher than most places in the country.

Our goal when we came to Texas was to win championships with nice kids who graduate. Because of our school and some great assistant coaches, we have been able to recruit players who can do that. One of the first things Coach Royal told me was that to succeed, we needed to rebuild a bond with Texas high school coaches. We have done that because these are the men who help form kids way before we ever see them. They are the heroes of our game of college football. High school football in Texas is part of the fiber of the state. In every small town on Friday nights, the whole town is involved. Kids either have a football uniform or a cheerleader's outfit from the time they are born.

History has always been important to me, and that's why we teach our players about the great tradition of Texas football. In our football trophy room, we proudly display the crystal ball national championship trophy of our 2005 team, but we also purchased replicas to honor the national champions of 1963, 1969, and 1970. A football program has no greater treasure than the men who have played the game before.

With a lot of help, we have been able to collect those BBs. Everybody in the athletics department, the alums, the lettermen, the administrators, the faculty, the grass roots fans of the state of Texas, and the high school coaches are all pulling for us to win because we are one of the faces for this state— not only in Austin and at The University but across the country.

Our unique colors, the burnt orange and white, our wonderful songs, and our hand signal—the "Hook 'em Horns" sign—are recognizable worldwide. When you travel to an area not expecting to see someone from home, you can readily pick out the person who's associated with The University of Texas. Traditionally, that's something that every other place in America is trying to be. It goes back to pride in who you are.

Finally, to be a Longhorn means, as Sally and I discovered when we got to Texas, you don't have to say, "Hello." Just say, "Hook 'em."

—Mack Brown

ACKNOWLEDGMENTS

BY ITS NATURE, THIS PROJECT IS UNIQUE in that the true authors are the 70 or so men whose stories you find within. Without them, this book would not exist. We were simply the keepers of their thoughts. Our job was to find them, secure interviews, transcribe those interviews, and then put their words into chapter form. It was, frankly, more of a challenge than simply writing a story; it was also tremendously rewarding.

To begin our thanks, we'd have to mention our spouses, Kim Scofield and Randy McEachern, and our families, for their love, support, and patience during the more than six months it took to finish this project.

We'd like to thank Triumph Books, specifically Tom Bast, for having the faith in us to accomplish this. And Alex Lubertozzi with Prologue Publishing Services, for his editing and layout work. Tony Barnhart of the *Atlanta Journal-Constitution*, who did the Georgia book for Triumph, gave us the blueprint and great advice on how to approach the interviews.

Special appreciation goes to Mack Brown and Darrell Royal, for their participation and support of the idea, as well as to DeLoss Dodds, Chris Plonsky, and Nick Voinis of the UT Athletics Department Administration.

John Bianco provided great insight to the more recent years of Texas football. His assistants Jeremy Sharpe and Thomas Stepp and administrative associate Margaret Tiedeken in the UT Media Relations area and Kasey Johnson in Mack Brown's office picked up the slack when Bill was on leave working on the book.

Also, thanks to Susan and Jim Sigmon and Joy Lawrence of the UT Sports Photography division for their efforts on the pictures, and to Carol Hastings of the Longhorn Letter Winners Association for providing addresses and phone numbers.

And we would be remiss without thanking Coach Greg Davis as well as the numerous administrative assistants and family members who helped connect us with the players who participated.

Finally, there were a few individuals, who because of communication glitches or availability issues, were not included because we simply ran out of time. Our thanks to them—Johnny Walker, Britt Hager, Lance Gunn, Nathan Vasher, Cedric Benson, and Derrick Johnson—all of whom agreed to participate, and hopefully will form the core of a future revised edition.

INTRODUCTION

When Jenna McEachern and I agreed to do this project, I'm not sure either of us knew the depth of the undertaking.

Both of us knew that personally, and professionally, we were immensely qualified for it. My love affair with Texas football spanned 50 years, from the time my parents first brought me to Austin from our home in Winters, Texas, to see a Longhorn football game. As a writer for *The Daily Texan*, the *Austin American-Statesman*, and an employee in the media relations area of the UT athletics department, I had written stories of the teams and the people of Texas football since 1961.

Jenna McEachern brought a wonderful perspective to the book. She is the daughter of a coach, the wife of a Longhorn quarterback, and a mother who has always been involved in sports. In the mid-1970s she was a Texas cheerleader. She used her degree in journalism to become an excellent editor, working with oral history projects for the LBJ Library. She also served as editor for *One Heartbeat* and *One Heartbeat II*, the books I did with Coach Mack Brown.

So, together, we agreed to be the gatekeepers of the personal memories of 70 or so former Longhorn football players who span the history of the sport at The University of Texas.

Howard Terry, who has given back way more than he received from The University, begins our chronicles. Terry came to Texas as a freshman in 1934, the year that rookie coach Jack Chevigny led the Longhorns to an historic victory over Notre Dame. Chevigny had played for Knute Rockne at Notre Dame.

From Terry's freshman season in 1934, through the 2005 BCS National Championship stories of David Thomas, Michael Huff, and Vince Young, there is at least one voice that speaks to every single year of Texas football for more than 70 years.

Bill Sansing, who was hired by D.X. Bible as the first sports information director at Texas in 1946, brings an invaluable look at such Longhorn legends as Bobby Layne and Blair Cherry, who are gone now, and were pivotal figures in the late 1940s. John Bianco, who 60 years later would serve in the same job Sansing held, assisted us in providing a view of the modern Longhorn.

Forty years separated the arrivals of Darrell Royal and Mack Brown, and yet the blending of their philosophy and friendship has been a major part of the history of Texas football.

In their individual stories, the former Longhorns who are featured here tell compelling stories of life as Texas athletes. But more than that, they also capture a picture of the history of The University of Texas. That is because universities are much more than bricks and mortar, and teams are much more than those portrayed in the latest computer-generated DVD.

These stories chronicle the lives of men who came from small towns and big cities, who played quarterback or linebacker or lineman or back or kicker. Some earned the highest accolades as players, others went on to great professional success away from the game. There are All-Americans and philanthropists.

There is Rooster Andrews, who cried because his draft board said he was too short to go when most of his classmates left in 1941 to fight in World War II. And Keifer Marshall, who played every down at center in the 1943 Cotton Bowl and then became a distinguished marine who survived the Battle of Iwo Jima.

And as each decade is packed with more former Longhorns, their stories mark the passages of Texas football, from coach to coach, from era to era. Names long forgotten live again through the reminiscences of their teammates and the memories of their youth.

The answers to the question "What does it mean to be a Longhorn?" are as diverse as the people who share them. So are the memories.

It is important to understand that the men who speak to us here are but a few of the legends of Texas football. To adequately reflect all of those living Longhorns would require volumes, even libraries. Instead, this group gives us a capsule look at a total picture. Hopefully, each will in some way touch the story of all of those we wish we would have had room to include.

So often, as time passes, we are left with no one to tell the story. It is then that historians and writers offer what they *think* happened. In the chapters of this book, we learn, from the men themselves, what they *know* happened. The history of Texas football has been well-chronicled. We know "what," and in this book, we learn "who."

The quarterbacks of the four national championship teams give insight into what brought them to that pinnacle. Pioneers and pathfinders speak to the historical significance of racial integration as a force in college football in the Southwest. Moments on and off the field paint a picture of college life—its hopes and its dreams.

The book comes at a perfect time for Texas because Longhorn football has never been more popular. Where Royal's teams dominated the 1960s and 1970s, Mack Brown has built the powerhouse of the first decade of the 21st century.

Darrell K Royal–Texas Memorial Stadium itself is undergoing a metamorphosis, with the new North End representing the most significant reconstruction in stadium history. Sellout crowds will reach nearly 100,000 to see the new versions of Texas Longhorns, those who one day will fill the pages of another book, in another time.

But, as we are reminded in these pages, the more things change, the more they remain the same. Kids are still just 18 years old when they come to campus, and while they may be more tech-savvy and bigger and stronger than their predecessors, their fears, hopes, and dreams remain the same.

That, in the end, is the beauty of college football. It is the spirit of Texas, and the excellence of goals reached for and attained. Encapsulated in basic four-year increments, these stories are a little piece of history, and a little piece of life.

All of which make up the grand mosaic of what it means to be a Texas Longhorn.

—Bill Little

★ ★ ★

I watched my first Longhorn football game in 1964, sitting in the "Knothole" section, where a ticket was 50 cents. I was nine years old and had no particular loyalty to Texas football, but after family friend and Longhorn fanatic Phil Zlotnick introduced me to the spectacle of college football at its finest—Big Bertha and Bevo, the Longhorn Band as it spelled out "Texas" in script, the expectation of victory, the fringe on the cheerleaders' uniforms— I was hooked. From that day forward, I set my sights on being a cheerleader at The University of Texas. There was no other school for me.

When I arrived in Austin, at long last, to attend The University, I was exhilarated by the variety of opinions and lifestyles and political ideologies and music to which I'd never been exposed. I was also pretty excited to get to know and work with men whose names were synonymous with The University and with excellence—Darrell Royal, Bill Ellington, Jones Ramsey, Cliff Gustafson, Mike Campbell, Frank Medina, Leon Black, and Leon Manley.

To work on this project with Bill Little, my friend for 35 years, was a delight. It was also humbling, for he is, without doubt, the singular authority on UT sports history. And as I talked with these former players, many of whom were friends from my college days, hearing their stories rekindled my own feelings of pride and awe at having been part of the Longhorn tradition. It was an honor to be the one to hear these men express their unabashed love for their teammates and coaches and to see their tears as they recounted just what it means to them to be a Longhorn.

Each story is unique, yet there is a common thread that runs through all of them. When faced with a choice of colleges, each of these "boys" had the courage to challenge himself to compete with the best and against the best. They courageously trusted their coaches to push them to their limits and beyond. They had the guts to step in front of 80,000 screaming fans to represent a school with impossibly high standards. They stoically subjugated their personal desires and goals in order to achieve success as a team.

To a man, they were challenged and changed forever by this tradition, this place, this "University of the first order." As Happy Feller noted, "Once you are exposed to the best, you never return to your old form." It's my privilege to present a snapshot of this continuum of excellence—*What It Means to Be a Longhorn.*

—Jenna McEachern

The
THIRTIES
AND FORTIES

HOWARD TERRY

LINEMAN/LINEBACKER

1935–1937

LOOKING BACK, I GUESS I WAS LUCKY. I was born and raised in Cameron, Texas, and I played high school football. I was not all that great a player, but I wanted to go to college. I had been invited by the Rice Institute line coach to come down and work out with the varsity in the spring of 1934.

They had me work out with the varsity, but the only thing I had resembling an offer for a chance to go to school was that if I would go to a junior college for two years, they would take me back at Rice. In hindsight, I can certainly see their thinking. I did have a visit to Texas A&M, but that wasn't productive, either.

Then, in the spring, one of our local teachers took me down to Austin to the C&S Sporting Goods Company. The teacher's friend there called Jack Chevigny. He had been the coach at St. Edward's University, south of the Colorado River in Austin, and he had just gotten the head coaching job at Texas. He came down to C&S Sporting Goods and met me. He must have been pretty desperate for football players, because I was just a 17-year-old kid. At that point, the junior college idea was the only thing I had.

Chevigny said for me to "come on down here, and we'll get you in school. You'll have enough money for a room and two meals a day." That was my offer of a scholarship, and I jumped at it. Anything was something in those days. We were in the middle of the Depression.

Howard Terry
started the Texas
Longhorn Education
Foundation.

When I came down as a freshman in the fall, we had probably 100 kids out there, and the freshmen didn't play on the varsity. But that fall of 1934 was pretty significant. The varsity had a pretty good team. Chevigny had played for Knute Rockne at Notre Dame, as had his line coach, Tim Moynihan. They believed in everything Notre Dame had ever done, and Chevigny tried to run his house that way.

It worked for him that first year, and it also helped a lot that he had 20 lettermen returning from the season before. In their second game of the year, the varsity went to South Bend and beat Notre Dame 7–6 in the Irish's season opener. It was the first time they had lost a home opener in school history. It was a big moment on campus. I remember going to Gregory Gym, where everybody was listening to the game. It seems almost like it was a closed-circuit showing, but it was only a radio broadcast in those days. The win gave the campus and the city something to be pumped up about.

The varsity went on to a 7–2–1 season, and they gave Chevigny a raise and a new LaSalle touring car at the team banquet after the season. But that wound up being his high point. My sophomore year, in 1935, I wound up starting in our first game against Texas A&I, which we won handily. But things did not go so well after that. We finished the season with a 4–6 record.

By my junior season, I was starting at guard and linebacker, and playing about 55 minutes per game. We opened with a tie and then a win over Oklahoma, but things fell apart in our game in Austin against Baylor. We had Baylor down 18–0 in the first quarter, and Chevigny took the starters out and told us to go shower. We were in the old dressing room under the west stands of Memorial Stadium, and as I was getting dressed, somebody came running in and said the score was 18–14 in the fourth quarter. I pulled on my pants and ran upstairs to the field just in time to see them win the game 21–18.

That game had more to do with getting him fired than anything else. He thought we had the game won, and he sent all the first team into the shower. We won only one more game that year, beating Texas A&M 7–0, but by then Chevigny had already announced he was not returning. On the part of the players, we probably would have liked to see him have more time, but as far as the public was concerned, there were pretty strong feelings, and there were certainly problems. Several players went to the athletics council meeting and spoke up for Chevigny, but it didn't make any difference. He left coaching completely. He went into the oil business and moved back up north.

Texas surprised a lot of people by hiring Dana X. Bible to replace Chevigny. Mr. Bible had coached at Texas A&M and Nebraska, and they paid him a whole lot of money to come to Texas. A lot of people expected immediate success because he had done that at Nebraska. But I think he failed to consider how valuable the players he had taken with him to Nebraska were. He didn't have that here, and it was a tough start for all of us.

There was one really bright spot my senior year, and that came against Baylor in Waco. We all remembered that they had beaten us the year before, and Baylor was really playing well in 1937. They had won all six of their games, and we had won only one game and tied one. They were hoping to go to the Rose Bowl, and there was even talk about a national championship. The game was even broadcast on national radio by Ted Husing.

But we really played well and surprised them. Hugh Wolfe, who was one of our best players, kicked a field goal in the fourth quarter to break a 6–6 tie, and we won 9–6. We didn't score a point the rest of the season, getting shut out by TCU and Texas A&M, but we did have one memorable moment concerning that Baylor game. When we got back to Austin, the "victory lights" on the Tower were lighted for the first time. The orange and white lights were turned on that day in 1937, and they've signaled a victory on the occasion of every win since. Mr. Bible didn't do as well as he thought he would the first year (we were 2–6–1), and he did worse the second (1–8–0).

After I finished school, I went to work with Procter & Gamble in Oklahoma. I wasn't close enough to the situation to know all that was going on, but when I could afford it, I became a supporter of the program. In those days, alums could help with recruiting, and I remember helping Mr. Bible get a player named Spec Sanders out of Cameron Junior College in Lawton, Oklahoma. Mr. Bible was not about to cross that Red River to get a player; he had a policy of not going out of state. He just would not take out-of-state players. That was one of his house rules. So I picked Spec up in Lawton and took him down to Wichita Falls to meet Mr. Bible, and he took him. He turned out to be a first-class running back who went on to play pro ball, and that 1941 team damn near won it all.

After Pearl Harbor, I went into the navy. I later learned that Chevigny got killed at Iwo Jima, and Tim Moynihan also died in the war. I didn't know it at the time, I was too busy trying not to get killed myself.

When the war was over, I made some investments, two or three moves that helped me a lot financially, and I was in a position to give something back to The University. It was a place where I started to grow up and get a good education that has helped me for the rest of my life. I don't know if that answers the question of what it means to be a Longhorn, but that's the way I remember it.

5

Howard Terry came to Texas in 1934, the same year Jack Chevigny became head coach. He played as a lineman and linebacker on Chevigny's last two teams and the first team of D.X. Bible. He was instrumental in forming the Texas Longhorn Education Foundation, and the Longhorn football locker room bears his name. He was inducted into the Longhorn Hall of Honor in 1988.

NOBLE DOSS

WINGBACK

1939–1941

IT WAS REALLY A CHANGING TIME when I came to The University of Texas, and looking back, we didn't have any way of realizing how much everything was going to change for everybody over the next four years.

In 1938 Mr. Bible was in his second year as the Texas coach. It had been a big deal when he was hired because he had been at Texas A&M and Nebraska, and they were paying him a whole lot of money during hard times to coach football at Texas. His first season, they hadn't been very good, but he had such a reputation, and The University was such an important place, that a whole bunch of us committed to come to school. There were 125 of us who were part of that 1938 freshman class. We had all-staters from all over Texas. They didn't have any limits on the number of scholarships, but times were hard, and we all needed money.

A scholarship meant $40 a month, but it was the first year in the new Hill Hall dorm, and the players had to pay the university $30 a month for room and board. The university held out $7.50 a month to pay tuition, leaving us $2.50 a month spending money.

We all thought pretty highly of ourselves, and the varsity that year was struggling. They only won one game. The varsity didn't have very many players, and people began making fun of Mr. Bible's defense, calling it "Ali Bible and his 40 Sieves." The only game they won that year was the last one, against Texas A&M, 7–6.

Noble Doss made "the impossible catch" to beat A&M in 1940.

Everybody kept talking about the freshman class being the future, so we started believing them. After we beat the varsity in a scrimmage that fall, we got together and chose a representative to go talk to Mr. Bible, to tell him we needed more money.

We all waited for his answer and were deflated when we got the report. In his unforgettable booming voice, Mr. Bible (who had a habit of smacking his lips before he spoke) sent back the message: "Tell the boys I will be glad to meet with them, one on one, each individually, at any time."

Not a one of us dared do it.

Mr. Bible was strict—very strict. He didn't allow any funny business, but he was the greatest teacher I ever knew. He taught us so much more than just football, and as we began playing as sophomores in 1939, things began to change for Texas football. Mr. Bible always pointed to our Arkansas game that year as the game that made the biggest difference. It was our fourth game of the season, and we had just lost to Oklahoma 24–12. The year before, Arkansas had beaten Texas 42–6.

Jack Crain was a little guy who had a lot of speed. In the Arkansas game in 1939, he returned a quick kick 82 yards to set up a touchdown early in the game. But in the fourth quarter, we were behind 13–7 with just a minute left to play. A lot of folks had left when R.B. Patrick threw a short pass to Jack, and he turned it into a weaving 67-yard touchdown. Then he kicked the extra point with less than 30 seconds left for a 14–13 win. I remember Mr. Bible saying, "That play and that victory changed our outlook—mine, the players', the student body's, and the ex-students. Things had been going pretty badly up until that game. The way was still long, but we had tasted the fruits of victory and we were on our way."

Mr. Bible was a tough coach, and he was a great motivator. Before our Texas A&M game in 1940, he brought out a poem called "It Can Be Done." The Aggies were defending national champions, and they were headed for the Rose Bowl if they won. They were undefeated in 19 games. But we had never lost to them in Memorial Stadium.

I'll never forget that poem: "Somebody said that it couldn't be done, but he with a chuckle replied that 'maybe it couldn't' but he would be one who wouldn't say so till he tried…"

They had John Kimbrough, who was a great back, but Mr. Bible thought if we could surprise them early, we would have a chance. He had put in a special play for that game, and on the first drive Pete Layden had a throwback pass to Crain that carried us to their 33-yard line. We ran another play that almost worked, but the pass was incomplete. But on that play, I realized I could get behind their halfback, who was big John Kimbrough.

They were playing a 6-2-2-1 defense, and when I went down and cut out, he picked me up. It was a down and out, a play we had run a lot during the year, so it wasn't something new. When I turned downfield, I got a couple of steps on him, but that's all. The pass was perfect. It worked good…real good. I think my momentum carried me out of bounds at the 1-yard line, and we scored on the next play. We had played just less than one minute and we were ahead 7–0. We held that lead the whole game. I was lucky enough to come up with three interceptions, and they never scored.

Our senior year, in 1941, we were really good. Mal Kutner was a great player at end, and we had Crain and Layden and some real good linemen. Things were really rolling. We had a big write-up in *Life* magazine, were unbeaten through our first six games, and were averaging almost 40 points a game.

I will never forget our Baylor game in Waco because we lost a chance at a national championship when I dropped a pass. We should have beaten them easily, but we had a lot of injuries. We had a 7–0 lead, and I ran a down and out—the same play that had worked against Texas A&M. I was open at the goal line, and the ball just went right through my arms. It would have been a 45-yard scoring pass, and we would have gone ahead 14–0. Instead, Baylor scored in the last seconds to tie the game 7–7. I have thought about that play every day of my life since. It was the national championship, and I dropped it.

When we got back home from Waco, the whole campus was crushed. I think we all started feeling sorry for ourselves and didn't get ready to play the next week. TCU beat us 14–7. It wasn't hard to get up for Texas A&M, though. We hadn't beaten them in Kyle Field, just like they hadn't been able to win in Austin. But everybody pulled together and we won easily, 23–0.

All season long, there had been talk that we would go to the Rose Bowl in Pasadena, California, but the tie and the loss put that in question. Mr. Bible had scheduled a game with the University of Oregon to close the season. While we were still hoping for the Rose Bowl, we turned down an invitation to the Orange Bowl. The Rose Bowl already had Oregon State as its host team, but since they had barely beaten Oregon, I think the people with the Rose Bowl were afraid of waiting for the outcome of our game with

Oregon. They didn't want to be embarrassed by taking us if we lost. And so they asked Mr. Bible to cancel the game.

Mr. Bible was a man of great character, and he told them he had never canceled a game with an opponent and didn't feel it would be right to do that. He said he'd guarantee a victory, but he wouldn't cancel the game. So the Rose Bowl invited Duke. We beat Oregon 71–7.

Ironically, nobody got to play in the official Rose Bowl Stadium that year. The day after we played Oregon, the Japanese bombed Pearl Harbor. The threat of war on the West Coast caused the game to be moved to Duke, in North Carolina, which had been invited in our place.

Being a Longhorn has been my life. So many of my friends came from those days at Texas, and I have been fortunate to live most of my life in Austin, where The University of Texas has meant everything to me. That's what being a Longhorn means to me.

Mr. Bible was everything I ever wanted in a coach. I can still see him standing in front of a chalk board, pointing with an old pool cue to plays, over and over again. He gave us a foundation in discipline and responsibility. We got a great education and a lifetime of memories.

Noble Doss still shares the Texas record for interceptions in a career and in a single season more than 65 years after he set them in 1941. A halfback and defensive back on the famous D.X. Bible teams of the early 1940s, he was long remembered for his famous "impossible catch"—an over-the-shoulder reception that set up the only touchdown in Texas's 7–0 upset of previously unbeaten Texas A&M in 1940. He is a member of the Longhorn Hall of Honor.

ROOSTER ANDREWS
ALL-AMERICAN WATER BOY
1941–1946

IT IS HARD FOR A LOT OF PEOPLE TO BELIEVE, but I was headed for Texas A&M just before school started in 1941. My dad worked for the railroad, and I had my bags packed, ready to get on the train for College Station from Dallas.

Malcolm Kutner and I had become friends, and he had been talking to Mr. Bible about getting me to come to Texas as a football team manager. The night before I was to leave for A&M, Mr. Bible called me and said, "Do you want a National Youth Administration job?" Those were jobs from the WPA during the Depression, and I had to have a job because there was no money for college.

I said, "Yes, sir. I sure do. I want to come to The University of Texas."

I switched my train pass to Austin, and Kutner met me at the station.

The pay was $16 a month, plus tuition, room, and board. I worked with the football team as an assistant manager and also had a job working with Mr. Walter Fischer, sweeping up at Gregory Gymnasium. I had no way to know that would be the beginning of a long relationship with The University of Texas. I was just elated to have a chance.

It was during that freshman year that I got my nickname. It was a Wednesday night, and Bull Cohenour, Buddy Jungmichel, Jack Crain, and Preston Flanagan came to my room in Hill Hall. They said they were recruiting me because they needed my help. There was a cockfight that night over in Bastrop, and those guys kept their fighting rooster, whose name was Elmer, in a

Diminutive Rooster Andrews was a team manager who actually drop-kicked an extra point in a game during World War II.

12

sycamore tree outside the dorm. Well, I was a freshman, and Bull weighed about 250 pounds, so when he said, "Elmer needs to go to Elgin," I said, "Yes, sir." I grabbed a flashlight and started up the tree. Elmer was at the top of the tree, and I was the only guy little enough to get to him without breaking branches.

Bull said, "Grab him by the ankle," so I grabbed him by the ankle. That's when Elmer pecked at me and caught me. The flashlight flew in one direction, and I flew in another, but I had Elmer. I hit the ground and broke my arm. They took Elmer to Elgin, and he won the fight. And that night, they told me I would never go untouched without being called "the Rooster." Later, when some bigger guys were picking at me, Bull Cohenour stepped in and said, "I'll tell you one gawddam thing, leave him alone, because he is the poppa of the rooster."

That first year was special, but it was also hard. We were unbeaten when Baylor tied us. But the toughest thing came when Pearl Harbor happened right after the season. Everybody was going to war, but they wouldn't take me because of my height—I was only about 5' tall. I called the army recruiter in Dallas and told him, "I've got to go." But they wouldn't take me. I had been captain of the ROTC in high school, so I knew what to do. The hardest thing I ever faced was watching my friends go.

It was during the war that the next thing that would stay with me the rest of my life happened. We were playing TCU in 1943. The year before, they had beaten us 13–7, so we were looking for revenge. We were way ahead— we eventually won 46–7—and Mr. Bible was emptying the bench. I had fooled around in practice, drop-kicking the ball. Mr. Bible said, "Who wants to join the contest?" I said, "I do!"

He looked at me and said, "You might win it! You might win it!" Of course, we were so far ahead, that wasn't going to be a factor. We were getting ready for an extra point, so he put me in the game. The crowd went crazy. And then I drop-kicked the ball through the goal posts. Everybody was happy except for Dutch Meyer, the TCU coach. He was insulted that Mr. Bible put the water boy in the game. Boy, was he upset. He even wrote me a letter, although later on we became good friends.

It was the next year that I met Bobby Layne, who became a friend for life. If you had to use one word to describe Mr. Bible, it would be "gentleman." If you had to use one word to describe Bobby, it would be "rounder." There are too many great stories about Bobby. There isn't time or space to tell them all here. He was just one of a kind. When he came back from the Merchant Marines in 1945, he almost brought Doak Walker with him, before Doak decided to go to SMU. There are a lot of stories about how SMU convinced Doak to go there after they mustered out in New Orleans. But the truth is, Doak's mom just told him she didn't want him down there in Austin with Bobby. He may have been a little wild, but he had the biggest heart I ever saw.

In 1945 we were playing Texas A&M over in College Station, and when we scored our last touchdown to make the score 19–10, Bobby convinced Mr.

Bible to let me in the game, and I threw him a pass for the extra point that made the final score 20–10.

Bobby was also a great baseball player, and later in a game in College Station he was pitching a game for the conference championship. He had cut his foot when we were horsing around a couple of nights before, but he didn't want to tell our coach, Bibb Falk. Bibb always sat at one end of the bench, so Bobby got down to the other end and told me to go buy him a six-pack of beer. He'd go out and pitch, and then come in and drink a cold beer. After six innings, he was still going and sent me to the store for more beer. He finished the beer, and the game, and pitched a no-hitter.

While I was at Texas, I was fortunate to become involved with the College All-Star Game, when the NFL champion would play a team of college all-stars in the summer after the school year. I made a lot of friends, and it opened a lot of doors. When I got out of school, I went to the Miami Seahawks as equipment manager. But I didn't stay long. In six months, I was back in Austin, and Ox Higgins, one of our former Longhorns, gave me a job traveling with C&S Sporting Goods. I had a special girl named B.J. who thinks she was the reason I came back in the fall of 1946, and since we married in the spring of 1947, I guess she was right.

There are other stories, like when Blair Cherry put me in a baseball game against Texas A&M, and when everybody fouled out and Bully Gilstrap put me in a basketball game and I had to play about four minutes.

All of those are memories of when I was at Texas, and then through the sporting goods business, I was able to maintain a close relationship with so many of the people. I guess that is the best answer to the question of what it means to be a Longhorn. It is about friends and relationships. And if you ask me what that means to me, it's "everything."

Rooster Andrews was one of the most popular figures in Texas athletics. He was a team manager and doubled as a kicker during the World War II years. He is a member of the Longhorn Hall of Honor.

KEIFER MARSHALL

CENTER

1943, 1946–1947

ONE OF THE REAL COLORFUL CHARACTERS of The University of Texas, Bully Gilstrap, was the line coach at Texas when he recruited me in 1942. My home was in Temple, Texas, which was close to Austin and The University. Several of my high school teammates had gone to Texas one or two years before. Bully was a very persuasive person and one heck of a coach!

I enrolled at Texas in January 1943 and moved into Hill Hall, the athletics dormitory. D.X. Bible, Bully Gilstrap, Blair Cherry, Clyde Littlefield, and Shorty Alderson made up our coaching staff. I had met Mr. Bible six years before at the First Baptist Church in Temple. He presented me with my Eagle Scout badge and was the main speaker for the event.

I was 17 years old, and many of the players and "older boys" (as Mr. Bible called them) were leaving to go into the service. By the fall semester, the Southwest Conference had made freshmen eligible to play on the varsity.

We had a lot of talent on that freshman team, including Harlan Wetz, Bobby Coy Lee, Jimmy Banks, Ray Borneman, George McCall, Jimmy Canady, and Joe Bill Baumgardner.

That fall, we had several good players from other schools transfer to Texas via the V12 Navy College Training Program and the V5 Naval Aviation Program. Our fall training started with freshman players from Texas and California, and other sophomore, junior, and senior players from all over the United States.

I was one of the several freshmen who started on the 1943 team. J.R. Calahan transferred for his senior season in the V5 program. He had been outstanding in his junior year at Texas Tech. The Navy V12 sent us Marcel Gres who was a great player from Santa Clara.

We lost one game to Southwestern University. Most of the seniors from Texas had transferred to the Marine ROTC units there. They had most of the 1942 Texas team, as well as players from Baylor, Rice, and SMU. Southwestern beat us 14–7. Many times they drove the ball up and down the field, but when they got to our 20-yard line, the Texas band would play "The Eyes of Texas," and those former Longhorns like Spot Collins, Harold Fischer, Jack Sachse, and others would stand at attention.

The 1943 team was led by captains Joe Parker, Joe Magliolo, and Ralph Park—all of whom were older players. We won the Southwest Conference in 1943 and played Randolph Field in the Cotton Bowl game. Randolph Field had many former college stars on its team as well, including Martin Ruby, who had been All-SWC at Texas A&M in 1942. I played center and linebacker at about 180 pounds. Ruby was almost 240 pounds and played middle guard, so I had my hands full with him! I played the entire 60 minutes of the game—the first, and maybe the only, freshman to do that in the Cotton Bowl game. The weather was cold and rainy, and Mr. Bible said that it was as bad as he had ever seen for a football game. We tied Randolph Field 7–7.

I went into the United States Marine Corps in 1944 and fought as a rifleman on Guam and the Battle of Iwo Jima. I returned to Texas in 1946 and 1947 on a football scholarship.

Being a Longhorn was something very special in my life. Mr. Bible always said that the two finest things a young man can do is to get a degree from a four-year college and to earn a varsity letter. He had a strong and profound influence on his players and turned out a group of successful men with good character. Tom Landry, who went on to coach the Dallas Cowboys, was an example of one of his "boys." Lessons learned in football and athletics in high school and The University of Texas helped me get through combat in World War II and have had a tremendous effect on my business career.

I got my BBA [bachelor of business administration] degree in 1950 and have owned an insurance company in Temple since that time. Being a Longhorn has helped me in my business and helped me develop mentally and physically. I was pleased when my son got a football scholarship to The University

Keifer Marshall became a marine and survived the Battle of Iwo Jima.

of Texas in 1969 under Coach Darrell Royal and experienced that same great feeling of pride in being a Texas Longhorn.

When we got back after the war, we had players who had entered The University between 1939 and 1946. Teammate Peppy Blount was a member of the Texas legislature. Also on the 1946 team were seven other players with ties to Temple—H.K. Allen, Terrell Allen, Ed Heap, Maxwell Jones, Red Simmons, Ben Procter, and Leslie Proctor.

In 1947, after Mr. Bible had retired, Blair Cherry became head football coach. Texas played the University of Oregon in Oregon. We made the first airplane trip that any Texas athletics team had ever made. Today, you can fly to Oregon in about three hours. In the fall of 1947 we left Austin early in the morning and flew to Denver, arriving there about noon. It was my first airplane ride, and the first for most of the players except the ones who had been Air Force pilots in World War II. We got off the plane to have lunch, and quite a few of us were air sick—probably the sickest was Bully Gilstrap. I remember him sitting on a bench at the airport and telling Blair that he was going to take a train back to Austin. Coach Cherry talked him into getting back on the plane with us, and we flew all afternoon, arriving in Oregon about 6:00 that night.

The team and the coaches had recovered by the next afternoon, and we soundly defeated Oregon 38–13. The game matched two of the great quarterbacks in college, and later pro football, with Bobby Layne playing for us and Norm Van Brocklin playing for Oregon. The trip back to Texas was a long but happy one!

After returning from the war and finishing my degree, my wife and I lived in an apartment complex on North Guadalupe Street near The University. Our neighbors were Rooster Andrews, Ralph Ellsworth, Dick Harris, Pud Evans, and their wives. All of these men were great athletes at The University of Texas.

Being a Texas Longhorn meant being with the best! I made many lifetime friends with my teammates and fellow students, including my wife, and we have been married almost 60 years.

Keifer Marshall is an honored veteran of World War II, having fought as a marine in the Battle of Iwo Jima. As a center and linebacker, he played every play—all 60 minutes—in the 1944 Cotton Bowl game. He is a member of the Longhorn Hall of Honor.

BILL SANSING

SPORTS INFORMATION DIRECTOR

1946–1949

THESE NOTES ARE IN RESPONSE to a request to reprise some memories of the late 1940s. Memories of that age are like a kaleidoscope—some images are crystal clear, others are misted by time. I was fortunate to have a front-row seat for these events. At the end of the war, Mr. Bible had the foresight to establish a full-time sports information office—the first in the Southwest. I was lucky enough to get the job, an example of what it means to be a Longhorn.

The years after World War II were part of a period of rampant change and transition for The University of Texas athletics in general, and football in particular. Consider that longtime iconic coach, D.X. Bible, delivered the head coaching responsibilities to his right hand for 10 years, Blair Cherry. Recall that Cherry—in a landmark change—elected to embrace the (then) new approach to the offensive strategy, the T formation. And without any experienced T formation quarterbacks! Remember that the quarterback he chose to learn the T formation became one of the all-time greats of the game—Bobby Layne. Today, any one of those changes would be *SportsCenter* features. But in 1945 and 1946, they all began to happen in rapid succession.

In many ways, the Bible-Cherry-Layne combination was the hallmark of the era. Layne made a sensational intro into the picture in the 1946 Cotton

Bill Sansing later helped Jack Nicklaus build his business empire.

Bowl game against Missouri. Only a freshman, he set bowl records that would endure for a generation. He personally scored 28 points (four touchdowns, four extra points) and passed for two more.

Then, the Bible era ended with an outstanding team of experienced players, augmented by some returned-from-the-war talent. My recollections of my job that fall included looking like mad for some decent housing for members of the team, many married, some with children. I begged, borrowed, and stole apartments, duplexes, rooms, and anything else available.

The '46 season started grandly but fell afoul by two traditional problems of this era—upsets by Rice and Jess Neely, and TCU and Dutch Meyer. In those days, an 8–2 season was no reason to celebrate. There were few bowl games. But the Longhorns rose up at the end to give D.X. Bible a going-away game to remember.

Mr. Bible had enjoyed a storied career at Texas A&M and Nebraska before coming to Texas, and the good-bye game against the Aggies was of special significance to the great coach. The Longhorns gave him a thrill with a 24–7 victory that wasn't as close as the score sounded. Texas A&M was held without yardage in the first half, and with only 27 yards of gains for the entire game.

Bobby Layne went on to become a member of both the College and Pro Football Halls of Fame.

Mr. Bible had made a remarkable record, turning the entire UT football picture from dismal to outstanding. The transition from Bible to Cherry was equally remarkable. Cherry had only assistant coaching experience at the college level, but he had a wide reputation as an outstanding football tactician. He started with a bang by switching from a successful single-wing to the new T formation.

I knew Cherry well. He was a next-door neighbor in my early days at UT, and I used to ride to the campus with him. He was a truly brilliant football strategist. His personality was hampered by a difficulty in accepting losses or media criticism, a trait that eventually forced him to leave coaching.

He identified Layne as his T quarterback from the start and gave him an incredible introductory training course. It included time at the College All-Star camp and visits to the Chicago Bears and Chicago Cardinals coaches, both newfound T formation specialists.

Layne made an awkward adjustment to the strange moves and subtleties of the T job, but his innate abilities would have worked with any offense. He later became a record-making NFL passer; he was a sturdy and strong runner, an accomplished place-kicker. But more than these, he was an inveterate competitor—at any skill—and born to win.

There were two interesting side shows during the Cherry-Layne tour. One was the annual "war" with the Doak Walker–led SMU Mustangs. Layne and Walker had been stars at Highland Park High and had planned to come to UT together. But wily Rusty Russell, an assistant coach at SMU, interfered, and Walker landed with the Ponies. The resulting Layne-Walker duels were a sight to see and remember, until the two eventually reunited in pro football.

A second supporting act in those years was in the person of Hub Bechtol, who was a brilliant target of Layne's passes for three of his seasons, leading to his selection as an All-American for three straight years, a rarity in Longhorn football history. He went on to a distinguished record in Austin political and community activities, and both he and Layne were eventually inducted into the National Football Foundation's College Hall of Fame.

Cherry and Layne's 1947 Longhorns wound up with a 10–1 record and had a clear-cut victory over Alabama in the Sugar Bowl game. New personnel dotted the field in 1948, and success was spasmodic, including one more unsuccessful duel with SMU and Walker. But an eventual 7–3–1 record earned them a much discussed bid to the Orange Bowl. Though roundly picked to lose big to a fine Georgia team, Texas beat them handily and left East Coast and Miami writers stumbling for excuses and apologies.

But it wasn't that game that stands out in my book of memories. As the Longhorns' sports information director, I was sent to Miami to find a place for Texas to have a pregame warm-up. Bowl games normally give teams a pregame practice, then insert 45 minutes of pageantry. Cherry had noticed this at the Sugar Bowl the year prior and was determined not to let it happen again.

The Texas team entered the field at the scheduled time, circled the field once, and abruptly departed. We had reserved an adjacent baseball park and used it at the regular time for the normal pregame workout. It was a major asset in the surprising win.

This collection of my memory clips hasn't spoken to the subject of what it means to be a Longhorn. Mine is encapsulated in those moments, before any contest, when the band strikes up "The Eyes of Texas." It's all there—the tradition, the memories, the sights, and the sounds. It stirred me decades ago, and it still does. Only a Longhorn could really grasp that and thrill to it.

Bill Sansing, who turned 87 in 2007, is one of the true legacies of Texas athletics. He was a team manager in the late 1930s, and in 1946 D.X. Bible hired him as the first college sports information director at Texas, and in the southwestern United States. His immense knowledge of the era, and those Longhorns who are no longer with us, qualifies him to tell their stories.

The
FIFTIES

JAMES CARROLL "T" JONES

QUARTERBACK

1950–1952

How did I get to Texas? The better question is, How did The University of Texas get to me?

I grew up on a farm just outside of Childress, Texas, near the Texas Panhandle. We were a small high school, and that allowed us to play all sports in the mid-to-late 1940s. My dream was to play college football and be on an athletics scholarship at a major university. I wasn't sure college recruiters could find athletes from small schools. After all, there wasn't any television, just radio and newspapers. Fortunately, several universities contacted me and invited me to visit their campuses. All of these were over 400 miles away. A scholarship was very important to my family. I lost my older brother to a football injury at age 15, and there were three of us boys left. We never asked, but we knew our parents couldn't afford to send us to school.

My family would listen to Southwest Conference football games on the radio each Saturday. There was one particular broadcaster named Kern Tips who was outstanding. When you listened to him, he made you feel you were there. His voice was special, and his unique description of players and the game was in a class by itself.

I decided to visit only three schools, and The University of Texas was, by choice, my last visit. It was a wonderful weekend. Blair Cherry was the head

Quarterback James Carroll "T" Jones was one of four Longhorn backs to earn All-SWC honors in 1952.

coach, and Eck Curtis was the offensive backfield coach—the person who recruited me and hosted me while on campus. He was such a gentleman, he made a great impression on me and my parents. Today, you would call him the offensive coordinator.

While on campus, I had the "gut" feeling that this is where I should go to school. I had no idea at the time that my commitment that day would be one of the most important decisions in my life.

Some way, I knew at a very early age that I wanted to be a football coach at a major university. That was my goal. The day I committed to Texas was one of my more meaningful moments…ever. I felt that I should major in business to back up my coaching career if it didn't work out.

Football at Texas was very, very special to me. We won a lot of games, two conference championships, and beat Tennessee in the Cotton Bowl game my senior year in 1953, in what was the first nationally televised New Year's Day bowl game.

After my sophomore year of 1950, Coach Cherry resigned and Ed Price became the head coach. Blair's resignation was a shock to everybody. We changed philosophy to some degree. Blair had used more of the pro-type T formation, with drop-back passing. Ed wanted to go back to more of a traditional split-T. It was an opportunity for me because Ben Tompkins, who was our starter in 1950, gave up his final season of eligibility to sign a baseball contract with the Philadelphia Phillies. I had taken just three offensive snaps in 1950.

The split-T required the quarterback to make decisions, and it took us a while to adjust to it. It was a simplified attack, yet a highly complicated one because the greater percentage of plays were switch-offs, or automatics, at the line. Either you called everything at the line or you could check off and go to another play. The quarterback had complete control of the offense in that he called all the blocking. When we got to the line, he would look over the defensive adjustments and call or change the blocking by number.

A lot of people used to joke that I got the nickname "T" from the formation. That was not true. It actually came when I was a baby and my brother used to point at me and say with a lisp, "Tee the baby."

In those first years of the 1950s we had some outstanding athletes, particularly on that 1952 club, which finished 10th in the country. Several were All–Southwest Conference, some were All-American, and some went on to the NFL. My senior year, every starter in our backfield made the All–Southwest Conference team, and we had seven members of our offense, including me, Harley Sewell, Tom Stolhandske, Phil Branch, Dick Ochoa, Gib Dawson, and Billy Quinn, chosen All-SWC. These were special people after the same goal—championships. Today, they are still special friends. Of course, as we get together today, our games and stories get bigger and better. This trend seems to be true with all ex-athletes from all universities.

After my eligibility ended, I had a two-year military commitment to serve our country. This was during the Korean War. Just before discharging, I wrote D.X. Bible, the athletics director at Texas, to tell him I was about to be out of the service and wanted his advice and help concerning my coaching ambitions. He contacted me and offered me an assistant coaching position at Texas. Wow! Another dream come true.

My first year was unbelievable in many ways. We won one game and lost nine. That's 1–9, and this had never happened in Texas history. We all got fired, and they hired a young 32-year-old as the head coach. That guy, of course, was Darrell Royal. Coach Royal asked me to stay on his staff. What a great experience we had together as a staff. Most of us were young, and four of those guys, Ray Wilsey, Jack Swarthout, Jim Pittman, and Charley Shira, all went on to become head coaches. Mike Campbell stayed with Darrell, and Coach Bob Schulze, who was the only other holdover from Ed's staff, stayed and coached the freshman team at Texas.

During my days with Darrell, he made coaching what I thought it was supposed to be and hoped it would be. Darrell was a great coach, whose record speaks for itself, and he remains today a great friend. I still owe him one for giving me a chance.

There is nothing as rewarding as working with young athletes and watching them mature and excel as young men. The close association with coaches and athletes is what I miss most about coaching—even to this day.

After coaching, I went into the banking business and then came back to Texas in 1980 as associate athletics director, working with my old friend, Bill Ellington, and staying on after DeLoss Dodds took over when Bill retired. My final position in athletics, as athletics director at Texas Tech University, gave me again the opportunity to be with and around athletes and coaches. After retiring from Tech in 1993, I was proud to be inducted into the Texas Tech Hall of Honor. Life and time work in mysterious ways for most of us. I had been truly blessed to be inducted into the Longhorn Hall of Honor in 1978.

Many people have asked me what it means to be a Longhorn. Most people would think this is a simple answer, but it really isn't. I always felt it was a very special privilege to represent The University of Texas. Every time I put on the orange-and-white uniform as a player or a coach, I was proud to represent The University. This responsibility was true off the field, as well. Whatever we had accomplished athletically and by name recognition was "on the line" everywhere we went, and as they say today, "it was 24/7." I have always tried to do my part to honor this great school. They found me and gave me a chance a long time ago.

James Carroll "T" Jones led the Longhorns to a victory in the Cotton Bowl over Tennessee after his senior season of 1952. He had the unique distinction of being part of a Longhorn team in which all four backs were chosen first-team All–Southwest Conference. He served as an assistant coach and later assistant athletics director at Texas, and as athletics director at Texas Tech University. He is a member of the Longhorn Hall of Honor and the Texas Tech Hall of Honor.

TOM STOLHANDSKE
DEFENSIVE END
1950–1952

I WAS BORN AND RAISED IN BAYTOWN, TEXAS. I played basketball and football at Goose Creek High School, but in Baytown and the surrounding area, football was king. I had offers to go to college, and, never having been out of Baytown, I was unaware of everything that was going on in the world around me.

I had made all-state and was being offered many scholarships. I was unaware of what colleges had to offer; I was in awe of all the attention that I was being given regarding my athletic abilities. I don't remember being directly called by a Texas coach. Most everything that was done was done through alumni, whom I became very attached to. They let me know that The University of Texas was their alma mater and they loved it. They offered me reasons they thought The University was where I should go to school. I didn't really make up my mind until I was visiting The University, and I realized the athletes and the football players were all living in an athletic dormitory. It was sort of a fraternity of athletes—football, basketball, baseball, and track, and they disciplined themselves. I was amazed at the camaraderie they had.

We were not really supervised. There was a live-in couple there, but they stayed to themselves and didn't venture into the dormitory. Ms. Griff was our house mother. At the time she was in her seventies. She would have prayer before every meal. She walked around, and if she saw anybody acting up,

30

Tom Stolhandske later became an attorney and Bexar County commissioner.

throwing food or anything, she'd scoot behind them, grab them by the hair, pull their head back, and give them a real lecture. In some instances, she carried a walking stick, and she'd strike you with this stick. Everybody loved Ms. Griff; she was a mother away from home.

In the 1952 season Frank Medina, our trainer, advised Ms. Griff to cut down on the amount of food we were getting. So she began to do this. One day we were at the stadium preparing for practice, and the team captain—it may have been Dick Ochoa, Bill McDonald, or Jack Barton—had been told the guys were hungry; we were starving. So he told Coach Price—bless his heart, probably the most level, easygoing man I've ever been around in athletics. He heard this and was concerned. About two or three days later, Coach got up—he had a way of putting his hands together and flexing his fingers—and said, "I've got good news. I listened to what you said the other day about y'all starving to death. I went to the Health Center and checked with the doctor. Guys, you don't have to worry; it takes a guy 32 days to starve to death." He won the battle, and we won the conference.

Frank Medina—the Little Indian—was our trainer. You didn't want to go see him. He'd been accused of being a witch doctor because if you got under his control for some kind of treatment, it was absolute horror. I'd walk into the training room and see somebody in the steam bath—locked in, can't get out, pounding on the door, trying to get out. If Frank put you in there for *x* minutes, you were going to stay in there for that amount of time, whether or not you passed out. He'd get you in the stadium and make you run to the top some 70 or 80 rows, back and forth, back and forth. And if you didn't do it, or he thought you needed more, he'd give you a dummy to carry. I injured my ankle in a game against Oklahoma, a slightly sprained ankle. We got back to Austin, and he said, "Come get some treatment." I said, "Frank, I didn't hurt my ankle, I just thought I did. Tape it up." So I played with an injured ankle. He wasn't about to get me in that training room and go through all that junk he made you do. It was beneficial, of course, but I didn't want to go through it.

We would often play hearts or spades in the dorm, then we'd lie around and talk; it was a lot of fun. One day Bill Harris, a communications major, rigged up a speaker from his room. He ran it down the wall and plugged it into the radio so that from his room he could interrupt the broadcast and talk over the radio. They were playing cards—this was during the Korean conflict—when all of a sudden, a voice on the radio said, "Pay attention to this important announcement. New York has just been bombed, and it appears there's going to be an invasion, perhaps from the West Coast. Make arrangements to get out of danger zones; there will be another announcement later." Then it goes back to the regular radio station. Well, one of the guys got so excited that he took off—I mean running. He jumped in a car— it wasn't even his car, he had borrowed it—and he headed for home, which was around Wichita Falls. He was caught in Georgetown going about 100 miles an hour. They were holding him, and we got a call to come make his bond. Well, of course, our man for trouble was Frank Erwin. He got him out and took care of that matter. It was hilarious to see the commotion it caused.

The coaching staff was adamant that we go to class and get passing grades. They were serious about seeing that you graduated, to the point that some guys would return as student coaches so they could have their education paid for. Going to The University and being enrolled is like the first step to heaven. You know you're going to the best school with the best people; the best place in the best state. That's The University of Texas.

The greatest thing that happened to me while at The University—and has been the greatest thing in my life since—was the introduction that I had to my wife, Betsy. We've been married for 54 years and have had three children. We've had a wonderful life together, and I wish to spend another 50 years with her.

I had a God-given talent to play football, and I recognize that. The other thing God gave me were the Texas Exes [former students] who directed me in the right path to conduct my life. I was amazed that the alumni were so interested in the athletes. Not only before you committed to Texas; they followed through with their concern while you were a student and even after your graduation. Although many have passed on, I still hear from some of these folks some 50 years later.

From 1949 to 1953 were the most wonderful, poignant years of my life. The professors were good, and they made me work for everything. I'm an optimist, you know…we can do it. We're The University of Texas. It was great satisfaction when I'd go to bed at night at Hill Hall and look over and see the Tower orange. I was just as thrilled this last year when I went to Austin and saw the Tower with the No. 1 on it. What I'm saying is, once a Longhorn, your blood is orange and it will stay orange. The greatest thing is the loyalty they gave me when I was there and the loyalty I've had from them since I graduated.

One of the bigger games was when we played SMU. They were No. 1 in the nation, and we were No. 2 or 3. We beat them something like 23–20. That game is vivid. I can still close my eyes, and the stands were just reverberating with all the screaming and hollering…burning the candles all week. We won some big games, and we had some heartbreak losses, but whenever you hear "Texas Fight" right before the kickoff, the hair on the back of your neck stands up, and you're excited because you know that you're representing The University of Texas.

We threw every now and then. I was blessed to have Ben Tompkins and T Jones as quarterbacks. Both were great. I don't know that I would have succeeded in football if it hadn't been for somebody like T Jones, one of the smoothest, smartest little quarterbacks that Texas has ever had.

Blair Cherry recruited me as a fullback. He came to me in spring practice my freshman year and said, "You can play as a fullback, but would you play end?" I said, "Coach, I'll play anywhere you want me to play." It was the greatest thing that happened to me as far as athletics was concerned. I was a starter from that day forward, and I started every game thereafter for three years.

One day Coach Price asked me to come over and talk with him. I didn't know what it was. I didn't think it was my grades; I just didn't know. I walked over there, and he said, "Tom, you've been selected to be on the All-America team, and I wanted to be the first to congratulate you."

Ed Price was a gentleman, a morally good person, and a good coach. He loved his boys, and the boys loved him. He believed people; he did not realize that there were people on his staff who were not loyal.

If there is a heaven on earth, going to The University of Texas is the first step toward going to heaven in Texas.

33

Tom Stolhandske was a three-year letterman for the Longhorns and earned All-SWC and All-America honors as a senior. He was one of the outstanding players on the 1952 team that defeated Tennessee in the Cotton Bowl, leading the team in receptions. He was inducted into the Longhorn Hall of Honor in 1976.

DELANO WOMACK

HALFBACK

1953–1955

I WAS RAISED IN AUSTIN, so I started going to games in 1947. UT had a "Knothole Gang," and we got in for almost nothing. I was going to University Junior High at the time, which is the building just south of the current field house. That's where I first started seeing people like Bobby Layne, Peppy Blount, Byron Gillory, Byron Townsend, Bud McFadin, and all those guys who played ahead of me. To be frank with you, when I first started going to games, I didn't even know what a football was. So when I went out for football at UJH, it was all new. We practiced across the creek, which was then the UT freshman field. We were down in one little corner with the junior high boys, and then all the big boys would come practice there.

I went to those games religiously in '47, '48, and '49. I had no idea that I'd ever be invited to play football at The University of Texas. That was a dream; we didn't think about it, we were not preoccupied with it. I didn't know where I was going to college until after my senior year in high school.

My one idol who was not a Texas guy was Doak Walker. SMU played the single wing, which was what we played at Austin High. I almost thought I'd go to SMU because of Doak Walker. Then I went out to the old Heep Ranch and visited with Mr. Herman Heep; he was an Aggie. But I did not want to go to A&M. I knew better than that already. I was dating Margaret Ann Olle at that time. Her daddy, Ed Olle, was business manager of athletics at Texas, but he never said one word to me about coming to Texas.

Coach Price and Bully Gilstrap had come to the house to talk to Mother and Daddy. Something told me that I ought to stay home and not go to Dallas. So after the Texas High School All-Star Game that summer, I announced that I was coming to Texas. My folks really liked Coach Price, and they thought he was a good man. They were right; he was a good man.

UT still had a freshman team, which was wonderful because you met a bunch of guys who were going to be teammates for a long time and friends for the rest of your life. If you were very good, you might have played both ways, but normally you played one way. But when you got to varsity, they switched to one platoon. They changed that NCAA rule in '53, and you had to play both ways. You couldn't just go play offense and come out on defense.

I was fortunate. I started as a sophomore because I could play both ways. I played safety my first and second years and linebacker my third year because they switched me from left halfback on offense to fullback my senior year. If you played fullback, you played linebacker. So that was a neat deal.

We played some great football teams. We played Notre Dame when I was a junior and Southern Cal when I was a senior. Of course, we played Oklahoma every year, and I'm unhappy to say that we got caught in their 47-game winning streak. We played respectably and weren't ever out of the game, we just lost.

We beat a wonderful Baylor team 21–20 in '53. That backfield is considered Baylor's best foursome ever. Those guys are immortal in Baylor's history, and we beat them. Remember, you couldn't sub after every play. So if the opposing team scored and you were on the field, you stayed on the field. In other words, you didn't have a separate kicking team.

Coach Price was a really good football coach. Baylor scored, and we needed to block the kick. Coach Price had Carlton Massey and me switch positions so that I went inside and Carlton rushed from the outside. Baylor let him go because they didn't think he was fast enough to get to the ball. They both took me coming in on the inside. That was very smart of Coach Price to devise that play. He said, "They're gonna take you, Delano, because you're gonna be quicker getting off of the line of scrimmage. And just for a second, they're gonna let Carlton go, and because he's taller [by about six inches] he's gonna be able to reach that long arm out there"—I can still hear him saying that—"that long arm out there and knock that ball down." And it worked! Carlton blocked the extra point, which eventually led to us winning the game.

I loved my teammates, and we still keep in touch. For the last 10 to 15 years before the opening football game, those who are in town will meet someplace for dinner and rendezvous. Our freshman year was 1952, so in 2002 Menan Schriewer, Herbie Gray, Joe Youngblood, and I had dinner together with a couple of other friends who weren't football players but were freshmen at the same time. We thought about it and said, "Do you guys realize it's been 50 years since we met each other? Fifty years!" It's been a lifetime bond.

I keep up with Menan once a month. Charlie Brewer, from Lubbock, and I were roommates. He and I see each other at least once a year. We went to the 50th anniversary of the Hook 'em Horns sign together. The Hook 'em Horns sign was initiated when I was a senior at the TCU game and Big Bertha was donated by Colonel D. Harold Byrd in '55, which was my junior year. That's pretty important to me to know that those two things are still there after 50-some-odd years.

There used to be a Southwest Conference Sportsmanship Award. Players were nominated by the coaches and officials, and when I was a senior, I was the recipient of that award. When I was at Texas, I also won the Longhorn Sportsmanship Award at the football banquet. I'm very proud of those two things.

When I went to Fort Worth to accept the Southwest Conference Sportsmanship Award, in the crowd were all those TCU boys who had beat us, costing us the conference championship. See, after we got beat by TCU in Memorial Stadium, I was so disappointed that, instead of walking down to our locker room, I went to the far end of the field and walked into the visitors' dressing room. Abe Martin was their coach, and they were all celebrating. I told them, "You guys played a wonderful game. I'm disappointed that we lost, but you guys played better than we did." One of their players—I think it was Hugh Pitts, their center—said, "Well, y'all gonna beat A&M for us?" I said, "I guarantee we're gonna beat A&M." My word. I cannot believe I told those TCU guys that we were going to win that game. A&M was No. 3 in the nation at the time, and they had beaten TCU. They had John David Crow and Bobby Joe Conrad and Jack Pardee and Gene Stallings and Charlie Krueger, and I guaranteed we were going to beat those guys.

But we did beat them. We went down to College Station and beat that good A&M team, Bear Bryant's team. We were running the split-T, and we had three backs—Fondren, Hawkins, and myself—and we each had over 90 yards of rushing. Coach Price did a good job in that game. He ran some plays

Delano Womack led the Longhorns in scoring in 1953.

he hadn't run before. He started some seniors who hadn't played a lot, and they responded, and we won the game 21–6.

So when I went to Fort Worth to get that award, eight of those TCU guys were sitting at the table in front of me. They were there to thank me for that victory because if we hadn't beaten A&M, the Aggies would have gone to the Cotton Bowl instead of TCU.

The bottom line is I got to play for a great university and didn't even realize it when I was playing for them. At the time you don't understand the magnitude of playing here. Today when I meet people and someone says, "Delano used to play at The University of Texas," they look at you like you're a god. "You played at The University of Texas?" Well, it was a long, long time ago. It was an honor, but it's more of an honor the older you get, to say you are part of that tradition.

I ended up marrying Margaret Ann, and her dad became athletics director after D.X. Bible and before Darrell Royal. There's a lot of Longhorns history in our family. My oldest son, Jack, walked on and was captain of the suicide squad at Texas. I didn't even know he was out there until Darrell sent me the letter to order tickets as the parent of a player.

The University has been awfully good to me. I got a degree there, and there are associations, not with just my teammates, but other guys I went to school with. I was a Phi Gam, and I've got lifetime friends who are Fijis. It's not all about football, it's about who you are and the friendships you make. I am so glad I was a Longhorn because I know I wouldn't have been as happy at any other school and I wouldn't have the relationships I have now. They've lasted a lifetime, and they're still there.

Delano Womack was part of a rushing tandem with quarterback Walter Fondren in the mid-1950s. He lettered three seasons, 1953–1955, and led the team in all-purpose yardage in 1954. He also received two awards for sportsmanship.

WALTER FONDREN

QUARTERBACK

1955–1957

IT WOULD BE AN UNDERSTATEMENT TO SAY that the period of the mid-1950s was a time of significant change. Not only for me but for The University of Texas and for college football.

Football was important to me, but it originally was not the deciding factor in my choice of school. I was primarily interested in going to a school that had a good geology program. That fit my family upbringing because that's where our roots were. My dad had gone to Oklahoma, but I had two sisters who had gone to Texas. I made motions about going to Oklahoma, but it was never really a consideration. I had pretty well made up my mind that I was going to Texas. The recruiting process was nothing like it is today, but I did take a trip to Oklahoma in the spring of my senior year in high school in 1954. The biggest thing I noticed was that I left Texas in the spring, and when I got up there it was still winter. There were no leaves on the trees. That kind of surprised me. I don't know why, but that stuck in my mind.

Ed Price was the Texas head coach, and he and Ox Emerson, one of his assistants, recruited me. There were no scholarship limitations for schools. I was fortunate in that I would have been able to go to school whether or not I had a scholarship. Initially, because of our financial situation, my dad didn't want me to take up somebody else's scholarship. But Texas didn't want that. They said they didn't have any limitations, and they didn't. Including me,

Walter Fondren was a quarterback/punter/kicker and the captain of Darrell Royal's first team at Texas.

although I had been a single-wing tailback, there were seven all-state quarterbacks on our freshman team. It was just a different time.

After my junior year, Coach Price resigned. We had gone through a disastrous 1–9 season. I don't think anybody worked any harder than we did, physically or mentally. But it was obvious we didn't have the horsepower to deal with the other teams. Opponents were standing in line…they couldn't wait to play us. The only game we won was against Tulane because they missed an extra point and I didn't. I think we won 7–6.

Coach Price was a delightful person and a wonderful gentleman. I mentioned earlier that it was a changing time in college football. I look at that as being involved in an era change in coaching. Coaches around the country were changing the face of football and how they coached it. Prior to that, we didn't have much structure in our coaches' schedule. If something didn't work, you kept working on it in practice, even if you didn't get involved in other areas that you were supposed to. There wasn't a practice schedule.

That was one of the first things we noticed when Darrell came. We had a lot of differences in what was going on, but the game was also played totally differently because of the platoon system. If you came out of the game in any one quarter, you couldn't go back in until the next quarter. Think how much the game improved when they did away with that. Think about the national championship game in the 2006 Rose Bowl with Texas and USC. What if either team lost their quarterback on the first play of the game, and he couldn't be replaced until the second quarter? What kind of game would that have been?

We didn't break up practices into time periods as they do today. It was more of a team workout. Sometimes we had pass defense drills, or pass-receiving drills, but we never broke into groups before practice, with the defensive ends and the offensive linemen and the defensive linemen and linebackers and halfbacks. We never broke up and looked at film on that basis. There was also a lot less structure in the teaching part of the game. Darrell started that, and that whole generation was bringing it in. It was like stepping out of one time zone into one that was advanced several years down the road.

Another thing that was difficult for me was that I didn't call plays in high school. I had played as a freshman and called plays, but freshman football at that point was just an afterthought. There wasn't a lot of attention paid to it. It always amazed me as to how Texas could field a freshman team and never beat anybody, but the varsity always had a fairly good record within the conference. Except for that 1–9 year, the bad years, since I was in school, have been six-loss seasons.

This era also changed coaching philosophy. I never had anybody explain to me, for instance (and it greatly simplified the game), that you had the ball only 12 or 13 times a game. How many times are you successful scoring? How many times does the defense stop you? How many times do you stop yourself with some sort of fumble or turnover? Darrell's "unfavorite" term was an incomplete or a dropped pass. It tickles me; I led the team in passing my

41

senior year at under 500 yards. He used to say, "If a guy's open, run down there and hand it to him." We even quick-kicked at that time. It was Darrell's philosophy to try for field position—try to get the ball in their end of the field and let them make a mistake so you could take advantage of a short field. That put emphasis on defense, sometimes more than on offense. Just before I came to Texas, the Southwest Conference was always referred to as "pass happy." I guess these things go in stages. I don't think I've seen anybody quick-kick in a bunch of years. I always thought, *Boy, wouldn't it have been fun to be able to benefit from three years with Darrell?* I was never envious of other generations. It's exciting to be part of something that has gone on to become what Texas has become since I've left. The only reason I've been envious is that I would have loved to have run the wishbone. That would have been fun. I didn't say I would have been successful, but it would have been fun, and I think the game's supposed to be fun. I admire Vince Young for understanding that.

Some of my best memories are the times I spent with Darrell, discussing football strategy. He would break the game down into various elements. I don't think any other coaches at the time talked about the importance of the kicking game, field position, and things of that nature.

Nobody kicked field goals, and I remember holding the ball in an Arkansas game when Darrell let Fred Bednarski, a soccer-style kicker from Poland, kick a field goal. It wasn't long, but I think it was the first ever kicked in college ball by a sidewinder. Everybody else was a straight-on kicker, including me. I tried Fred's style once, hit about six inches behind the ball and chili-dipped it. I almost broke my knee, and they told me I couldn't try that anymore.

Another thing that was changing was the academic standard of The University itself. There wasn't much emphasis on academics until Darrell came along. He hired the first athletics academic counselor and gave a "T" ring to those who lettered and graduated. He said, "If we recruit all these kids, and they fail out of school, they aren't any good to us." Of those seven all-state quarterbacks we signed my freshman year, there were only three left when I was a senior. It was during that time that they first changed the grade requirements and they tightened down the screws academically.

That is part of what it means to be a Longhorn: there is a great sense of pride in having been a part of a great winning tradition that has done things in the right way. I used to have arguments with people about recruiting violations, and they would ask me, "You think Texas doesn't violate recruiting rules?" I kept telling them that if they gave me proof of illegal recruiting, I would turn us in myself. That's the way I felt about it and still do. Being a Longhorn is being part of something that has not only recorded a great record but conducts itself with a great deal of class.

The game has changed. I laugh when people learn that I led the team in kickoff returns. Can you imagine Vince Young being involved in returning kicks? He would have been great at it, but no one would risk that today. The facilities are so much better. We had a small training room inside a dressing room that's been there under the west stands since the stadium opened.

Having been a part of Texas football always amazes me. Every now and then, even after all these years, I still get handed a little helmet or a football, and I'll be asked for an autograph. That's not me…that's The University of Texas. A while back, I got a chance to play in the British Amateur Golf Tournament. Several reporters were asking questions. One of them—he may have been with the *Stars and Stripes* newspaper—asked me, "Didn't you play football at The University of Texas?" That's the reach of playing football at Texas. Here I was, getting ready to play golf in Scotland, and that's the question he asked. That pretty well answers what it means to be a Longhorn.

43

Walter Fondren was Darrell Royal's first starting quarterback at Texas and a three-year letterman, from 1955 through 1957. He was an All–Southwest Conference selection in 1955 and the Most Valuable Player on the 1956 team, as well as co-captain of Royal's first UT team in 1957. He is a member of the Longhorn Hall of Honor.

BOBBY LACKEY

QUARTERBACK

1957–1959

I GREW UP IN WESLACO, IN SOUTH TEXAS, and I always wondered how Texas could beat Texas A&M, even when A&M had the better team. Well, my sophomore year at Texas, Sunday night before the game on Thanksgiving, we all went to this Boy Scout house out in the country. It was the most tear-jerking thing I have ever seen in my life, when the senior football players talked about the game with the Aggies. That was such an emotional evening, if you couldn't get ready to play football then, I don't believe anything else could get you ready to play.

We went over to College Station and played A&M on Thanksgiving Day, 1957. It was Darrell Royal's first year, and Bear Bryant was A&M's coach. They had been unbeaten until they lost to Rice the week before we played them. John David Crow was the Heisman Trophy winner, and we beat them 9–7. I was fortunate to be able to kick a field goal that will linger on with me for the rest of my life. It was a great occasion, a wonderful victory for Coach Royal and The University of Texas. That's one of the most memorable moments.

There was a lot of irony in that because I had no intention of going to The University of Texas. There were a number of good quarterbacks who graduated from high school in Texas in 1956, including Charlie Milstead [who went to Texas A&M] and Don Meredith [SMU]. Each Southwest Conference coach who came to recruit us would show us the names of the guys they

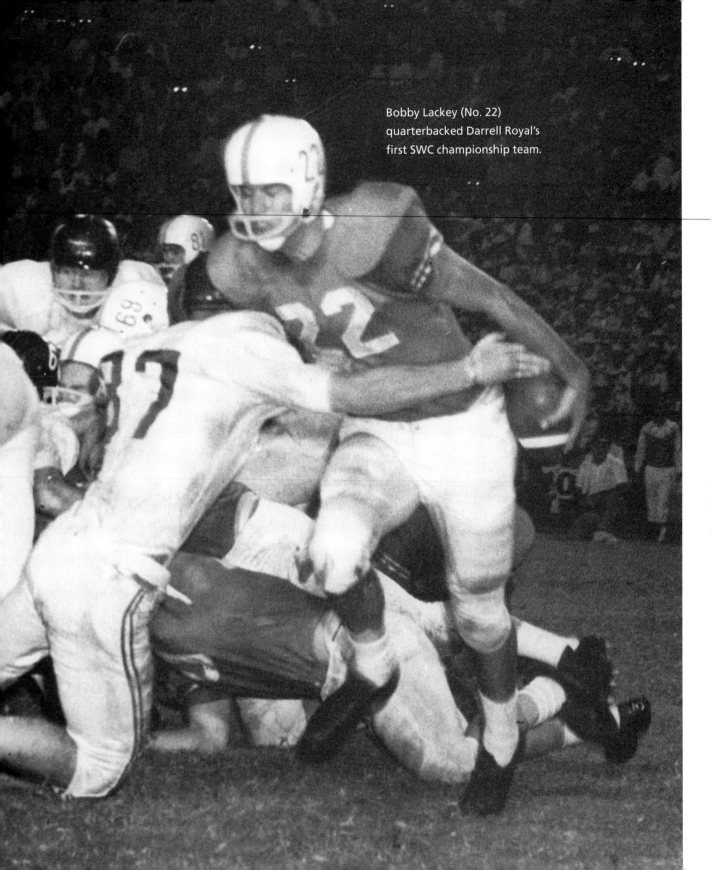

Bobby Lackey (No. 22) quarterbacked Darrell Royal's first SWC championship team.

had at quarterback, and our name would be at the top. When they went to the next guy, his name would be at the top of their list.

I didn't know where I wanted to go. I visited Texas and SMU. Baylor and Rice were after me. But that spring, a friend of mine took me to Austin to see the UIL Boys High School Basketball Tournament. I said, "Man, how could you not want to come to this place? You've got the state basketball tournament here." A little later, some guys from Weslaco invited me to come up to the Texas Relays, which was during Round Up [a spring campus celebration]. We really had a good time. Charlie Brewer and Johnny Tatum, who were football players, were members of the same fraternity as my friends. I knew a girl who was going to Texas, and Round Up and the track meet made the whole weekend awesome. I enjoyed it so much that I said, "Hey, I just gotta come to this school. If they want me, I'm coming." That's what convinced me to go to The University of Texas.

Darrell was an excellent motivator and coach, and he had some great assistants. Jim Pittman, Charley Shira, and Ray Wilsey all became head coaches someplace else. Mike Campbell could have, but he didn't want to leave, so he stayed there. The backfield coach, Bob Schulze, and T Jones moved to the varsity when Darrell came in. I thought if T had stayed around, he might have been the next head coach at The University, but he quit and went into business…great guy, Longhorn all the way.

Darrell wasn't very well known at the time. He'd been moving around different places. I'd watched Coach Price's workouts, and when we had our first meeting with Coach Royal, you just knew things were about to change. He had a charisma about him and a certain cockiness that rubbed off on you. He was so sure of himself at a young age.

We ended up with a lot of sophomores playing football in '57. Coach Campbell once told me that our freshman class was one of the best classes they had in their 20 years at Texas. He thought the Steve Worster class was probably better, but our class was one of the best, especially when they came in as new coaches. They had excellent players. It was not easy under Coach Royal his first few years here. During two-a-days in '57, we had guys off the '56 ballclub that went 1–9 who were leaving without even cleaning their lockers out. It was tough because all we did was eat and sleep football for two weeks.

The other memorable game would have to be against the Sooners in 1958, when we beat then 15–14. That was the first year of the two-point conversion. Don Allen, a good friend of mine, was our fullback. He scored two

46

points, and those were the only two points he scored while he was at The University. But what a two points he made that day. He was one-on-one with their linebacker, and he got in and scored. The shot that sunk the Sooners was a pass that I threw to Bobby Bryant for a touchdown. Then I got to kick the extra point. I also intercepted a pass at the end of the game—a one-handed sideline pass. If they had had instant replay, I might have been out of bounds. But it was an interception, and we ran the clock out and beat the guys 15–14.

We beat 'em—that was the turning point for Coach Royal at that time. It was the first victory we'd had against Oklahoma in five or six years. That thing kind of runs in cycles—it seems like we win five or six times and they win five or six times. We'd worked very hard—the coaches had done an excellent job of preparing us for that game. We worked out two hours in the morning and two hours in the afternoon, and kickers and punters and anybody who had a speciality had to be on the field earlier because Coach Royal wasn't going to waste time for you to stand around out there and punt or practice kickoffs or extra points during practice. Drills were so organized that when that whistle blew, you knew exactly where you were supposed to go next. It was so organized that, for two hours, you were busy the whole time. We did lose a lot of those guys off the '56 team.

I thought we had a darn good football team in 1959. We were undefeated until we played TCU; but we got beat in a blizzard, 14–9. We had a lot of good sophomores coming on. We had a tough game against Texas A&M. We were behind 10–0 at halftime. Coach Royal told me, "This half is yours. Go out there and take charge and see if we can't score some points." I pretty much played the whole second half and never came out until the end of the game. I started throwing the ball quite a bit and beat them up with that same quick pass that we used against Oklahoma. Then they started knocking our ends down, and our back was open. We won 20–17, tied for the conference championship, and went to the Cotton Bowl.

We had played in the Sugar Bowl on New Year's Day of 1958 against Ole Miss. We worked out so hard before that bowl game, we were happy when game time came, and we didn't want to play any more ballgames. In 1958 we had a chance [to go to a bowl game], but the players didn't want to go. So in 1959 we were supposed to be representing the conference, but we went in and said, "Coach, it was so tough—we're seniors, and we don't want to have to work out like we did when we were sophomores." He said he thought maybe he had made a mistake, and it wasn't going to be that way. He told us we were going to enjoy it—and we did. He wasn't as hard or tough on us in the workouts for the Cotton Bowl as he was in the workouts for the Sugar Bowl. He had mellowed a little bit. That's why I say that Bear Bryant had nothing on Coach Royal when Bryant took those guys to Junction. Darrell knows that…he knows exactly what I'm talking about.

We had a good game with Syracuse. I felt that we were probably as good as they were. We made a mistake or two and let them get a win, but it ended up as a nice season for us. I think that helped his recruiting over those first three years.

What does it mean to be a Longhorn? First, you get a good education—one of the things you have to look forward to. Usually—most always—Texas has played good football, sometimes great football. It means a lot to be an alumnus where you can be proud of what's going on. There are so many alums that, if you make a name for yourself, those people remember you throughout. Here I am, nearly 70 years old, and I have people who remember when I played. It's a heck of a nice feeling when somebody comes up and says, "I remember." I don't think you get that at the smaller schools. Those are rewarding experiences. The orange blood is in my body—it's not red, it's orange. I love The University of Texas and I love what it stands for.

Bobby Lackey was the quarterback for Darrell Royal's first Southwest Conference championship team in 1959. He led the team in scoring in 1958 and 1959, and was an outstanding punter. A three-year letterman (1957–1959), he played on Royal's first three teams at Texas. He was inducted into the Longhorn Hall of Honor in 1977.

BOBBY GURWITZ

HALFBACK

1958–1960

A LOT OF THINGS HAVE TO DO WITH LUCK, and I just happened to be lucky enough to be in Darrell Royal's first recruiting class at The University of Texas. I was lucky enough to choose Texas. To make it more confusing, I almost chose it for the wrong reasons, and I just got lucky.

My brother was in law school in Austin, so I had a little comfort zone there. The only other school I even thought about was Rice. Although my father graduated from Texas A&M, that wasn't one of my choices. I finally decided that Texas was the place to go, mostly because I had a comfort level there. Coach Royal just happened to be the right person for me, so that's why I say I was just lucky to get there.

Coach Royal is responsible for developing more people over the years than anybody I know. Every time you talk with somebody who played for him, half the time they'll say, "This is what he did for me...." To me, that is really special.

When I came to Texas, I think I was playing seventh-string right halfback, and it seemed as though everybody was 6'4" and weighed 230 pounds. I didn't think I'd see the light of day, and I was close to right. I played one down my freshman year. Then the other guys started to evaporate over the course of my freshman year. What you came to understand was that, if you went all the way for Coach Royal, he would go 110 percent for you. If you didn't, then you might as well just turn in your jersey, because if you weren't putting out

Bobby Gurwitz clinched the 1959 SWC championship with a pass interception against Texas A&M.

100 percent, he wouldn't have anything to do with you. It was all about work habits, sticking to something, and having a plan.

My plan almost got derailed in the fall of my freshman year in 1957. An Asian flu epidemic had hit the campus. It was so bad that the Longhorn band, which was all male at the time, didn't have enough people to march at the Oklahoma game in Dallas. So they agreed to allow women to fill in, and they've been marching ever since. I came down with the flu, and all of the hospitals in Austin were full, so I went home to get well, and it took about a week. My roommate neglected to tell anybody where I was, so when I got back, I was not on the coaches' A-list. They sent me to be cannon fodder for the varsity, and I spent most of the season there. Every drill they could put you through that wasn't fun, I was involved with. It was just survival, but it taught me a lot about playing the game; it taught me a lot about being tougher than I was, and it taught me to stick to it.

Darrell had a great staff, but T Jones may have been the one who was most responsible for making me into a football player because he was not nice to me. I think that's what helped me develop into the type of player I became. I certainly wasn't very large. I was fairly fast, but there were people who were faster. T taught me about learning to play the game.

We weren't the most talented offensive team back then, so Coach Royal's plan was to play defense. We'd kick on third down. We did things that nobody would even think about doing today. And of course, we all know how he felt about passing. We didn't have the guns to outrun or be more athletic than somebody, so what he did was figure out ways to outsmart the other team with his defense. The first couple of years, we survived on that. That was his plan, and it worked very well.

We learned that, when our opportunity came, we'd better be ready for it. My sophomore year, we were playing at Georgia in our season opener. Wally Butts, the Georgia coach, had inserted a new quarterback named Fran Tarkenton, who had pulled them to an 8–7 lead late, with about seven or eight minutes left in the game. I was a third-string halfback. I was sitting on the bench, and I hadn't been on the field.

Suddenly, Coach Royal called me over. "Gurwitz," he said, "get in there and return the kickoff." I barely knew where my helmet was. Of course, they kicked the ball to me. To this day I don't remember how far I returned it. It may have been to the 25-, 30-, or 35-yard line. But I stayed in as we started the drive, and we drove all the way. It was the early part of September in Texas—it was hot, and everybody was tired. I was fresh, so I handled the ball a lot on the drive. We had a fourth down at the 1-yard line, and our quarterback, Bobby Lackey, called my number. I scored with about a minute remaining. We won the game 13–8.

That could have been the highlight of my career. It was really exciting. My hometown newspaper, the *Three Rivers News*, even had that on the front page. It's funny how memories are. Things that happened almost 50 years ago are more important to me now than they were then. In the Texas A&M game my junior year, in 1959, we were fighting for a share of the Southwest Conference title and the Cotton Bowl berth. We had fought from behind and had just gone ahead 20–17 late in the fourth quarter.

They had a play where their receiver went out and up the sideline. Two or three of us wound up in the end zone, and the ball came down in the middle of us. I was fortunate enough to get my hands on it and be the one who caught the pass instead of the fellow who was supposed to be receiving it. They say the legendary radio announcer, Kern Tips, first called it "complete for a touchdown!" But he then quickly said, "No! It's intercepted by Gurwitz in the end zone!"

Those are just a couple of the memories of playing for Darrell and all the things that we accomplished. It was a long way from Three Rivers, where Charley Shira, one of Darrell's assistants, sat at our kitchen table and talked about playing football at Texas. I was also a basketball player, and I think that's one of the reasons Darrell recruited me. I was all-state and all-tourney, but Three Rivers is a very small town, and I don't know how they found me.

Coach Royal changed a lot of things when he came to Texas, and one of the first was that he brought discipline to the program. The year before I came, the dorm where the players lived was a wild place. He came in and changed all that. The year before I got there, they would tear up the dorm. But when he got there, he cleaned it up. Anybody who didn't want to behave, didn't want to act like a gentleman, didn't want to obey the rules was gone.

The people who did things the right way, if they needed an extra six months or a year of college to get their degree, whatever he had to do, he'd help them get their degrees. There were a number of guys who didn't play, some of whom didn't suit up. But he gave them that extra year as a student-coach so they could finish.

Having played at The University of Texas is like a badge of honor. There isn't a year that goes by that someone doesn't come up and mention it to me. That's something you'll always have. You don't realize what you are building when you are 18, 19, 20 years old. You never realize that it carries you on through your life. Everywhere I go, someone is reminded that I was a football player at Texas. It's that simple. It's a great feeling. I don't carry a card that says I played at Texas. I just wear that "T" ring that Coach Royal gave us, and that is identification enough.

The success carries with you in your work and in your family life. I think my most exciting moment in sports was when my son, Brad, played on his basketball state championship team in the 1980s.

When I finished my senior year at Texas, Coach Royal was coaching the North-South All-Star Game, and he invited me to play in it. I had to turn it down because I was getting married two weeks after the game. I have probably regretted that most. But we've been married for 47 years. And Coach came to the wedding.

Bobby Gurwitz was one of a stable of running backs for Darrell Royal as Royal began his Texas coaching career in the late 1950s. Gurwitz was a three-year letterman whose game-saving interception in the end zone preserved the Longhorns' 20–17 victory over Texas A&M in 1959.

The

SIXTIES

JACK COLLINS

HALFBACK

1959–1961

MY DAD WAS A THREE-SPORT LETTERMAN at Texas in 1934, 1935, and 1936, so I grew up hearing about The University of Texas and his experience there. From an early age, I enjoyed listening to Texas football. They had an announcer back then named Kern Tips; he could make it seem like you were watching the game in person.

When I was a sophomore in high school, Texas wasn't doing very well in football. That was toward the end of Coach Ed Price's career, and Texas won one game that year. The way they do it now, they practically start recruiting kids in junior high school, but it was different then. I had no idea I'd ever be able to play college ball. I grew a lot between my sophomore and junior year, and that was the year Texas had recruited Darrell Royal to come to UT.

When I was a senior, it was between Oklahoma, SMU, and Texas. That was during Bud Wilkinson's heyday, and Oklahoma was really good. Texas hadn't beaten them in something like seven years. But I decided to come to Texas. I was part of Royal's second recruiting class. I'd say it was my family history and Coach Royal's influence that got me here.

First of all, Coach Royal won. He had that going. He was all of 33 or 34 back then. It was probably his youth and enthusiasm that impressed me. He seemed organized, and he seemed like he knew what he wanted to do. Of course, he was a lot younger than Bud Wilkinson—Bud Wilkinson had coached Royal.

Jack Collins was Darrell Royal's first All–Southwest Conference running back.

55

Freshmen were not eligible at that time. We had about 70 people in that freshman class. I remember an assistant coach telling us, "In four years, there probably won't be but a handful of y'all that will be graduating from here." That was hard to believe. It turned out we had a few more than that. We had a real good recruiting class, and there were about 10 of us who went through together, not redshirting. We got to play early, got to play quite a bit as sophomores, and had a lot of success.

My sophomore year, we played our first game at Nebraska. This was before Nebraska was as strong as they were in later years, but they were still pretty good. I didn't know I was going to start until about three minutes before the game. The first play of the game was "Cornhusker right." I played left halfback, and on that particular play, the quarterback lined up under the center, but the snap was to come directly to me. Well, it did and hit me right in the face. Fortunately, it bounced right, and I just fell on the ball. After that I was fine. But before, it was one of those deals where my legs were just shaking.

After that Nebraska game, we came home and played Maryland. That was the first game that I played in Memorial Stadium. We got the ball on the 20-yard line, and on the first play of the game—the first carry—I went 80 yards for a touchdown. It was all downhill from there.

Texas hadn't had a lot of speed in the past, and that's what Royal tried to get. Our team had a lot of guys who could run pretty well. People weren't used to us doing that, so that helped us, too. We were still playing one-platoon football and had limited substitutions, so we played both offense and defense. I played safety on defense. By the time I was a senior, they had gotten a little bit more liberal, but you still had to work out at both positions because you couldn't just send someone in, then take them out, then send them back in. If they went out, they had to stay out for a certain period of time. We were in pretty good shape, but we weren't the size of the players today. I was about 190–195 pounds, which was big for a back then but is not considered big today.

We were Southwest Conference co-champions my sophomore year, and we played in the Cotton Bowl. That was the first time Texas had done that in about six years. We played Syracuse, the No. 1 team in the nation. We played them a good game, but they won 23–14. The only two games we lost that year were to TCU and to Syracuse.

Winning the Southwest Conference championship two years and playing in the Cotton Bowl were the highlights for me, from a team standpoint. My senior year we played Ole Miss, and we won that game. We were ranked No. 1 all year and had beaten all our opponents by probably three touchdowns. Then we lost to TCU 6–0. I'm 66 years old, and you'd think after all these years… But I think about that game every year. That was 1961. It was a fluke; I still don't know how it happened. TCU had won three games that year; they beat us and tied Ohio State, but then they couldn't do anything after that. Our team came close, but it was two years later that Texas finally won the national championship.

I still see Coach Royal. Back when you were a player, you thought he was God. You're just real impressionable. He had a lot of young assistants, and I think that's what helped make him a success; most of them became head coaches, like Jim Pittman. He's the one who recruited me and he coached at Tulane and TCU. My position coach was T Jones. He was the freshman coach, along with Bill Ellington, and they moved on up to the varsity when I became a sophomore. We were fortunate to have Ellington and T Jones compared to some of those other guys. I think we got away with more.

Lan Hewlett was the academic coach, and we all had to sign these "cut" slips saying that you went to class every week. One week—the week of the OU game—I didn't go. I cut a class. And I remember having to run stadium steps with Frank Medina at 6:00 in the morning. I mean, I don't care if you were a starter or what. You didn't get by with that. Frank Medina used to lock the guys who were overweight in the sweat room and wouldn't let them out. I remember him taking some guys up to Round Rock and just letting them out of the car. They probably hitched a ride, but he wanted them to walk back to Austin to lose weight.

The University of Texas is a quality school, and to be a Longhorn is to have a sense of pride. The way Coach Royal ran the athletics department was first class. I don't ever recall Texas being under any suspicion of doing things wrong during that time, and the way DeLoss Dodds has run it since then has carried that on. A lot of people hate us, of course. They may hate us, but I think they also respect us for the way the program is run. Texas has always done a good job of dodging those bullets. We've spent a lot of money and taken great pains to try to do it right. I feel a lot of pride in that integrity.

57

Jack Collins led the 1959 Longhorn team that earned Darrell Royal his first Southwest Conference championship. He topped categories for rushing, receiving, total offense, and all-purpose yards, and earned All–Southwest Conference honors. He is a member of the Longhorn Hall of Honor.

MIKE COTTEN

QUARTERBACK

1959–1961

M Y DAD WAS WITH THE HIGHWAY DEPARTMENT, so he and my mom fol- lowed construction projects around the state. When he went overseas in 1943, my mother and I lived in Amarillo because she was a Panhandle girl. When he came back in 1946, we moved to Austin—I was six. At an early age, I was interested in sports and became aware of Texas.

The first recollection I have about my excitement about Texas was an Orange Bowl game when I was about eight years old. That would have been the 1948 team that played in the January 1949 Orange Bowl. There wasn't any television; I listened to it on the radio, and it was just real exciting.

A couple of years later—I would have been 10—I sat in the Knothole Sec- tion, which was in the north end zone, and watched the Texas-SMU game when Freddy Benners was the SMU quarterback. He was a passer, and it was the most exciting game I'd seen up to that time.

I went to University Junior High School. I think it's now the UT School of Social Work, but it's the building just south of the stadium. I played foot- ball at UJH, and our football team had a little area down on the south end of what used to be the freshman field where we practiced junior high football. The freshman football team and also the varsity used to practice there. So I got to see the teams and be around them.

In those days, two-a-days started September 1, and we weren't in school yet. I used to hang around two-a-day practices at the old baseball field, Clark

Mike Cotten led his team to a Cotton Bowl victory over Ole Miss and later became a marine who served in Vietnam.

Field. I would sit on the fence and watch and take my camera. I've got a great picture of T Jones—I guess it would have been his senior year. It was a shade-tree break, and he's lying on his back with his head resting on his helmet, and he's got a cup of water. It's a great picture.

I just kind of hung around and followed it and became interested in Texas football. Then I became an athlete myself and started preparing myself to try to get a scholarship to The University.

When I was 13 and 14, I played Pony League baseball. I was fortunate to be picked for a team that was coached by T Jones and Bill MacDonald. Bill probably spent more time with it; T, of course, was the quarterback and ultimately was my coach when I was a quarterback on the freshman Longhorn team. Bill was a center on the same 1952 team that T played on. Bill was a co-captain and became a real big influence on me, personally. He became a lawyer himself, and he's been a very influential person in my life.

I went on to Austin High School and continued to follow Texas. Coach Campbell recruited me, and I didn't visit another campus. I never left Austin. I wasn't interested in seeing other schools because I knew what I wanted to do. I talked to a couple of coaches, but I didn't take any trips. I didn't want to waste anybody's time.

Bobby Nunis was a teammate of mine and was an all-state running back. We announced on the first day we could announce and got it over with because we were both playing baseball.

In those days, Texas still had a freshman team. I played on the freshman team, and T Jones was the assistant coach to Bob Schulze. My first year on varsity was 1959. Coach Royal came to The University in 1957, when I was a senior in high school. And he was 32 years old.

We were 25–5 over three seasons, which was pretty good at that time. Nineteen fifty-six had been a bad year. When Coach Royal came in 1957, they were a very competitive team. That team went to a bowl game; I think they played in the '58 Sugar Bowl. The '59 team played Syracuse in the Cotton Bowl. The 1960 team went to the Bluebonnet Bowl. Then the 1961 team went to the Cotton Bowl as the Southwest Conference champions.

In those days, the Cotton Bowl was the end of the rainbow. That's what you played your season for, to get to the Cotton Bowl.

My most memorable experience was being elected a captain. The team had an election, and Don Talbert and I were elected. I was very proud to be a captain of that team, a Texas team. We were the ones who did the coin flip and we were the ones who led the team on the field. I was very proud of that.

There were two games that were memorable to me. One was our 1961 game against Arkansas, played in Fayetteville. Both of us were 4–0, and Arkansas had a very good team, with Lance Alworth. We had a shaky start. We fumbled either the kickoff or the first play, I can't remember. But they fumbled it right back to us. So we started anew on the 20. Then we proceeded to move the ball up and down the field, making first downs and long drives. It was just a quarterback's dream, or at least a quarterback who played for Coach Royal. I mean, ball control, field position—we had it. We ended up beating them 33–7, and it was the best game that I ever quarterbacked.

The Cotton Bowl game against Ole Miss was a good game. They were a very good team and had some outstanding players, several of whom went to the pros. Coach Royal, as he did on a number of occasions, put in some special plays. And I'm satisfied that those were the plays that helped us defeat Ole Miss.

When I think back, I realize I was just so blessed to be able to play for Coach Royal, a legend. In those days, quarterbacks called their own plays, which is kind of hard to believe. Of course, we didn't have that many plays, so you couldn't miss it by much. But we met with Coach Royal virtually every day—there were three or four of us—during the season to go over field location, down and distance, and what plays to call, given the down and distance. Like second down and six—what are the plays we've got? When you were on the field calling plays, that clicked in. I'm not going to say they didn't run plays in every once in a while, but we had the proper play to call ingrained into our heads. We relied heavily on a power sweep. We didn't throw much until my senior year.

My sophomore year, substitutions were very limited. It was virtually one-platoon football. If you started a quarter and went out, you couldn't come back until the next quarter. As I recall, there were two exceptions. You could freely substitute two people, and we substituted for our quarterback and our offensive fullback. In other words, when the ball changed hands, those positions would either go out or come in, depending on the situation. When we were on defense, I went in for the quarterback. I played safety, which was the position of our quarterback. Don Allen, a linebacker, a defensive specialist, substituted for our fullback. So those two could move freely, but everybody else, if they came out, they couldn't come back in for a while.

I didn't play any more defense after my junior year. My senior year I was strictly an offensive player. They were still going both ways, but the substitution rules were starting to loosen up.

We didn't do any off-season training. And as I recall spring training, you had 30 days to get 20 workouts in. It was a more compact deal than it is now. Spring training was a pretty good workout. My junior year was not a satisfactory year. Our team lost three games, and that was just totally unsatisfactory. So in preparation for our senior year, we had a hard spring training. That senior group worked extremely hard, and it paid off. We came back in September 1961, ready to go.

The first thing about being a Longhorn is just the experience of being part of that team. You come together as freshmen, from different areas and backgrounds. You come together for the purpose of playing hard and winning and representing the school. You befriend athletes in other sports and you pull for them because they're also representing you. Beyond your own class, the four years you were involved yourself, you become part of the tradition that preceded you. Texas has a very rich tradition in athletics and in academics. You want to follow that tradition, and you want to lay the groundwork for those who will follow you.

Now I'm a fan. I'm one of thousands of fans who are Longhorns, who never played, but who support the team and love the school.

Mike Cotten was the quarterback of the 1961 team, widely regarded as one of the best Darrell Royal teams in history. Cotten was an All–Southwest Conference selection, and he also was the MVP of Royal's first bowl win, a 12–7 triumph over Ole Miss in the 1962 Cotton Bowl. He is a member of the Longhorn Hall of Honor.

BOBBY MOSES

END

1959–1961

WHEN YOU LOOK BACK OVER THE YEARS of Texas football, particularly over those early years of Coach Royal, when I played, you'll get a lot of different perspectives. When Mack Brown came to Texas in 1998, and they were looking for someone to help with contributions, I agreed to have my name on the Trophy Room in Moncrief-Neuhaus, the football building, with one stipulation: I wanted to share that space with Mike Campbell because I wanted to recognize how close together and of one mind that Darrell Royal and Mike Campbell were. Mike, of course, was Darrell's longtime assistant.

A long time ago, I was playing golf at the El Dorado Country Club in Palm Springs, California, with three legendary coaches, John McKay, Chuck Knox, and Colonel Earl Blaik. It was after Coach Royal had retired, and they all wanted to know how Coach was doing. And then they wanted to know how Mike Campbell was doing.

I told them, and after a while as we sat and visited after our round, I asked them, "What kind of coach, in y'all's opinion, was Mike Campbell?" McKay and Knox both answered, "Mike Campbell was the greatest defensive mind of our era."

And when I look back on my life, I realize what an impact he had on me. I had come to Texas the long way. I was born in Houston, but my dad had

Bobby Moses was named the outstanding defensive player in the 1962 Cotton Bowl win over Ole Miss.

gone to a boarding school called Deerfield Academy in Deerfield, Massachusetts, so that's where I went to high school. I had enjoyed some success on the football field, and I had always wanted to come back to Texas and play football if it was possible. Fortunately for me, I had some speed, and Coach Royal was always very, very big on speed.

When I arrived on campus, we had 70 scholarship freshmen. Today, they have a maximum of 25. That was in 1958. And I guess I got an early answer to the question of what it means to be a Longhorn a couple of years later.

In 1960 we were playing at Maryland in our second game of the season. Our team was staying at the DuPont Plaza Hotel in Washington. At our team dinner on Friday night before the game, Coach Royal always invited special guests. Our two guests were Lyndon Johnson, who was the majority leader of the U.S. Senate and a candidate for vice president, and Sam Rayburn, who was the powerful speaker of the House of Representatives. Both of those gentlemen impressed on us the importance of representing our state.

It was a powerful evening, and Coach Royal impressed on each of us that we had a responsibility in the game. He told us to choose somebody on the other team tomorrow and kick his butt. The next day, when the referee was ready to mark the ball for the first snap of the game, my friend Ed Padgett, who was one of our tackles, stood up and pointed to the guy across the line from him and said, "I have chosen you for today, and after this game, if you haven't had enough, we'll get on the goal line and finish it up."

We won 34–0.

I was fortunate to be at Texas with some extraordinary people. The class I came in with won two Southwest Conference championships and finished with the 1961 team, which many people think was Coach Royal's best team. At the beginning of the year, nobody realized how quick the team was, but we wound up winning every game except the TCU game. It takes a lot of good things and a lot of good football players to make things like that happen, and you can also lose it on a freak bounce of the ball. TCU crossed the 50 one time and scored; we were inside their 10-yard line six times but couldn't score. That's when you really appreciate Coach Royal, because as hard as that loss was, he was able to show us how to hold our heads up and go on. "That's football," is what he taught us.

After that game, we went on and won the Southwest Conference, and we played in the 1962 Cotton Bowl game against a highly thought of Ole Miss team. After the 1957 season, Texas had played Ole Miss in the 1958 Sugar Bowl, and Ole Miss had won decisively, 39–7. In 1960 we had played Alabama in the Bluebonnet Bowl, and it brought together two good friends, Coach Royal and Bear Bryant. We tied 3–3. That was the closest Bear ever came to beating Darrell. A Bear Bryant–coached team, whether it was at Texas A&M or Alabama, never beat a Darrell Royal–coached team.

Ole Miss was a really good team in 1961, and it was a close game, and I guess I was fortunate. I always had a very wonderful teacher in Mike Campbell, and through the years we did become great personal friends. We were leading 12–7, and Ole Miss had a fourth-down play on about our 3- or 4-yard line. They had about a yard and a half to go to make a first down, and they came around my side. Somehow, I slipped a block and tackled the quarterback to prevent them from making it. The media said that was the play of the game. They gave me way too much credit and voted me the outstanding defensive player of the game.

I learned a valuable lesson that day. Before the game, Coach Royal gathered all of us—the defensive ends, linebackers, and defensive backs—and said, "The last time we played these guys, it was a track meet, and we lost every race. I know they don't have one person who can outrun you guys, so I don't expect to see you lose one race today." Coach Campbell was standing right beside him, and he started talking in that Southern drawl of his.

"Now forget everything that we ever taught you, and just play football," he said.

That was a lesson about life. You can't go through life trying to do everything somebody teaches you. Pretty soon, you have to take over and take care of yourself. Those things that you have been taught become part of your instincts. As I look back as I get older and older, I realize that Coach Royal had a corporate structure in a lot of areas. He was the first fellow to hire a "brain coach" in Lan Hewlett, who was our academic counselor. He realized that it was one thing to recruit the best, but if you didn't keep them in school, it didn't do any good. Lan Hewlett was there to make sure we got the right instructions from tutors and also to go to class. The next thing I noticed was that Coach Royal was the ultimate manager. He was kind of like the conductor of the train. He had Coach Campbell running the defense and a bunch of really good coaches in charge of different sections. Coach Royal just oversaw. He did not come down and try to take over their positions, he managed to make sure everybody was doing his best and doing it the right way with the best assets he needed to do his job. The corporate world works that way. You have the guy who's running the program, and everybody has to do their job and come together to work as a team.

A Longhorn is a lot of different things. You know you are playing for The University and the state of Texas. You have a tremendous amount of alumni who care what you do, and at that age, you sometimes don't realize it. When I came back to Texas to play, I knew that if I was willing to help myself, they would help me. To be a Longhorn is being in that moment when you are a player, but it is also what you gain after you leave school that you can build on. The guys whom I played with are still my friends today, and no matter what we've done since we've been in school and no matter what each one has accomplished, we're still friends and still remember how we were. We played with poise and charisma and we beat a lot of teams before we ever came out of the locker room by just being who we were.

Bobby Moses was named the outstanding defensive player in the 1962 Cotton Bowl game victory over Ole Miss, helping Darrell Royal to his first bowl victory as a Longhorn coach. He was a consensus All–Southwest Conference selection in 1961, when he led the Texas team with 14 receptions, five of which went for touchdowns. He is a member of the Longhorn Hall of Honor.

JAMES SAXTON

RUNNING BACK

1959–1961

FOR THE RECORD, I'D LIKE TO GET ONE THING STRAIGHT: I did not chase jackrabbits. But I did catch cottontails.

Obviously, there is a difference. They say jackrabbits can run about 50 miles an hour. The little cottontails scoot, but they don't fly. At any rate, that part of the story is true. I was working on a ranch in the summer near Kaufman. I was mowing alfalfa, and the rabbits were running everywhere. I kept watching them, and they were running in circles. So I just stopped my tractor and got off and cut through the circle and caught one. I told a friend about it, and he didn't believe me. So a guy from the local paper came out to see if I could catch another one, and I did.

I kept doing that until I cut my finger badly on a mower blade, and that was the end of chasing rabbits. But by the time the story grew, they had me chasing jackrabbits all over Texas.

I came to Texas in 1958, Darrell Royal's second season. He was the only reason that I came to Texas. When I went on my first recruiting visit, he made me feel like I was the greatest thing that ever walked. I weighed 145 pounds as a running back in Palestine High School in East Texas.

Coach Royal told me that he wanted me to be a running quarterback. I had never played quarterback in my life, but he had a way of making you believe him. I told him I had never played the position, but he said, "Don't worry, I'll teach you the position."

National Football Foundation Hall of Famer James Saxton still holds the Texas record for yards per carry in a season.

The two things I remember most about my recruiting visit were Coach Royal and the fact that they took me to Hill's Café and I had a Big Sizzler steak. But the quarterback thing was the big talk of the school when I got back home. It was interesting. I was born in College Station. Texas A&M recruited me but didn't offer me a scholarship. I committed to Texas but had not visited anywhere else. When I got back home, someone from Rice was talking to me every day.

Carol Ann, who was my girlfriend and would eventually become my wife, was going to SMU. My mother had raised me, and I was getting pressure from my mother and my aunt, wanting to know why I was so set on going to Texas. Everybody was telling me, "They say they want you to play quarterback, and you're not going to play quarterback at Texas." I kept listening to them, and they were saying either Coach was crazy, or he didn't know what he was doing. So I was ready to de-commit. Finally, I got enough guts to tell Coach Royal I wasn't coming.

"James," he said, "I'm coming through Palestine, and I want to talk to you. I don't want to talk to your mother, your sister, your aunt…none of the women in your family."

Sure enough, he drove up to Palestine with Jack Swarthout, who was recruiting that area. Swarthout was one of his young assistants. He would go on to coach many years as the head coach at the University of Montana. The two coaches came to the door, and I sat down with them.

"James," said Coach Royal, "I told you I would give you an opportunity to play quarterback and I still mean that. We want you there, and you are going to play quarterback, and we want you there."

I said, "Yes, sir. Let's go."

My mom had raised me the best she could, but I didn't have a manly touch to what I was doing. Coach Royal became that male influence in my life. He and I just hit it off. He was my mentor for four years. So the first day of practice my freshman year in 1958, Coach came over to me on the first play and said, "James, I made you a commitment. Now, the first thing you've got to do is to learn to take a snap."

It sounds funny now, but I remember being really tentative when I walked up behind the center and stuck my hands between his legs to receive the snap. You can imagine how that felt to a teenage boy who had never even thought about that. But I learned to do it, and I learned to play quarterback my freshman year.

Outside of football, things were going pretty well. Ma Griff, the lady who ran the dining hall, was cooking meals that were good, and I was putting on weight. I think I got up to a rousing 165 pounds by my senior year. And we were doing some exciting things on the field. As a sophomore, I played with Mike Cotten behind Bobby Lackey, and we tied for the Southwest Conference championship. We were running the wing T formation, and I was exactly what Coach had promised. I was a running quarterback.

In fact, I ran so much I almost had the most embarrassing moment of my life at the Oklahoma game in Dallas. My freshman year I had been bruised a little, so I wore a corset under my uniform. I was in on a series, and we kept moving the ball. The corset was slipping. I kept looking to the sideline, but Coach wouldn't take me out. When we were learning new plays, Coach Royal would say, "This is a new pass play, but James, when you are in the game, don't call it." So I finally got out of the game by throwing a pass that went out of bounds.

Now, here I was, in the middle of the Cotton Bowl, with the corset down around my knees. The only way to fix it was to take off my entire uniform. I had to take my clothes off in front of 70,000 people. So a couple of the managers got some blankets and held them up around me so I could change clothes. All the time, I kept imagining what was going to happen if somebody came out of bounds and ran into the blankets. But fortunately, that didn't happen.

Jack Collins had an outstanding year as our halfback our sophomore year, so you can imagine my shock when Coach Royal called me in and told me he was moving me back to running back. We had Jack, Jerry Cook, Tommy Ford, and several other runners. I never dreamed they would make that change.

"Look," Coach said, "I have a guy in you sitting on the bench who is averaging nine yards a carry. I'd be stupid to leave you there."

So he moved Jack to wingback and moved me to running back. By our senior season in 1961, we had one of the most productive offenses in the country. But it wasn't about me, it was about Jack Collins. My senior year I had a lot of long runs, and on every one of them—you can look at the film— Jack threw the key block. He was at the line of scrimmage, he was downfield. When I think of what Jack sacrificed for me—he should have been an All-American, and all of the things that have happened in my life because of athletics should have happened to him. That's what he did for our team, and I was the beneficiary of it.

A lot of people who have watched Texas football for a long time believe that our 1961 team was one of the best ever. We were No. 1 in the country, and a national championship was a realistic goal. We had two games left, against TCU and Texas A&M. My cousin had been a track star at TCU, and before the game he called me and gave me a warning.

"Jamie," he said, "there's a bounty out on your head among the TCU players, and they are going to knock you out of the game." I thought he was kidding. "I'm just telling you," he said.

Early in the game, I had broken free for a 45-yard run down to the TCU 10-yard line, and as I was getting up, a TCU player came across and hit me in the head with his knee. That was the last thing I remembered until I woke up in the third quarter, and my cousin was sitting beside me on the bench.

"You SOB," he said. "I told you they were gonna get you."

We struggled the rest of the way. They crossed the 50-yard line one time, on a flea-flicker pass that went for a score, and won the game 6–0. It seemed impossible to believe that the best team of its era, the No. 1 team in the nation, and a team leading the country in both offense and defense, was beaten by a team with a losing record. But it happened.

As for me, I was blessed. I didn't know what the Heisman Trophy was when I was playing at Texas, and by my senior year I was one of the finalists for it. I made All-American, and one of the great thrills of my life came several years ago when I went to the mailbox and found a letter from the National Football Foundation, telling me that I had been named to the College Football Hall of Fame.

The Texas Cowboys, a service organization on campus, has a motto that says, "Give the best to Texas, and the best will come back to you." I gave everything I had, and it has kept following me through my life. In football, in business, in parenting. To be a part of an organization that had such a presence in athletics and dignity in everything—it has been an honor to be part of that endeavor.

James Saxton, Darrell Royal once said, was like turning loose a balloon and watching it dart about. But in 1961 he ran, as they say, "north and south." He was a consensus All-American, averaging 7.9 yards per rushing attempt his senior season. He finished third in the Heisman voting, and has been named to the National Football Foundation's College Hall of Fame and the Longhorn Hall of Honor.

DON TALBERT

TACKLE

1959–1961

WE HAVE A WONDERFUL TALBERT TRADITION, and one of the things we are the proudest of is the Talbert legacy. Coach Royal, fortunately or unfortunately, had a Talbert in his program for 10 of the 20 years that he coached.

It started with me, then Charlie came along. He was as good an athlete as ever played in Texas City High School, and in the state of Texas for that matter. Then Diron followed, and he was a bull in a china closet. He killed everybody.

We were transplanted Texans. We were born in Mississippi, and then we traveled around some and wound up down at Texas City. We were all big, and there were none of us boys—there were four of us—who were scared to take that last biscuit off the table. We didn't really know a lot about The University of Texas, or the rivalries between Texas and Texas A&M and Oklahoma.

I was a sophomore when we moved to Texas City, and my senior year we moved up from Class AAA to Class AAAA, which was the largest in the state. We played Galena Park, Baytown, and Baytown Lee, and a lot of guys from there went to UT. In those days, they had, like, 125 scholarships, and whoever quit, left, or got run off could be replaced with another player. My freshman year was Coach Royal's first year. I was playing spring ball in high school, and right then you couldn't sign with anybody. Coach Bob Schulze had been around, and I really didn't know whether they were offering me a scholarship or not. I was a big kid, and they had offered me a half of a scholarship to play basketball down at Lamar Tech. They told me they'd filled up all the scholarships at Texas, and I didn't think I was going to get one. So I decided I'd go to a junior college and see if I could work my way into getting into a big school.

One Friday night—I remember it very well—I was filling up the old family car, and I was going to drive up to Tyler Junior College to try to get a scholarship with Coach Wagstaff there. I got a phone call about 6:00, and it was Coach Schulze. He said, "What are you doing, Don?" I told him, "I got the old car ready, and I'm leaving early in the morning to go to Tyler to talk to Coach [Floyd] Wagstaff." He said, "Why don't you go in to your coach, get the film of the best game you played, bypass Tyler, and drive to Austin?" He said to try and be there by 10:00. So I got a film of our Spring Branch game, and I got Ed Padgett to go with me. I drove down old highway 71, and when we got to Austin, we went to Gregory Gym. That's when I first met Coach Campbell, Coach Shira, and Coach Pittman. They were all sitting on the steps outside Gregory Gym. They took the film and went in to see Coach Royal. They told me to go have lunch at the chow hall with the guys.

The coaches came in, and Coach Schulze told me Coach Royal wanted to see me in his office at 1:00. So I walked over to his office and walked in. There was Darrell. He looked like he was young enough to play with us. He asked me what I really thought of The University of Texas. I said, "Oh, Coach, that would be great…I'd love to play here." He told me he had looked at the film, and that I looked like a pretty tough, competitive kid, and that I did well in the game. He offered me a one-year, or day-to-day, scholarship. He told me that as long as I could play, I could stay at The University of Texas. So it was pretty impressive for me. I was real excited.

Then he said, "Let me ask you something…you ever have any relatives in Lewisville, Mississippi?" I said, "Yeah." He said, "Did you ever have a cousin named Birddog Franklin Talbert? I coached Franklin, ol' Birddog, at Mississippi State. He was a pretty good competitor. I hope you're cut out of the same mold as him." I said, "Coach, I'll do everything I can to keep my scholarship, and do whatever it takes to get the job done." The Darrell Royal era had kicked off, and the Talbert tradition had begun. I broke my leg and missed a year, but that wound up leading to one of my highlights because it allowed me to be a captain on the 1961 team, and that was Coach Royal's real kickoff

Don Talbert and his rugged brothers, Charlie and Diron, became Longhorn folk legends, once causing a local tavern to post a sign that read, "No Shoes, No Shirts, No Talberts."

team. That year, I was lucky enough to make a couple of All-America teams, and that gave me the chance to go on to play a few years in the pros.

Between the three of us brothers, we were at Texas from 1957 through 1966. As you look at the result, the Talberts never lost to OU, and we never lost to A&M in our varsity years at Texas. We were lucky, and we were happy for what our legacy was at The University of Texas, and what the Talbert tradition is. At the time Coach Royal got there, everybody in the Southwest Conference wanted to beat Texas. They had had some great teams and great tradition in the past, but when Darrell got there and the Darrell Royal era started, Texas football changed. In his regime he won three national championships. I was lucky that I was a guy who helped start that era. I'm happy for that, along with all of my teammates—the Saxtons, the Cottens, the Collinses, the Padgetts. We made Coach Royal the Coach of the Year in 1961. We were just one game away from being national champions. All the guys who were sophomores that year made him Coach of the Year and won the national championship in 1963. Texas football was on its way.

As I got back in the pros, there were a lot of guys who said, "Hey, man, I sure would have liked to play for ol' Darrell." I told them, "You might have wished you'd played for him, but your ass would have had to get in high gear to do that."

I think most folks would say that the Talbert brothers haven't changed a bit since they played at Texas. We loved helping start that era, and what we have left as a legacy is that we have a "Varmint Brothers Association" that was created through some of the tricks and BS that we've pulled through the years. You have to have the complete endorsement of the three brothers to get in. All three of the Talberts have to vote, and there is no election on a split vote.

Each year, we have a get-together out at a secluded place in West Texas, and we invite guys to come out as prospective Varmints. So far, we only have 10 members of the Varmint Brothers Association: that's my dad, Slim Talbert; Coach Royal; Mike Ditka; Tommy Nobis, a good friend of ours named Ken Bailey; Ed Padgett; David McWilliams; Charlie and Diron Talbert; and me. So the group's pretty limited.

We almost lost Mike Ditka on one trip when we put a live jackrabbit in his bed. It hadn't been shot. We caught it in some headlights one night down on Governor Dolph Briscoe's ranch. They were down there playing cards and carrying on, and Ditka was raising hell with everybody. So I went in and got the rabbit and tied its legs together and put in his bed, right between the pillows. Mike had had a few snorts, and he came in and laid his head down on that rabbit, and he thought it was a rat. You could have heard him holler all the way to Mexico City. The group's pretty limited, but we still have a lot of potential Varmints, and we have a lot of associate guys who are still under critique.

We've had great fun, and all of the coaches—Campbell, Shira, Pittman, and Schulze—were unbelievable. Coach Royal had guys who got the job done. You just didn't waddle around out there on Darrell Royal's football team. You came to hit, to run, to win games.

The Talberts touched a lot of years of Texas football, and we've carried on the fight. We don't back down from no Aggies, but we have some good friends who are Aggies. John David Crow is a great guy, and Jack Pardee was Diron's best man in his wedding. We know what their tradition is and what it means to beat the Aggies. The same is true with the OU guys. We've got friends from Oklahoma.

What does it mean to be a Longhorn? Aside from the Talbert legacy, we think we started something. Not many guys get a chance to play for the guy whom the stadium is named after. And what it really means to us was to take it to the level it was, and where it stayed, and continues to stay in the Mack Brown era.

Don Talbert was the first of the three Talbert brothers to play at Texas. He was named All-American and All-SWC in 1961 and served as a co-captain on a team that employed the "flip-flop" offense, where the linemen switched sides based on where the wingback lined up. He played eight seasons in the NFL and is a member of the Longhorn Hall of Honor.

DUKE CARLISLE

QUARTERBACK
1961–1963

I'LL NEVER FORGET BILL ELLINGTON, because if it hadn't been for him, I might never have been a Texas Longhorn.

When I was in high school in the late 1950s, Oklahoma was coming to the end of their 47-game winning streak. They had a quarterback from Texas, and Bud Wilkinson was one of the top coaches in the country. I started following Oklahoma during that winning streak, and because of their success, I became a fan. Besides, there was a guy from my hometown of Athens, Texas, who was two years ahead of me who had picked Oklahoma over all the schools that recruited him.

I met Eddie Crowder, who had been a quarterback at Oklahoma in the early 1950s. He would later be the head coach at Colorado, but at that time he was recruiting our area for the Sooners. He was a nice guy and stayed in touch as I went through high school. I became more and more convinced that Oklahoma was probably where I wanted to go. In those days, I had a chance to go to the Texas-Oklahoma game in Dallas pretty regularly, and in 1958, I was at the game and saw Texas upset Oklahoma. Then, when I was a senior in the fall of 1959, Texas beat Oklahoma again, and this time it wasn't an upset. They just beat them because they were the better team.

That spring, the coach who recruited my area for Texas was Coach Ellington. He was a really good guy and a fine person. He was kind and patient, and he spent time with my parents, and they got to know him. Everybody thought a lot of him. And he caused me to rethink this thing.

I only had one visit, one-on-one, with Coach Royal, but that was enough. It was in the spring of my senior year, in his office in Gregory Gym on the UT campus. He asked me where I was thinking about going, and I said, "Well, one of the schools I have thought about a lot over the recent years is Oklahoma." And he said, "I can tell you that we've beaten them the

Duke Carlisle (No. 11) led Texas to an unbeaten season and its first national championship in 1963.

last couple of years, and I feel confident that we're going to be winning on a regular basis from now on. I've got some good football players in here, and there's a good class coming in that you'd be a part of who are going to be good players, and we're going to do well."

I had been around Coach Wilkinson a couple of times, and he was a likeable guy, but the way Coach Royal said that that day, I walked out of Gregory Gym thinking, *You know, I really think this is going to be the place to win football games.* I talked to Coach Ellington after that and committed to Texas.

Sure enough, when I got there in the fall, there were a lot of good players in the group they had recruited that year. Scarily, it included five other quarterbacks. We had a good freshman year and won all our games, and it turns out he was right about the players who were already there because they were outstanding. The guys who followed were, too. Because of that and the good coaches that he had, we did, in fact, win just about all of our games.

In fact, it is amazing to think how close we came to winning four consecutive national championships. In 1961 we lost to TCU 6–0, and that was our only defeat. The 1962 team was probably the weakest of the four, but it had been No. 1 in the country, and only a 14–14 tie with Rice kept it from winning it all. In 1963 we were the national champions. And in 1964 only a failed two-point conversion in a 14–13 loss to Arkansas kept them from winning another.

People ask me what my biggest thrill was, and obviously, it was all of that success, including when we were seniors winning the school's first national championship. The games people remember the most positively from that season are the Oklahoma game, the Baylor game, and the Navy game in the Cotton Bowl.

Early in the season, we were playing Texas Tech in a night game on the day that Oklahoma had played Southern Cal, which was the defending national champion. Oklahoma pretty well overwhelmed them, and it was no fluke. I remember watching the game and being worried because Oklahoma definitely had the better team. I remember we were all thinking that we had our work cut out for us because they had an enormous amount of talent.

When we played them, they'd moved up to No. 1, and we were No. 2, so it was a huge game in the country that year. We knew it would be a hard road if we lost to get back to that spot. So everybody was as excited and ready to play as you could possibly be. Things went well for us that day. We got some breaks and took advantage of them, and everybody played hard. It ended up being a game that wasn't close. We won 28–7. I don't know that we covered the betting line in any other game, but we did that day.

We had moved to No. 1, and we were moving along. Baylor had maybe the most high-powered offense in the country, and they were also a good defensive team. With Don Trull at quarterback and Lawrence Elkins as a receiver, they were an excellent club. We had some chances to score some points but didn't, and then we scored a touchdown. It was 7–0, and it appeared we were going to close them out with a first down inside their 15 with not much time left. But we fumbled, they started a drive, and in the course of two minutes, they moved down the field to our 20.

Coach Mike Campbell was in the press box, and after we fumbled, he suggested to Coach Royal that I stay in the game at safety. It was probably just a hunch. It was interesting because Jim Hudson had had a fabulous game and a fabulous year. And I am convinced that the result would have been the same if he had been in there. Joe Dixon, our halfback, always kidded that I saved him on the play, but Joe played it exactly right. He was on Elkins and he had to protect the outside. He was supposed to get help inside, and I was fortunate enough to be there and intercept the ball. It was the only defensive series I played all year.

Through the years, that interception has gone down as one of the great plays in Texas history, and I have tried to point out that it is remembered because it happened in the last seconds in a low-scoring game that was 7–0. The most impressive thing about that game was our defense held that offense scoreless. No one else came close to doing that.

The same was true of the Navy game in the Cotton Bowl. We had already been declared national champions because the bowls didn't count in the final poll then. But it was a thing of pride. It wouldn't have been much consolation if we had lost the game and tried to say we were No. 1, anyway. We had had a poor game against Texas A&M, and a lot of the Eastern press had criticized us. So with all of that, we were a little more excited than we might have been for a bowl game. We played like we had against Oklahoma, and won 28–6. Interestingly, the two games that were not close that season were the games that involved a No. 1 and No. 2 match-up.

Again, our defense held Navy and Roger Staubach without a touchdown. It is true that Coach Ellington or someone had picked up Navy's defensive signals, but they were easy to figure out. It was like Coach Royal said, their signals looked like a guy on an aircraft carrier signaling for planes to come in. Still, it wasn't about the touchdowns we scored, it was about the points they didn't.

Coach Ellington and his family continued to be a major part of my life, as did a guy from my hometown, Frank Denius. My family had known Frank's family in Athens, and when I got to Texas, he and his wife fed me Sunday dinner nearly every week, and we have maintained that friendship all of these years.

Looking back, playing with the guys I played with and being a part of that experience, I was lucky. Timing is everything. It was, in fact, the time to be headed to that school—not the only time, but certainly one of the very best times, because you couldn't have asked for things to work out better. It ended up being a great place to get an education. I got both my BBA and my MBA there and met a lot of great professors and a lot of other students who have become lifelong friends. The whole experience was great. It's hard to know, particularly when you're 18 years old and making a decision like that. But it's been fun to be a part of the organization since then and to continue to support the teams in all sports nearly 50 years later.

Duke Carlisle quarterbacked the Longhorns to their first national championship in 1963. He was part of a three-year record of 30–2–1 from 1961 through 1963. He was an Academic All-American who was chosen to the Longhorn Hall of Honor in 1979 and the Cotton Bowl Hall of Fame in 2000.

DAVID McWILLIAMS

CENTER

1961–1963

UNTIL MY SENIOR YEAR AT CLEBURNE HIGH SCHOOL, I hadn't planned to go to college due to a lack of finances. I'd planned to graduate from high school, join the military for two years, come back and work for the Santa Fe Railroad shops in Cleburne, and set my trot lines for catfish in an area called Goat Neck on the Brazos River. There were plenty of fish, rabbits, squirrels, and homemade stills to supplement your income.

I was surprised when colleges started offering me football scholarships. No one on either side of my family had ever graduated from college, so I had no favorites.

I started contact football in the fourth grade, and for eight years in Cleburne our team had won approximately 95 percent of our games. In my senior year we were state co-champs with a 20–20 tie against an Emory Bellard–coached Breckenridge, Texas, Buckaroos team.

I had two criteria when I was a choosing a university: the program had to have a winning tradition where I had a chance to be on a national championship team, and the academics had to be strong.

I made several campus visits and had narrowed my choices to Texas and Oklahoma. Both had winning football programs and both were tops in Petroleum Engineering, which I had thought would be my major. I knew that it would be easier for my parents to see me play at Texas than it would be at Oklahoma. The academics at Texas had an excellent reputation and, being from Texas, I felt the job opportunities would be good with a degree from UT. Lastly, I chose Texas because of Coach Darrell Royal, Coach Mike Campbell, Coach Jim Pittman, and Pat Culpepper.

On December 27, 1963, I was up in the "T" Room when Coach Royal walked in. I could tell by the expression on his face that something was wrong. He walked straight over to me, and I asked him, "Is it my mother, my dad, or my brother?" He said, "You need to call your dad," so I called him from the "T" Room. He told me that my mother had had a severe stroke and was in a coma.

Coach Royal had already arranged for a private plane (John Holmes's plane out of Houston) to fly me to Cleburne. My dad picked me up at the airport, and I got to see my mother, but the doctor said she had no chance of recovery. Dad said he and my mother had agreed that if this should happen to either of them, they would "pull the plug," or not leave the other on life support. So, at age 46, my mother was gone. One of the many thoughts battling my emotions was whether I should play in the Cotton Bowl on January 1, 1964, against Navy. Coach Royal had told me it was my decision and he would support me either way.

My mother loved football, and I felt she would want me to play. I knew she would have the best seat in the stadium. It was one of the best decisions I ever made.

I played offensive guard and linebacker in 1961, and I remember in the TCU game pulling outside the block for quarterback Mike Cotten on a bootleg pass/run. I turned back inside to block a TCU defensive player—which is not what I was supposed to do—and the outside man forced Mike to throw the ball incomplete. We went on to lose 6–0, and we dropped from the No. 1 national ranking.

After the game, Tommy Ford, Scott Appleton, and I told our parents we did not feel like going out with them that night. We sat on the steps outside Moore-Hill Hall, and we made a pact that we would do everything we could to win the national championship before we left. I truly believe this is why we did win it in 1963.

We had been so close to winning it all in 1961, and we were ranked No. 1 in 1962 until we had a tie game. Our seniors were determined to win the national championship in 1963. All throughout the summer, Captains Scott Appleton, Tommy Ford, and I wrote our teammates, telling them to be sure to work out, to report in shape, and to be ready to play every week in every

David McWilliams was a tri-captain on the 1963 national championship team and later served as both an assistant and head coach at Texas.

game. At halftime of our A&M game, we were trailing. The halftime pep talk was calm and decisive and was led not by the coaches but by the seniors. Our talk in the huddle was, "We will not lose it again," and we didn't. Thank you, 1964 seniors.

I'm really proud of the fact that the freshman squad of 1960, during their four years at The University, posted a record of 35–2–1 and had a graduation rate close to 90 percent.

My mother's dream was that I would get a college degree, and my dream was to accomplish this for her. Walking across the stage in May of 1964 to accept my diploma—a BA with honors in mathematics—and knowing she was not there to see it was another real "gut check" for me, my dad, Dennis, and my brother, Barry.

Once you attend The University of Texas, you are truly a "Longhorn for Life." As I look back, I realize that Longhorn football has helped mold every aspect of my life since 1960.

One of the greatest lessons Coach Royal taught us from the first day we walked on campus was that the lessons we learned that would help us be successful in athletics would also help us in our academic and personal lives.

The lessons I learned didn't come only from winning but came mainly from the pride instilled in us by our coaches and by the great traditions created by those Longhorn players before me. I learned I had a responsibility to live up to the motto, "The pride and winning tradition of the Texas Longhorns will not be entrusted to the timid or weak." How valuable this was, and later on I made sure that our children learned the same thing about the McWilliams family name. I learned self-confidence and how to compete in a fair and honest way.

I was given a great academic education that also included discipline, hard work, and teamwork. Even today I can hear Coach Royal demand, "Don't bitch at the officials." I gained mental toughness to help handle the tough times in my life as well as a "gut check" toughness to deal with the really serious problems I would later face.

My favorite saying of Coach Royal's is probably, "What I gave today, I have. What I kept today, I lost."

The Texas Longhorns gave me everything they had every day, and I try to make sure every day that I give it to others so I don't lose it.

David McWilliams has served The University of Texas in various capacities of Longhorn football for almost 50 years. He was the center and tri-captain of the 1963 national champions, returned in 1970 as an assistant coach, and served as head coach from 1987 through 1991. He is a member of the Longhorn Hall of Honor and serves the athletics department as head of the Longhorn Letter Winners' Association.

TOMMY NOBIS

LINEBACKER

1963–1965

PEOPLE ASK ME HOW I GOT TO TEXAS. Highway 35 was a two-lane road when I made my first trip up there. Now it's an interstate highway. Times have changed.

I was very fortunate my senior year at Thomas Jefferson High School in San Antonio that I had a good season. I caught the eyes of several major colleges in the area, including The University of Texas.

I did get recruited by Oklahoma. I was very fond of their coach, Bud Wilkinson. He had a pretty good track record of putting out some young men who went on to be pretty good coaches, and early on I had thought about wanting to be a coach. Some guys wanted to be a conductor on a train, or fly a plane, or be a carpenter and build a house. But my thing was I wanted to stay in sports and coaching.

I really had a lot of admiration for Coach Wilkinson, and the OU program was winning a lot of games. But you know, when you cross that Red River and go into Oklahoma, it's different. When I started hearing people say negative things about not just The University of Texas but the state of Texas, I couldn't handle that. I don't know how they got so many Texas boys, and they still do, to go there when the attitude is what it is about the state of Texas. It's amazing that a kid coming out of Texas would go to Oklahoma with some of the things that they say about our great state. And I didn't want

Linebacker Tommy Nobis (No. 60) is recognized as perhaps the greatest defensive player in school history.

to put up with it. I knew I belonged somewhere back in Texas, and of course, I was leaning all the way toward the school in Austin.

Charley Shira had the San Antonio recruiting area, and people who knew Coach Shira knew he was a likable, great man. To me, he was like Hoss Cartwright, that big ole character from *Bonanza* on TV. He was a quiet guy who walked with a big stick, and he really had a lot of respect from everybody once they met him and found out what he was all about.

They didn't have any limits in scholarships, but they probably had more people than they needed when I was coming out of high school. I was probably one of those who if they didn't get, it wasn't any big deal. Coach Shira was bringing Coach Royal to visit, and that was a big thing for my parents, to have Coach Darrell Royal come and visit our house. My mother cleaned the house for a couple of days to get ready. I had to help her. I guess that's why I remember it. But we got the house all cleaned up for the coach to come in.

Basically, what he told us was that there was a scholarship up there, and they'd like to see me consider coming to UT. He said he knew there were a couple of others I was considering, and if I chose to go there, they'd wish me the best. I knew The University of Texas was going to continue on with an outstanding program without me, but it made me feel good that I did get an invite, and I certainly made the right decision when I did get the invite.

89

What I noticed when I got to Texas was the good-looking women. Now, anybody who played in that era of the '60s and '70s knows that the academics were tough, so it was hard just trying to stay eligible and pass your work. The game plan the coaches had to keep us on point was to keep us busy, and they certainly did that. We had football, trying to keep up with your school work, and occasionally going out. We did find time to have a good time, though. It was demanding trying to hold your position and staying eligible, and I worked pretty hard at each.

We won a national championship my sophomore year of 1963 and lost a one-point game to Arkansas that cost us another in 1964. I guess my biggest memories are the true excitement of game day in Memorial Stadium—to stand out in that stadium at the start of the game, with the people standing up and singing "The Eyes of Texas." I will remember those afternoons forever. It was a big motivator, and the whole scene kind of put things in perspective. You felt like you were not only playing for yourself and your teammates, but it gave you the feeling that you were playing for a lot of people. That song got me going.

I was really fortunate to play in two of the greatest bowl games in our school history, and both had particular meaning. In 1963 we had already won a national championship when we went into the Cotton Bowl, but there were a lot of media people and fans in the East who favored Navy. I was a sophomore, but I still remember the tradition of playing an academy and its being such a big game. We had Scott Appleton, and they had Roger Staubach, and they were two of the most famous players of the time. It was a big, big football game back in that era, and we won handily 28–6.

Then, after my junior year, we played Alabama in the first Orange Bowl night game. For me, that game was special because of what I was thinking of doing with my life, and at that time, I was thinking about coaching. Two of the greatest coaches who had ever been in the college game, Bear Bryant and Darrell Royal, were coaching, and just to be a part of that was special. You had two great universities, where football meant so much to the alumni, the students, and the faculty. When you put those two teams out in the arena, you have all of those factors—the history, the tradition, the popularity— going. You could feel that.

Everybody remembers our stop of Joe Namath at the goal line to preserve the win, but as a player, it didn't make any difference if Joe Namath or somebody else was the quarterback. We were excited about playing that football game. When I think about having played against Roger and Joe, I realize what we accomplished. We played against two NFL and College Hall of Famers, and won both games. Then when I went to the NFL, I was suddenly playing against pros like Johnny Unitas, Bart Starr, and John Brodie. That was the era of guys I grew up watching, and all of a sudden, I was playing against them.

Going into my senior year in 1965, we kind of started out on the same path we'd been going down. To that point, we had lost one football game in my three years. We beat Oklahoma and seemed headed to a pretty good year. But things turned around at Arkansas. We fell behind 20–0, then came back to take the lead, only to have them overtake us 27–24. The game was real close. We had played them so well. It was hard to understand. I was a senior and I was supposed to be a leader.

I will never forget that year. I learned then that you should never take anything for granted. Did we work hard enough? Our opponents were going to be as good athletes as we were. They were big, fast, strong, but we thought we'd outwork them. Now, there were a lot of questions. I thought I had worked hard enough, I thought as a team we'd worked hard enough. The coaches had us prepared, but things happened. That's football. If there is any one year in my life I would like to relive, it would be that.

We finished the season at 6–4 and were invited to play in the Bluebonnet Bowl. We didn't belong—not that we didn't deserve a bowl bid, we just didn't belong. I was limping around a little bit, I had hurt my knee earlier in the Oklahoma game. As I said, I'd just like to go back and do that one over.

It's been a long time, but it was certainly a special experience. If you crank up "The Eyes of Texas" and "Texas Fight," I still get goose bumps. You have a feeling that you are representing all that tradition. Coach Darrell Royal was a great football coach, and his most valuable talent was to surround himself with good people. You can go down the list and look at the ones who were there when I was in school, and they were not only good football coaches, they taught positives about life. It was not only all the X's and O's of the sport, they taught us how to do right on the field, in the classroom, and in all things. There are a lot of challenges when you are that age, but they were great teachers and they made a difference in our lives.

Tommy Nobis is widely regarded as the best defensive player in Texas Longhorn history. He won the Outland Trophy in 1965, and as a lineman and linebacker had the distinction of finishing seventh in the Heisman Trophy voting. A member of the *Football News*'s all-time All-America team, he is a member of the Texas Sports Hall of Fame, the College Football Hall of Fame, and the Longhorn Hall of Honor.

BILL BRADLEY

QUARTERBACK/ DEFENSIVE BACK

1966–1968

THE FIRST RECRUITING TRIP I TOOK out of Palestine High School was to Texas A&M University in College Station. Barry Stone, who was 6'4" and weighed 235 pounds, was from Kilgore, and he and I went together. Barry opened the door of the coach's office, and we went into his office. I was behind Barry, and I don't think the coach saw me. He grabbed Barry by the shoulders and rather aggressively pushed him up against the wall and yelled at him, "You wanna be a Texas Aggie, don't ya?"

I kind of slid in and thought, *What in the world is going on here?* This was our first visit. We got out of that meeting, and I said "I'm not sure I want to do many more recruiting trips if they are all like this."

The year was 1965. Texas had won the national championship in 1963, so after visiting Austin, we didn't do any other trips. I kept all the letters that the coaches back then had handwritten to me. I still have them in a scrapbook.

One of my best friends in Palestine was a guy named Bill Hall. I wanted him to come to Texas with me. I stopped by his house the night before I was going to leave for Texas. Bill had already enrolled in Sam Houston State Teachers College. He was a manager on our football team in high school and ran the high hurdles in track. I wanted him at Texas, so I called Coach Royal and told him that I had a good friend and I would really appreciate it if

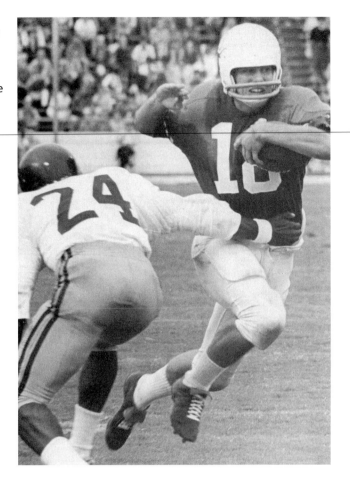

"Super Bill" Bradley was a legend in Texas high schools before he ever came to The University.

Coach could help him get a job so he could come to Texas. Coach told me that he couldn't give him any money, any room and board or anything, but if he could come down on his own, he'd see about letting him work as an assistant student manager. So I talked Bill into coming, and we loaded into his 1956 Chevrolet and headed for Austin. When we got there, I got my blanket and pillow, and Bill headed for those old green army barracks that used to be down by Waller Creek near the stadium. That was the least expensive place to live. So there I am, living high in Moore-Hill Hall, the athletes' dorm, and Bill's down by the creek. Neither one of us had any money, but I got three meals a day, so every three squares I got in Moore-Hill, I always made an extra plate and took it down for Bill. Now, Bill was getting his three hots, and he had his cot.

But Bill Hall was a steady worker, and he kept moving up. By the time we were seniors, he was carrying the headphone cords for Coach Royal. I was a captain with a suite, and Coach Royal let Bill move in with me. Bill wound up staying for a fifth year, was a manager on the national championship team, and now is one of the largest Dairy Queen franchisees in Texas. Just shows what you can do if you'll work at it.

I have wonderful memories of having meals with Ma Griff, the lady in charge of the dining hall. Coach Royal was one of the first who enhanced the idea of his players living in the dorm with other students. There is a lifetime of memories of guys in the dorm because there were players three years above you when you were a freshman and three years below you when you were a senior. These were unbelievably great people.

The first years I was at Texas were bittersweet. Our freshman class came in with a lot of publicity. I had played in the Big 33 game, a high school all-star game between Texas and Pennsylvania. Bobby Layne and Doak Walker were the coaches for the Texas team. I had a good game, and afterwards Doak said they needed to look under my jersey to see if I had a big S on my chest. That's where I got the name "Super Bill." For a long time, I struggled with that because it was hard to live up to. But now I appreciate it and even sign autographs with it.

Our first two years did not turn out like we had wanted. The 1966 season I got hurt, and we finished 7–4 after winning the Bluebonnet Bowl. The next year was labeled "The Year of the Horns," but it was anything but that. We lost our last game 10–7 to Texas A&M and finished 6–4. Coach Royal was in no mood to go to a bowl game, so we stayed home.

The next year we changed offenses and went to the wishbone. I was the quarterback to start the season, but I couldn't operate the offense very well. We tied Houston in the opener and lost to Tech in the next game. I wasn't paying very good attention, and I wasn't holding up my end of the bargain as a quarterback. James Street, who is a fantastic man and to this day is one of my best friends, wound up coming into the game in Lubbock.

We got home late, and there was a knock on my door early the next morning. They told me Coach Royal wanted to see me in his office. Now, when you go to a coach's office, three things can happen, and all of them are bad. Coach Royal was sitting behind his desk, and he was kind of twisting and leaning, and finally he says, "Bill, we are gonna make some changes around here, and we're gonna start with you. We're moving you out as quarterback.

Now if you want to come back out, we'll find a spot for you." They moved five other players, but the quarterback move got most of the attention.

When we came out the next Monday, everybody was watching me to see how I would respond. I was a captain. This was supposed to be my team. Now, I was fourth- or fifth-team wide receiver. I was punting, holding for kicks, and actually did some kicking off. I was staying alive. My dad had brought me up to never quit, so I figured I would do something to lighten things up. We were in sweats that day, so as I came out to run a practice route, I undid the string on my sweat pants. We had a ton of media, and everybody was watching. As I ran, my pants slid down to my ankles. That broke the tension on everything. People were waiting to see how I was going to handle all of this, and I became a team leader that day.

James was a great operator of the wishbone. When he started operating that deal, it changed football for a decade. I went on and played some receiver over the next several games, and one day we were short of defensive backs. Coach Mike Campbell, who had given that offense a pretty good defense to go with it, had a chaw of tobacco in his cheek. Coach Royal was up on his tower, watching practice.

"Hey, Darrell," Coach Campbell said as he stopped practice. "You using ol' Bradley down there on offense?" Coach Royal said, "No." Coach Campbell said, "Well, send him down here." I walked down to the defense and lined up at right corner, and it changed my life.

By the time we played Texas A&M at the end of the regular season, we were as good as any Texas team had ever been. The year before, we had lost to the Aggies in a game that gave them the conference championship and knocked us out of it. I had thrown four interceptions, and they weren't very nice to us at all. So when A&M came to Austin, we were ready. Chris Gilbert, Corby Robertson, and I were the captains, and I was the spokesman. I'll never forget that moment. The referee was going through his deal. Now, Chris and Corby are classy guys. The official did his introductions. "Captain Bradley, this is Captain Hobbs [Billy, of A&M]....Captain Bradley, Texas A&M is the visiting team, so Captain Hobbs will call it and get their choice of the coin toss." Hobbs called heads, and the coin came up tails.

Now, Billy and I wound up being roommates for five years when we were both with the Eagles in Philadelphia, but at this point there was no love lost. I was really focused. I hadn't shaved in three days. Now, the official was talking again.

"Captain Bradley, Captain Hobbs called heads and it's tails, so it refers back to you. Do you want to receive the ball or choose an end to defend?"

I looked him straight in the eye and said, "We don't give a shit."

The official was startled, and he turned back to Hobbs, and then turned back to me and said, "No, Captain Bradley, you have to make a choice."

I said, "I said we don't give a damn…okay, we'll just take the ball."

When I came off the field, Coach Royal walked over and said, "Bill…what are you doing out there?" I said, "Don't worry, Coach, we're gonna kick their ass." And we did, 35–14. I had thrown four interceptions the year before, and this year, I intercepted four of their passes. It was sweet revenge. We went on to beat a really good Tennessee team in the Cotton Bowl and finished one of the best Texas seasons ever at 9–1–1 and third in the nation.

If the question is, "What does it mean to be a Longhorn?" you don't need to be asking me because I'll start crying. It means the world to me. It's what I am. I was an All-Pro safety at Philadelphia, and I have had a chance to coach at a lot of places, both pro and college. But being a Longhorn is a lifetime of memories. The best way to describe it is, that's who I am. I'm Bill Bradley, the Longhorn.

Bill Bradley was known as "Super Bill" in his long career as a safety with the Philadelphia Eagles in the NFL, where he was a three-time All-Pro selection and twice led the league in interceptions. At Texas, he played quarterback, wide receiver, defensive back, and also punted. He was a tri-captain of the 1968 Longhorn team, and is a member of the Longhorn Hall of Honor.

CHRIS GILBERT

RUNNING BACK

1966–1968

I CAME TO ATTEND THE UNIVERSITY OF TEXAS for two basic reasons: Coach Royal and The University of Texas alumni. Coach Royal visited my family and me at my home and made a great first impression. He was friendly, an excellent communicator, and convinced my parents that UT was the best place for me to attend college. What he initially did not do was convince me that he really wanted me to come to Texas.

Most coaches told me that I would start immediately if I came to their school. Some coaches even told me they would make me an all-conference or All-American player. Some even offered me financial perks and incentives. Coach Royal offered me a full four-year scholarship and nothing else.

Because Coach Royal's approach was so low-key, I wasn't really convinced he wanted me to come to UT. In talking with him, I mentioned the things other coaches were saying and offering, wondering if he would match their offers. He did not. What he did tell me was that he promised he would give me a hard look and a chance to make the starting team. That was it! I thought about that for a long time, and at first I thought he didn't really want me that badly. The more I thought about his offer, it finally came to me that he did want me, and that none of the others could deliver on their word that I would be an All-American or anything else. All anyone can do is to provide you with the opportunity to succeed. I came to the conclusion that Coach Royal was one of the most honest coaches I had ever met. He knew he could

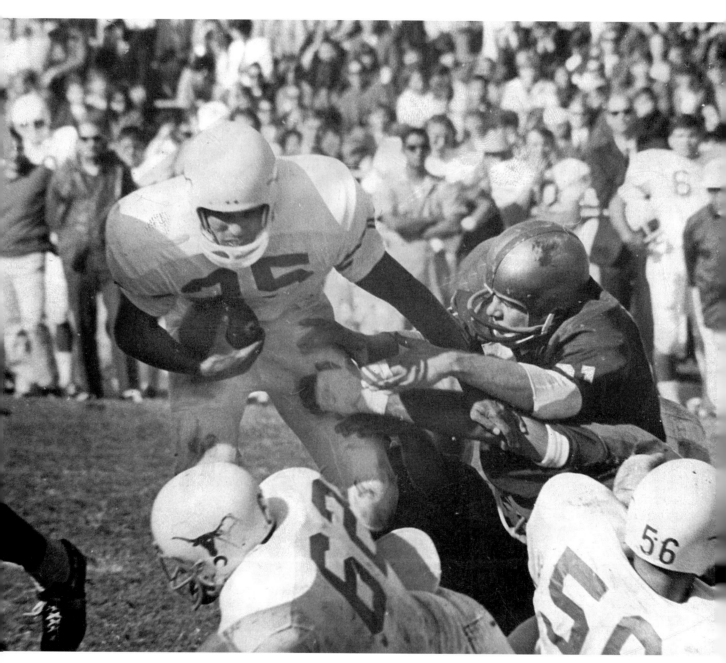

Chris Gilbert (No. 25) became the first back in NCAA history to rush for 1,000 yards in each of his years of eligibility.

deliver on his promise. How could those other coaches deliver on their promises?

A University of Texas alumnus named Weldon Smith invited me to attend a dinner on March 2, 1965, at the Rice Hotel in Houston, Texas. Texas alumni from all over the world celebrate this day as Texas Independence Day. When I walked into the ballroom of the hotel, I was overwhelmed with the hundreds of friendly UT alums who were in attendance. Many of them went out of their way to introduce themselves and to tell me they hoped that I would attend UT. Coach Royal was the main speaker for that evening's program. He made a point of introducing me as a part of his speech, and he told everyone he hoped I would choose to attend The University of Texas. The audience responded with a loud cheer, and it sealed the deal for me. That is how I got to Texas.

Receiving a college scholarship was special to me. In return for being given a scholarship, I felt an obligation and had a desire to help make The University of Texas football team the best team in the nation. It took four years to reach that goal.

Our football teams had disappointing seasons for the first three years I attended UT, but things changed my senior year. We had a great senior class in 1968 that led a talented group of underclassmen to the beginning of the longest winning streak in the history of The University of Texas.

99

Two equally meaningful moments occurred for me that season. The first moment came at the end of the 1968 game against A&M. The game was played in Austin, and Texas dominated the game from start to finish. We won the conference championship that day, and as the game ended, I stood on the field and looked around the stadium like I had never done before. I remember thinking that we truly had a great team and realized I would never play another game in this great stadium. It was an emotional moment for me. But we did have one more game to play, which brings me to the other memorable moment.

On January 1, 1969, Texas played Tennessee in the Cotton Bowl. Texas dominated the game from the kickoff to the final whistle. For all practical purposes, the game was over by halftime. Everyone on our team got to play. Texas ended up third in the nation that year. As players, we felt that there was no team in the country that could beat us. We felt, as did many of the Longhorns faithful, that at that point in time we were the best football team in the nation. The 1968 football team started what would eventually be the longest winning streak in Longhorn history.

At the end of the Tennessee game, I remember thinking that I had fulfilled my personal obligation of four years earlier. I had earned my scholarship and had reached my goal of helping make The University of Texas football team the best team in the nation. It was a sweet moment and one that I will never forget.

You don't have to be a UT football player to understand what it means to be a Longhorn. There are hundreds of thousands of UT alumni who feel as I do. They love Texas for many reasons—some personal and many commonly shared. The University of Texas is a great institution that has a profound effect on the state of Texas, our country, and the world. Alumni enjoy going back to the campus to reminisce and see how The University has developed over the years. Many alums give back to The University because The University gave so much to them. As Longhorns, we think of The University as family.

Chris Gilbert is a member of the National Football Foundation's College Hall of Fame. He was the first player in NCAA history to rush for 1,000 yards in each of his eligibility years. He was a three-time All-SWC player and a consensus All-American in 1968. He was a tri-captain of the 1968 Longhorn team and is a member of the Longhorn Hall of Honor.

BOB McKAY

OFFENSIVE TACKLE

1967–1969

WHEN I WAS IN HIGH SCHOOL and got called to the coach's office, I figured I'd done something wrong. Actually, I'd done a lot of stuff wrong, but I didn't know I'd got caught. This particular day, I went to the football office. It was dark, and there was a guy sitting at my head coach's desk with his feet up on the desk watching film.

He said, "My name's Coach Campbell. I'm from The University of Texas, and I'd like to talk to you about playing football."

I couldn't say anything but "Yes, sir," and "No, sir." I was as scared of him as I was a man with a loaded shotgun. It was a big deal that he was there. I was so thrilled that he could find Crane. Crane, Texas, isn't much bigger than the table where I'm sitting. He and Coach Royal came back later, and it was like a parade. Everybody in town wanted to see Coach Royal. I'd visited several other schools, so Coach Royal got right to the point. He said, "We've got a scholarship if you'd like to have it, but if you don't, we've got somebody else that will take it." I said, "Well, that solves that problem right now…I'll take it."

I wasn't smart enough to know I wasn't supposed to come to Austin and play. I thought I could play with anybody. That's what you get for being an 18-year-old kid and dumber than hell. I didn't know if you came down here from a Class AA school that that was unusual. They don't recruit kids like that. Leo Brooks was from Kermit, and I was from Crane. We showed up,

Bob McKay was an All-American tackle on the national champion team of 1969.

and we each weighed a whopping 220 pounds. The biggest thing for us, and the thing college players miss today, was the dorm. You showed up here, 60 of you, and became lifelong friends.

There was always something going on in the dorm. There were 16 of us on the second floor. As freshmen, every time Coach Royal would have a meeting with us, he'd sit there and talk. Then he'd say, "All right, I want the second-floor wing to stay here. Fellows," he said, "every time we come by the dorm, I don't care if we leave the office at 9:00 o'clock at night or 2:00 o'clock in the morning, your lights are on. What in the hell are y'all doing?" "Studying," we said. Then our grades came out, and he said, "Yeah, you've been studying real hard." We barely stayed in school.

A reporter from San Angelo asked Leo and me, "What was Coach Royal like?" Well, now, he's a good friend. But when you were in school, nobody went by his office just to shoot the bull. When you went by his office, you went at a high rate of speed because you didn't want him to know who you were. At practice, if he came off that coaching tower, you hoped to hell he turned right and went over toward the defense, because if he turned left, that meant you'd screwed up and were fixing to get your ass chewed.

In my time at The University, I went in his office five times. Four of them weren't worth a damn. The fifth time, he took me in there and told me that I made All-American and asked me not to tell anybody. My parents showed up two weeks later, and he told them, "Congratulations!" They said, "For what?" He said, "Bob made All-American, didn't he tell you?" I said, "Coach, you told me not to tell anybody, and I ain't told a soul."

I really believe the dorm made our team. We were there all the time. We knew who was going to work hard and who wasn't. And the one who was going to cheat you now was the same SOB who was going to cheat you later. If he'd quit now, he'd quit later.

In the spring of 1968 we went through a real hard time. We hadn't done well in 1967, and everyone was determined it would be different. Anyone who stayed, played. We were just hoping we'd live through one more day. It was full speed from the time we crossed the creek to the practice field until we got back across the street. It was just, who wanted to stay? The day I tore my shoulder up was the happiest day of my life. I had to go to the hospital for an operation, but I had lived through one more day of practice.

I'd lay there at night in the dorm and listen to kids leave. I don't know how many quit, and a whole bunch of us went to the hospital. But it worked. We had a hell of a team. Things like that brought us closer together. It was the friends that we made, and it wasn't just on our team. That's how I met Bobby Layne, Joe Parker, Rooster Andrews, Harley Sewell, and the people who made Texas what it is.

We played for our teammates and our coaches. We all respected Coach Royal, but we didn't want to disappoint Coach Willie Zapalac and Coach Leon Manley, our line coaches. We reached down and got whatever we needed to succeed. In 1969 we were No. 2 in the country, playing SMU in Dallas, and we were behind 10–7 at halftime. They had Chuck Hixson throwing the ball. We wound up winning the game 45–14 and running for 611 yards on the ground. We got to play the whole game, and each one of our backs had over 100 yards rushing.

We got beat our sophomore year at Texas A&M, and they left the score up on the scoreboard all year long. They were supposed to win the conference in 1968, and we beat them at our place and won the league ourselves. In 1969 we went back over there, and we scored every time we had the ball. It's stuff like that that you remember; we never thought we were going to lose a ballgame. Even when we were behind at Arkansas in the "shootout," it never, ever entered our minds that we'd lose. Everybody talked about what a good offense we had, but we had to have a pretty good defense. You can't lose the ball seven times and still win the ballgame.

The reunion we had with the Arkansas players in 2004 was a lot of fun. We didn't know any of those kids, but now we've become real good friends. Bruce James, the boy I played against, and I talk to each other all the time. Street and I spoke at the Little Rock Touchdown Club in 2006. It was the craziest thing you've ever seen. We went to dinner the night before, and this sportswriter told me we ruined his life when we won that game. He said he was so disappointed that two days after the game he enlisted in the service and went to Vietnam. I told him he had to be crazy to take things that seriously. "They were killing people over there," I said. "This was just a football game." It was one of those things that's wasted on kids who are 19 and 20 years old because it doesn't seem like it's that hard to get when you are doing it.

Football is a faith-based game. You have to have faith that you are going to do your job, and the next 10 are going to do theirs. You don't want to be the one to let anybody down. We were going to play Notre Dame in the Cotton Bowl, and they had this giant tackle named Mike McCoy. I had never seen a human that big in my life. He was a nice guy, very polite, but I told Mike

Dean, our guard, who weighed barely 200 pounds and was going to have to block him, that he was huge. But Mike Dean was just like the rest of us. It never entered his mind that he wasn't supposed to kick his ass, and he did.

We believed in ourselves and we believed in each other, and we know today, just as we did then, that if a guy's in a bind, all he's got to do is call.

Coming here, you think that's what is supposed to happen. You believe that if you work hard, you're going to do what you're supposed to do. When I got here, I just wanted to play. After you're playing, you think, *I'd sure like to make all-conference.* And then it all falls into place. You're an All-American and play eight years in the NFL. For a kid from Crane, Texas, that stuff doesn't happen.

Bob McKay is one of the most decorated offensive linemen in Texas history. A three-year letterman from 1967 through 1969, he was a consensus All-American and an all-SWC choice in 1969. He was part of Longhorn teams that won two Southwest Conference crowns and a national title. He was a first-round draft choice and played nine years in the NFL. He is a member of the Longhorn Hall of Honor.

TOM CAMPBELL

HALFBACK

1968–1969

M Y TWIN BROTHER, MIKE, and I were average high school football players at Reagan High School. I was not recruited at all, not by one
school, not by one junior college, not by anybody. We knew we were average players with average speed, but we were like a lot of high school players;
our high school careers were over, but the football was still in us.

I have to admit, we thought that with Daddy's [Mike Campbell, UT defensive coordinator] connections and with all the scholarships colleges had available, maybe somebody would give us a mercy scholarship. That didn't happen.
But we'd been admitted to Texas, so we were going to UT and walk on.

One day after recruiting was over, Daddy walked into our bedroom and,
"Well, Darrell has a couple of scholarships left over. You two can come out
there and stay as long as you want." We were ecstatic.

That August, we were as low on the totem pole as any walk-on could be.
When Mike and I graduated from high school, we weighed about 162–163
pounds. All we did our freshmen year was hold the dummies. The freshman
team played five games, and we got in one game. We got more playing time
than most walk-ons but only about three or four plays more. But we didn't
quit.

It got worse in spring training. They had more experienced dummy-
holders than we were, so we sat on one knee on the sideline and occasionally
traded knees.

Tom Campbell had two brothers who played for the Longhorns, all sons of legendary defensive coordinator Mike Campbell.

The only football I got during spring training that year and two-a-days my sophomore year were "shit" drills. My dad ran them, and they were just awful. They made basic training seem like Camp Longhorn in comparison. Daddy didn't consider it punishment; he knew that among all those guys sitting on the sideline in blue shirts were some football players, and he was looking for them. That's where Mike and I learned to play football. We were then up to about 170, and if the guy across from you weighed 220, that was your tough luck. Daddy knew if you had the right fundamentals, you could play with guys who were bigger than you were. I learned how to play football in that south end zone of Memorial Stadium. Without those drills, I never would have played.

That's where a lot of guys lost their heart for it. There were all-staters who thought they were above that so they just lost their hearts. Mike and I got mad because we saw all these guys that they'd tried hard to recruit, and we weren't that impressed with them. But they'd passed over us. I had a chip on my shoulder and something to prove. Well, we kept working our way up. Other guys would either quit or flunk out, or they went backward while we went forward.

Next thing I knew, I was on third team. I set a goal that, by the time I was a senior, I'd be able to sit on the sideline in an orange jersey instead of up in the seats.

On Monday after the OU game, they told me I was making the trip that week. I said, "How can this be? My goal was to do this by the time I was a senior. Here I am, a sophomore, and I'm on the traveling team. It cannot get any better than this." Then I said, "I hope to God I do not get into this football game, because I don't know what to do."

I don't know why, but right before the Arkansas game, I was moved to second team. They handed me No. 84. Well, the guy who had been second team before me had worn 84. The next home game, I opened the program to see my picture, and there was No. 84, all right—the other guy. I intercepted a pass in that game, against Rice. The announcer said that the other guy intercepted the pass. My own mother thought he'd intercepted that pass. After the game, I went out with my friends, and they didn't know I'd intercepted the ball. They didn't even know I'd been in the game.

I played behind Mike Perrin, who was all-conference his sophomore year. In the next-to-last game against TCU, Mike hurt his knee, so I played a lot. The next game, we were playing A&M, and I was thinking, *Good God. I'm nowhere near capable of starting against Texas A&M.* My dad knew it, too, so he moved someone over to start in front of me.

We went into spring training, and Daddy had changed the defense. Now I was left outside linebacker and my brother was the right outside linebacker. Heck, we were happy. Mike Perrin never recovered from knee surgery, so they put another guy in front of me. That was okay with me; it was the right thing to do.

We tied Houston that year 20–20. The starter played most of the game, and I got in some. Now, every Monday I'd look at the depth chart because I was never fully confident that my name would be there. On Monday following the Houston game, I looked, and my name wasn't at second-team left outside linebacker. My heart just sank. I looked at third team, and I wasn't there. I wasn't at fourth team. I wasn't at right outside linebacker. I even looked at the defensive backs. I was really panicking. I looked again at the left outside linebackers, and the name listed at second team was the guy who had been first team the week before. "If he's second team, who the hell is first team?" I looked up, and there was my name. That was the biggest shock of my life.

Even the coaches were befuddled by how well we were doing. They thought that Mike and I were slow and were just hard workers. I intercepted two passes in the Cotton Bowl and knocked down a bunch of others. I was covering their fastest receiver. My own coach came up to me after the game and said, "Tom, I never knew you were that fast." I said, "Coach, maybe everyone else is just slower than you thought." I was tired of getting insulted by the coaches.

They moved me to defensive back in the spring. It was a completely different position, but I was faster than they thought I was, and I figured I could do it. But I had a lot to learn. And, boy, did my dad chew me out a lot because I kept making mental errors.

Most parents, when the game is over, will say, "Good job, son. I'm proud of you." Well, all this has gone on, and Daddy had never said one word to me, not even from his coach's point of view. It didn't bother me because that's just the way he was. His attitude was, "If you did something good, you know it. You don't need to be told."

One Sunday I was at my parents' house, and the phone rang. Daddy answered the phone, and it was a one-sided conversation, which was not unusual for Daddy. He started giving some short responses, and I realized that a parent of another player was chewing him out about me. Finally, Daddy had had enough of it, and he said, "Look, lady, I know that Tom is no damned good, but he's the best I've got." That was the first of two compliments he ever gave me at The University of Texas.

We just got better and better. I got Defensive Player of the Game in the Cotton Bowl. I intercepted two passes and it was on national television. First game of my senior year, I intercepted a pass on national television. I intercepted a pass in the Tech game. We played Oklahoma on national TV, and I intercepted a pass in that game. I intercepted a pass in the Rice game and in the Baylor game. We played A&M, and I intercepted a pass on national TV. Then I intercepted a pass against Arkansas in the Game of the Century.

All this time, Daddy did not say a word. He threw compliments around like they were manhole covers.

Playing Notre Dame in the Cotton Bowl for the national championship, I intercepted a pass with about a minute to go, and we won that game. I came off the field, and Daddy did not say a word to me. As I was walking to the bus, Daddy waved me over to introduce me to someone. This is when he gave me my second compliment. He said, "Tom, I don't know what you're going to do with the rest of your life, but it ought to be on television."

There was a lot of pressure on us, starting on defense. But our being first team put a lot of pressure on Daddy, too, because he had to defend his decision to put us on the field. How do you put into words what it means to begin as a walk-on and one day become a starter, intercepting passes to win a national championship? One thing it means is that my father was proud of me. He never said it, but I knew that he was.

Being a Texas Longhorn has opened doors and created opportunities that I never dreamed possible. How many men who played college football can say that they played alongside their twin brother, had their father—a football genius—as their defensive coach, and won a national championship?

I'm now meeting the children of older UT football fans who know who I am because their fathers told them about the 1969 season. To tell my story today is as exciting as it was 30 years ago. I realize how unique it is; consequently, I honor the story always and give credit where it is due. I thank my father and mother who taught us so much and bled orange. I thank Darrell Royal who welcomed me and gave me an opportunity, and I thank my God, Jesus Christ, for constantly reminding me who is really responsible for what happened in my life to make it so unique.

Tom Campbell and his twin brother, Mike, are the sons of longtime Longhorn assistant Mike Campbell. Tom was an All-Southwest Conference selection in 1969 and was named the outstanding defensive player in the 1969 Cotton Bowl victory over Tennessee. He made two game-ending interceptions to close out the Arkansas game and the Notre Dame game in the Cotton Bowl to preserve the Horns' national championship in 1969.

JAMES STREET

QUARTERBACK

1967–1969

MICKEY MANTLE AND I WERE SITTING AROUND talking about sports in general one night, and he asked me, "Do you ever sit and watch those plays that you made and think that it really wasn't you…that it was somebody else that you are watching? That was a neat hit, or a great catch, but you don't think of it in the vein that it was you doing it?"

The Texas-Arkansas game in 1969 is obviously the game I get asked about the most. People want to talk about the call, the pass play, and all that stuff. As I watch those old tapes, that's sometimes how I feel.

When I came to Texas, I had no earthly idea what playing football for The University of Texas would be like, or even what going to The University of Texas would be like. Coach Russell Coffee had recruited me, and he'd come into town and take me to the local steak place for dinner. On signing day, Coach Bill Ellington came in, and my mother and I went out to the airport and signed.

I thought I knew what I was getting into. When I was being recruited, I came down to a freshman game and sat in the press box with Coach Royal. Bill Bradley was the quarterback, and he was unbelievable. Coach Royal told me he figured other schools would throw Bradley up to me a lot. And then he said this: "If you go somewhere else, you'll never know whether you could have played with the best and competed for a position with the best."

James Street, unbeaten as a Texas quarterback, also lettered in baseball at Texas.
His son, Huston, was the MVP of the 2002 College World Series.

I remember walking out and saying, "I think I can play with these guys. But, boy, that guy was awful good."

Still, there was a piece of me that had no idea what it was all about. I think when I got here, I expected the players all to be better because they were college players. I thought they'd have to be a lot better than some of the guys we'd played with in high school. I didn't know whether I was good enough to play.

During the summer between my senior year in high school and my freshman year at Texas, I was working on a farm in East Texas. That was the summer when the sniper, a guy named Charles Whitman, got up on the UT Tower and shot all those people. I was already afraid, thinking I was going from Longview, Texas, down there to that big school in Austin. And when that happened, my lord! They had people carrying guns and shooting people on campus. This was just craziness. Why was I going down there? Really, that was just the naïve person that I was, growing up the way we did in Longview. It was obviously a catastrophic event which is remembered by people 40 years later, and it could have happened anywhere. But it scared me.

When I went to my first practice, I was told to go over to a part of the practice field where the freshman quarterbacks were. There were 16 quarterbacks in that line. A lot of those guys ended up playing other positions, but they came from high schools where they were quarterbacks, because the quarterbacks were usually the best athletes on the team. We had more than 90 players on the freshman team, and 80 of them were on scholarship.

I think the fact that freshmen were not eligible for the varsity was a good thing. You came down here to this big, huge school, and you're thinking about classes, where you go, how do you find them—some never found them. With freshman ball, you had a chance to move slowly into the program. Now kids come out of high school, and they're automatically talked about being a starter as a freshman. Back in those days, you were a freshman, and all the upperclassmen talked to you like you were a freshman. I had come intending to play both baseball and football, and after that year, I felt like I could play at The University of Texas.

Coach Royal taught us far more than just football. He wanted to make sure our hair was cut right, that our shoes were shined, and that our fingernails were clipped. How basic can that be? But for a head coach the stature of Darrell Royal, that's what he taught you. He used to tell us all the time

113

when we dressed and went on trips that we were representing ourselves, our families, and our school.

At the end of the season of 1967, it was clear nobody was satisfied. We had finished with a 6–4 record and had lost a chance to win the conference in the last game with Texas A&M. It was that summer that Emory Bellard designed what became known as the wishbone.

Coach Bellard called us quarterbacks together late that summer, and he went through a play from the formation, showing us what it was going to look like. We went out on the field and walked through it. And if you had talked to Bradley, myself, Eddie Phillips—all of us—I think we would have said, at some point, "You can't do it that way." And I don't know if it would have worked because at the time, they had the fullback one yard behind the quarterback. Once they moved him back, it allowed you to read the defense. In our third game in 1968, Bradley had a tough game at Texas Tech, and I became the quarterback. It wasn't like a "battlefield promotion," as Coach Mike Campbell used to call it. We were struggling, and Coach Royal grabbed me and he looked for a minute as if he were having second thoughts about putting me in. Then he looked me straight in the eye and said, "Hell, you can't do any worse. Get in there."

As it turned out, we won the next 20 games, from early 1968 through 1969. Coach Bellard worked with me on a day-in and day-out basis. I never heard him say a cuss word, and I never heard him get mad or raise his voice and start hollering at somebody. He'd always say, "Don't worry about the outcome of the game. Just stay steady in the boat, and play every play like it's the big play." That's a pretty good philosophy to use for life—don't worry about where you're going to be 10 years from now, let's play today and play today like it's the big day of our lives.

Which, I guess, gets us back to that Arkansas game. As the years go by, I appreciate more and more the ability of Coach Royal to make that call. It was fourth down, and we were behind 14–8. Coach Royal had to make the call, never once thinking about what history would or wouldn't have to say about it. He thought the play would work. He'd talked to Randy Peschel, and Randy said he thought he could get behind the defender, so he made the call. Being in business now, sometimes I have to think about the results. If the results are not going to be positive, what kind of reflection is that going to have on me? Coach Royal never thought about that. It was just the right call at the right time.

When I threw the ball, Terry Don Phillips of Arkansas knocked me down. I was trying to look through legs and arms to see what happened, and I saw the referee signaling "catch." I just didn't know at that point in time whether it was an interception or a catch by us. The same feeling gives me chills today.

I went through a unique time period in having the opportunity to come to The University of Texas. I didn't realize how strong that was, getting a chance to play for Darrell Royal and play with teammates who have gone on to win their own awards and are lifelong friends. The first year, I didn't appreciate it as much as I do today. Basically, I was lucky—lucky to get the opportunity, lucky to play on a national championship team, lucky to play for Darrell Royal. I got to meet two presidents and do some things I could never have imagined. I've had a great life, with a great wife and great kids and a nice career.

That's why, sometimes when I think of Mantle's story, I look at the film and wonder if, after all, it's really me.

> James Street went 20–0 as the Longhorns' starting quarterback and was famous as the first successful quarterback of the wishbone offense. His dramatic, come-from-behind victories over Arkansas and Notre Dame in the 1969 season secured his place in Longhorns history. As a pitcher, he also led Texas to three SWC baseball titles. He is a member of the Longhorn Hall of Honor.

TED KOY

RUNNING BACK

1967–1969

EVERY AUGUST, IN MY PRE-ELEMENTARY school days, my dad, mother, brother, sister, and I would go to Austin to watch some of the football practices at The University of Texas. We'd stay at the old Commodore Perry Hotel in downtown Austin. Coming from Bellville, Texas, that was a huge event. We would proceed twice a day, in the morning and again in the evening, to go out and watch my heroes practice.

I grew up being a University of Texas Longhorn fan. My father had gone to The University of Texas, my mother had gone to UT, and to me, there was no other school. So those trips to Austin were natural, and they were just the top of the pyramid. As time progressed, my brother Ernie went to UT as a student-athlete. Following him by a couple of years, my sister went to UT as a student, so to that point, my entire family had gone to The University of Texas. My dad had played both football and baseball, and my brother Ernie had played football.

My senior year in high school, it came time for me to select where to go. Fortunately, I was able to look at schools as a student-athlete—as a football player and as a student. I honestly looked at a number of other universities because I thought, "You know, I've never even considered other schools, and there may be something out there that is more appealing to me as an individual, rather than just following in the footsteps of my family." So I made an honest evaluation. But I kept comparing every school to The University

Ted Koy's run set up the Longhorns' winning touchdown against Arkansas in 1969. Ted's brother and father also played for the Longhorns.

of Texas, and to me, there was none better. So looking back, I am very fortunate and thankful that I did that with my decision.

The late 1960s was a time of change and then success at Texas. There are many memories, but if I had to pick just one, I'd have to go to the closing moments of the 1969 Texas-Arkansas game, No. 1 vs. No. 2—the "Big Shootout," as it's been called. It was a very tough, hard-fought game on both parts, and at the end, we won 15–14. And as I remember those last fading seconds on the clock—I was part of the offense, and we happened to be on the field as the clock ticked away—I remember the feeling so well. It was not so much a feeling of triumph but rather one of completeness.

My thoughts raced back in the moment to my freshman year when I stepped onto the practice field for the first time as a freshman football player at The University of Texas. There were literally more players on that football field than there were in my high school in Bellville. I'm sure I was like all the rest of the kids. We all thought, *How in the world am I going to fit into this enormous program?* The freshman year was followed by the sophomore year in which we had a 6–4 season—which by UT standards was not acceptable. It happened to be the third year in a row in which, during the regular season, Texas had gone 6–4. That spring Coach Royal said, "We will never be 6–4 again," and he meant it. That spring training was a grueling one. We had two-plus hours of contact, and it was rock 'em, sock 'em. The survivors were the ones who made up the team. We were "Medina-ized," named for our trainer, Frank Medina, who was in charge of the off-season and conditioning program. I recalled the camaraderie that developed under the intensity of making a football team. My junior year of 1968, we had more success. We had gone to the wishbone, and by the end of that season, we were as good as any team in the country.

Then my senior year had been such a fun time, and all the hard work had paid off in an undefeated season and a national championship. As I recall the last seconds ticking off the clock, where we were declared the No. 1 team in the nation, it was not a feeling of triumph but of full appreciation of the road that I was very fortunate to have been on.

When people ask me what it means to be a Longhorn, I believe the answer is part of a tradition of excellence. I go back to my second grade year in Bellville Elementary School. My heroes were players at The University of Texas. In 1955 if somebody had come up to me and said, "Ted, you can go over in this room and meet the president of the United States, Dwight Eisenhower, or you can go over to this room and meet Walter Fondren, the quarterback from The University of Texas," in a heartbeat I would have gone to see the Texas guys. Not in defiance to the president, but that's who my heroes were.

As I look back, I can see that the responsibility of carrying on that winning tradition is on each generation of players. When I was a player, there was a sign that said, "The Longhorn Winning Tradition Will Not Be Entrusted to the Timid or the Weak." That's a pretty good summary of the responsibility and the privilege of being able to carry on the winning tradition, the tradition of excellence, that is so symbolized by The University of Texas. And that's not only in football but in academics and other athletics, as well.

And it carries on after you leave. I chose to become a veterinarian and went to vet school at Texas A&M. I'd say that the Aggies, in good spirit, gave me a very difficult time. They certainly accepted me as a veterinary student in their professional curriculum, but so many of the faculty were, and still are, die-hard Aggies, that they gave me a very hard time, and I probably gave them a hard time, too.

I lost my dad right after the Longhorns' Alamo Bowl win in 2006. He was 97 and the oldest living Longhorn letterman. I idolized him and what he represented, and again, to me, he represented The University of Texas. He had played pro baseball with the Brooklyn Dodgers and St. Louis Cardinals, and he epitomized UT athletics. It was through him and his friends who were athletes in the early 1930s, that I first learned about The University of Texas. I saw in them the genuine camaraderie, and I witnessed it a second time with my brother. I saw three different eras of Texas football. And through that, I came away with a healthy understanding of the tradition and excellence of UT football and what it means to be a Longhorn.

Ted Koy came from a legacy of Texas Longhorns, joining both brother Ernie and father "Big Ernie" as Longhorn lettermen. He was the tri-captain of the 1969 national champion Longhorns, and his 11-yard run set up the Longhorns' winning touchdown in their 15–14 comeback victory over Arkansas that season. He played five seasons in the NFL. He is a member of the Longhorn Hall of Honor and serves on its vintage selection committee.

HAPPY FELLER

KICKER

1968–1970

Growing up in the small German town of Fredericksburg, Texas, with a population of approximately 3,800 at the time, made playing at Texas a seemingly unreachable goal. When I was growing up, our family got to attend one Texas game. I was in elementary school, and we decided to make it a mini-vacation. We got up early and drove to Austin. We enjoyed a nice lunch and then we walked to the game. As we approached the entrance gate, my dad turned to my mother and said, "Mother, I sure wish we were back home by the piano." Mother replied, "Why is that, Lorence?" Dad replied, "Because that's where the tickets are." Well, the good news is we bumped into Mr. Bob Rochs outside that gate. Mr. Rochs was the business manager of the athletics department. I heard him ask Dad, "Do you remember your seat numbers?" Dad didn't, but I sure did. I had been personally admiring those tickets ever since I first saw them. I don't recall ever seeing tickets so beautiful. Anyway, I quickly relayed the section, row, and seat numbers, and Mr. Rochs allowed us in without our tickets.

I'll never forget the first day I arrived at The University of Texas. My parents drove me down from Fredericksburg. Our freshman coach, Mr. Bill "Duke" Ellington, was greeting the parents and players as we arrived. I noticed my dad approach Coach Ellington and say, "I'm concerned about Happy. He is from a small town, and I'm afraid he will get lost at this big school." Coach Ellington put his arm around Dad's shoulders and said, "Don't

Happy Feller kicked the winning extra point in the Longhorns' 15–14 "Big Shootout" victory over Arkansas in 1969.

worry, Doc. We will take good care of Happy. He will do just fine." Coach Ellington not only lived up to his promise, he still remains one of the finest human beings I have ever met in my life. I don't believe I ever saw Bill mad, nor did I ever hear Bill utter one curse word the entire fours years I was at Texas. That statement in itself is quite remarkable.

I would be remiss if I didn't mention Frank Medina. Frank was our trainer. He was a full-blooded American Indian. He was also a world-renowned trainer, and he trained many Olympic teams throughout his career. He was our conditioning coach, our off-season conditioning coach, and he ran and administered the summer training requirements and expectations. In the summers it felt like I received a letter every other day from Frank, outlining that week's training requirements. He was thorough, tough, and fair. Under Frank's supervision, there was never a game where we were out-conditioned by our opponents. Without question, Frank Medina was a huge unsung hero in the many successful seasons at The University of Texas.

As I reflect on and take stock in what it means to be a Longhorn, so much of my character makeup today is a result of my Longhorn experience. When I came to Texas, I was by and large a country bumpkin. Naïveté would be an understatement. Having the opportunity to come to The University of Texas and the privilege of playing football for this legendary program was a dream come true for me. But what I gained from this experience was beyond my wildest dreams. We won a conference championship in 1968 and won national championships in 1969 and 1970. I was exposed to the leadership skills of the great coach Darrell Royal. I learned the rewards that were possible through hard work and self-discipline taught by Frank Medina. And I learned kindness, thoughtfulness, and humility from Bill Ellington.

Being a Longhorn not only provided me unforgettable national championship memories that only a handful of places could provide, but the talented professionals of the athletics department unknowingly transformed me personally, professionally, and spiritually by exposing me to a pattern of excellence by which they lived their lives. Longhorn football is all about being the best. When you are exposed to the best, you somehow never return to your old form.

Happy Feller kicked the extra point that gave the Longhorns the national championship in the 15–14 victory over Arkansas in the "Big Shootout." He was an All-American in 1970.

The

SEVENTIES

EDDIE PHILLIPS

QUARTERBACK

1968–1971

I T WAS LATE IN THE SUMMER OF 1968, and our offensive backfield coach, Emory Bellard, had asked those of us who played quarterback for The University of Texas to meet him for breakfast in the Varsity Cafeteria. It was then that Coach Bellard told us about a new formation he was thinking about. In the spring we had run the stack I formation, or power I, with Chris Gilbert in the primary deep position at tailback. But Coach Bellard had quite a presentation for us that morning. He used everything on the table, the salt and pepper shakers, the sugar bowl, whatever else he could find, to lay out a formation where the fullback was just a yard behind the quarterback, and there were two running backs. The formation didn't have a name, but the way he described it, it was all based on blocking schemes and reads. It was different from anything any of us had ever seen.

I had watched Texas when I was in high school. They had a successful program, especially in the years of 1963 and 1964. They had a national caliber team. I was from Mesquite, and Texas got a lot of publicity in Dallas because they usually played three games there: the Texas-OU game, the SMU game, and the Cotton Bowl game. I still remember going to the Texas State Fair and hearing the fans at the OU game, and I still remember how exciting it was to listen to the game on the radio. That's when Texas became my favorite team.

I'm not sure if you really ever know if you are Texas material. I played four sports in high school, and I just played. All of a sudden, during my senior

"Wizard of the Wishbone," quarterback Eddie Phillips later became the son-in-law of legendary coach and former Longhorn, Tom Landry.

year, people started calling. I didn't even know if I would play college ball until my senior year. When they started calling, I was flattered that The University of Texas was interested in me. That was always my very first choice.

Of course, we all know what happened to that breakfast with Coach Bellard. They tinkered with the formation, moving the fullback back another yard so the reads were easier, and it took off. In that season of 1968 it became known as the wishbone. After two games, Street had become the quarterback, and he was a good part of the wishbone. When we started, we had Steve Worster, our fullback, real close to the quarterback. It got to where you didn't have enough time to run the play and read the defense—funny the difference a little bit of adjustment can make. We did have the element of surprise. People didn't know how to defend us, and that was good for James and me both. Defenses always catch up, though. All we really had were two plays one way or one the other. Bellard was a stickler for mechanics. I can still recite the routine, "Take the ball to your chest...."

James was our starting quarterback for 20 games, and we won all 20. The one thing I knew when he left was that I was prepared to be the starting quarterback. I had paid my dues. I worked hard and I knew the mechanics. I think I could have run the wishbone in my sleep, I really do. But the question always gets back to number one: Could I lead the team? And I followed a pretty good football player in James Street, so the second question was: Could I make the big play in the big game? Because that's what James did.

In the first game I started, against California, it was nice to start off successfully when we won going away. It didn't put James behind me, but I needed to have a good start, which I did. Then the third game of the season, the UCLA game, validated that there was at least one play, in one game, where we did make the big play.

By then we had won 23 straight. UCLA threw a defense at us that we weren't prepared for, and quite frankly, we didn't do a good job of adjusting to what they did. We weren't very successful in moving the ball. The defense they ran—if you put it into a "sound defensive category"—probably wasn't. It was more of a surprise, but the surprise worked. We had to fight for every yard we made. It was a fairly low-scoring game. They were leading 17–13, and we were running out of time.

We had the ball at their 45-yard line with about 25 seconds left. We ran a play over the middle that was a pass to Cotton Speyrer, our All-American split end. We had tried it twice before because we had seen on film that it worked against them. They had a very aggressive defense—gosh a'mighty, they had great athletes in their secondary. But sometimes a great athlete will bite on something, and it just so happened that that time they bit on the tight end coming across, and we hit the big play to Cotton for the touchdown. Tommy Woodard was our tight end. He was supposed to go down 15 yards and come across. He deviated and went down 20 yards, and I think Tommy's going across deeper caught the eye of their free safety. Even though it wasn't planned, it just happened. Of course, Cotton made a great catch and turned it into a great play. But that's football. If you go back and look at James's pass against Arkansas, it was a great call, but it was defensed, and it took a perfect pass to make it work. The same was true in the Notre Dame game in the Cotton Bowl. James's pass to set up the winning touchdown was behind Cotton. That was the only place it could have been thrown and not be broken up.

The season of 1970 was a storybook year for me, and it had a bittersweet ending. We were awarded a national championship by the coaches before the Cotton Bowl game with Notre Dame but lost the bowl game to end our winning streak at 30 games. I thought Notre Dame had a better team the year before, and we were just as good as we were the prior year. The only thing that sticks out is that it seemed like we always had 80 yards to go. We had horrible field position the whole game, which means we had to march and not make mistakes. We put the ball on the rug nine times and lost five of them. Even though we moved the ball, you can't sustain our type of offense with those mistakes.

It was bittersweet for me personally because I did set an individual total yardage record, but I was the least of their worries. They always talked about using a "mirror" defense, but the mirror defense didn't beat us. They tried to cover me man-to-man with a free safety. I got lots of yards. You would have thought there would have been some scoring in the second half, but there wasn't. They were ahead 24–11 at half, and that was the final score. All things come to an end, but it was hard for me. I was having a good game. Then I turned around and was the quarterback when the winning streak ended.

For some reason, I get smarter the older I get. When you are at The University of Texas, you take it for granted.

All of those memories came back to me when I was inducted into the Longhorn Hall of Honor in 2005. That meant a lot for a couple of reasons.

First, it is a great honor, and second, because I was able to join my late father-in-law, Tom Landry, the longtime coach of the Dallas Cowboys. He was quite a man, and he was proud to be a Longhorn.

I remember being on the sideline at that UCLA game before we pulled it out. Bobby Wuensch, our All-American tackle, was always keyed up. He had a little talk with me and said, as only Bobby could say, "Eddie, we are gonna win this game." He left no doubt about what my responsibility in that was. I don't think I have ever heard an eruption like the crowd that day when we scored. It went from dead silence, and it was like someone turned the microphone on for 66,000 people all at one time.

That was the voice of The University of Texas. We have tradition and high expectations. And the principles that I strived for when I was playing transferred into what I'm trying to do in the business arena. If I can meet those and validate those, I'm just a step away from excellence, and that's what it means to be a Longhorn.

Eddie Phillips was the "Wizard of the Wishbone," operating the run-oriented offense to the 1970 national championship. He set a single-game total offense record with 363 total yards against Notre Dame in the 1971 Cotton Bowl game. He was co-captain of the 1971 Texas team and is the son-in-law of the late Tom Landry, former Dallas Cowboys coach and a fellow Longhorn. He was inducted into the Longhorn Hall of Honor in 2005.

JERRY SISEMORE

OFFENSIVE TACKLE

1970–1972

I PLAYED THE TROMBONE IN THE SCHOOL BAND when I was in the fifth and sixth grade. I loved music. I could hear the music well and could differentiate between notes. You could play a note and I could tell you, "That's an A." I wanted to play the piano so badly, but as I grew, my fingers wouldn't fit between the black keys. You have to move between the black keys or you don't play "Fur Elise."

So, the piano died, but the music stayed. When I made my schedule for junior high, I scheduled band for sixth period. On the second day of class, the coach said, "Where's Sisemore?" One of the kids said, "He's in band." "What? You swear? He's in band?" The coach showed up at the band hall, and I tried to hide behind my trombone. He saw me and growled, "Sisemore, you're coming with me." That was the end of the music and the beginning of football. I didn't want to play; I didn't want to work hard and I didn't want to go through the pain. I was 5'2" and 150 in the seventh grade. By ninth grade, I was 6'4" and 185. It was like *zoom*—overnight. You know how it goes from there. I was very blessed.

My senior year, we had a coach who had been a walk-on quarterback at Texas. One day he asked me, "Sisemore, where you going to college?" I told him I'd sure love to play for Coach Royal if I could. That Friday night, Emory Bellard showed up at my game in Plainview wearing his white trench coat and smoking a pipe.

Jerry Sisemore is a member of the College Football Hall of Fame and was named to the Cotton Bowl Hall of Fame in 2007.

My mother had gone to Texas Tech, and she wanted me to go there, too. "No, ma'am. Coach Bellard said I could go to Texas if he could get me in. That's where I want to go." She said, "Well, the folks from Tech called and they want you to come visit." So I went down there, just to say "hey" and to do it for my mother. I was looking at my watch the whole time, thinking, *When can I leave?* I guess that was a visit, but that was the only place I visited besides The University.

In the middle of all the recruiting, I asked my dad what he thought I should do. He told me, "Well, if you go play for Coach Royal, you'll live in the state and you'll be close to home. And he's not gonna lie to you." That was my dad's take on the whole thing, which was pretty solid. And Coach Royal didn't lie to us. I appreciate it even today.

After I'd committed, Coach Royal came to town to get Dad to sign the national letter of intent. Dad built water wells, and he was out working in the field, and Coach Royal had to go find him. He told Dad, "I need your signature on this letter so we can get Jerry signed up to come to Texas." My dad said, "Why? He told you he was coming and he does pretty much what he says he's gonna do."

When you show up at The University, you're all grunts. Nobody's a super-star in Coach Royal's program. You think you have an idea of the traditions at Texas, but once you get here, it's so much stronger than you ever imagined. When we were freshmen, the varsity was vying for the national championship, and we wondered, *How will we ever beat these guys out? How will we ever carry on the rich tradition here?* So you start sweating about that, and then the old farts come around and start talking to you about what it means to be a Longhorn.

One sweet thing about Coach Royal was his assistant coaches. That coaching staff was good, right down the middle, rock-solid. Willie Zapalac— "One-Way Willie"—was my coach. You did not want him mad at you. You found out real quick what it took to make him happy. Rather, what it took to make him not mad; I don't know if he was ever happy. Willie'd go eye-to-eye with you. And if you went eye-to-eye with Willie, you were going to get your butt kicked.

And Frank Medina. "What are you saving it for, son? What are you saving it for?" We'd run the stadium steps and had to do it 10 times. It's only 75 steps to the top of the stadium, and at first we thought, *It's probably a nice view*

up there. By the time we got to the eighth time, we were crying. We'd jump rope and punch the bag. This was off-season with Frank. After the workout, everyone else would go to dinner, and he'd get the fat boys in there with weight vests on. They'd do sit-ups with dumbbells, and he'd count to 500. "What are you saving it for, son? What are you saving it for?" It was a gut check. But what a beautiful, wonderful guy. You knew you were in good with Frank if he invited you back to his office. That was sacred turf, believe me. He'd give you a cookie that his wife made. But, "Don't ever come in my training room except to get taped. I don't want you hurt. I'll tell you when you're hurt."

My senior year against Baylor in Waco, I sprained my ankle—just ripped it right before halftime. So Frank used about six rolls of tape on it. We were in the third quarter when he finished taping it. "Okay. I've wasted enough tape. What are you saving it for?" He said, "I'm going to lock this door, Sisemore. Are you going to sit here locked in, or are you coming with me? But if you go out there, you're playing." He was that kind of guy. He could push you further than you wanted to go. I didn't want to go back in, but I had no choice; I wasn't getting locked in there. I knew he was just trying to push me. So I finally said, "Okay, push me. I'm in." Guys loved him; you knew where his heart was. Frank was a large part of the attitude adjustment at The University of Texas. Coach Royal was a genius. He had great assistants in place, and every one of them had a place to be, a specific reason for being there.

We weren't supposed to win anything our senior year; we were dogmeat. We'd been horrible the year before. We were ranked down at the bottom because A&M was the big dog. We started winning, and then we got to Oklahoma. They were favored by 28 points, and with about four minutes left in the third quarter, they were ahead 3–0. We called a quick kick, and I did not do what I was supposed to. So my guy blocked the quick kick, and they scored. I think it ended up 27–0, and that was my dumb thing that I can't get rid of. I still think, *Man, what an idiot time to choke*. I still kick myself. That was the worst.

But it all ended with the Cotton Bowl, beating Alabama. It doesn't get better than that. That was the best. You know when Coach Royal gives his final speech to the team? Well, I've been told that I gave the speech. I don't know what I said, but we won. Of course, it was hard not to win with Travis Roach, Rosey Leaks, Alan Lowry, and Doug English. How could you not win?

The most valuable experience was just the guys, the teammates, some of the stupid stuff we got away with. By the grace of God, we're still here. Playing with the guys was the most important part of it. Coach Royal demanded that everyone was on the same level. No one was going to beat his chest or jump up and down. You weren't going to act like you did it by yourself. It bonded us together, and that's why everyone's still close. The University is different because of Coach Royal—his way, his life, his values—and we all respected that. Look at the respect he gets today, especially from those who played for him. It's pretty special.

It was a great time to be young, and it was a great time to be at Texas. A day doesn't go by when I don't think about the good stuff. My word, 37 years later, people still talk about all that. Was I blessed or what? I was in the right place at the right time through the whole thing. From the farm, to Plainview, to Austin, to Philadelphia. It was like a fairy tale. UT couldn't have been any better for me.

Jerry Sisemore's career as a football player at the college and professional level spanned 15 years, from his sophomore year in college in 1970 until his last year in the NFL in 1984. At Texas, he was a two-time consensus All-SWC and All-American, and a finalist for the Lombardi Award. He was named to the College Football Hall of Fame in 2002. His pro career with the Philadelphia Eagles spanned 12 seasons and included selection to two Pro Bowls. He is a member of the Longhorn Hall of Honor.

JULIUS WHITTIER

OFFENSIVE END

1970–1972

IWAS A SMALL-TOWN BOY. San Antonio was my world, and I had no clue what was going on outside it back then. I thought when I got through playing in high school, I'd be pumping gas somewhere. I had ADD (Attention Deficit Disorder), so I took life one day at a time. Not in a spiritual manner; I looked at it like, "Today's it. I'm going to have all the fun I can."

When I finished my senior season at Highlands High School, I had no idea colleges were looking at me. They were sending me letters, but I didn't know it. My mom and my coach conspired against me. They deprived me of this knowledge. They both probably knew that I was susceptible to arrogance, so after we'd lost the bi-district game, my coach called me in. He said, "I talked to your mom about this first, but these are yours," and he handed me two grocery bags full of letters from schools all over the country. He said, "Those are yours, but I want you to read this one first," and he handed me a letter from Coach Royal. That's the one I fell in love with. I don't know what happened to the rest of them.

Coach Mike Campbell came to the house and offered me a scholarship. My mom and dad stood back and let me choose. They didn't tell me everything negative they'd heard from friends, colleagues, or teachers who expressed concerns about Texas because they'd never played a black. "Nobody's ever gone to school there on scholarship. If you do go, you'll be buried at the bottom of

Julius Whittier was the Longhorns' first African American letterman and went on to become an attorney.

the roster." My parents said, "You go where you want to go," although my dad was scared for me. He'd known some guys who struck off into "white" territory and paid for it with their lives.

I came to Texas because it was big-time football 80 miles from home. And I loved central Texas. I was in the right place at the right time. I think it was divine—of God—because there were enough white people up there, if they'd wanted to kick my ass, they could have done it. Coach Royal was the right coach; Mike Campbell was the right recruiter; and the group of guys that was there was the right group. A few of my colleagues let their tongues slip, but I was comfortable that they didn't mean me any harm. I didn't care that some had ideas that were antithetical to integration. I didn't care.

The kids on campus were a delight. I enjoyed going to class. The profs let me raise my hand and spout out my ideas. I blew my Afro out and majored in philosophy. In those days, no one on the football team took anything past philosophy 101. That was an introductory course, and while everyone else thought it was just a grade, it blew my mind, so I decided to major in philosophy.

I had to do my study halls because all of my philosophy classes required an average of five papers a semester. I was blessed with a great tutor. The athletics department provided tutoring for difficult courses, and since I was the only one majoring in philosophy, I had my own tutor whenever I needed him, Peter Ayo. I learned more from him about constructing a paragraph than I ever learned in English. That's what got me into law school, the fact that I did so well in philosophy. I didn't do well in much else.

As a sophomore, I subbed for Mike Dean and Bobby Mitchell. I had to move from linebacker to guard to do that, but I was trying to move up the charts so I could get on the field. I knew the roughest part of football would be two-a-days, so I committed myself to being in shape. I told myself I was not going to be dragging butt during two-a-days.

When I got up there, I was at the top of the fitness chart out of everybody—running backs, wide receivers, everybody. Mike Presley and I were first and second in the testing every year he was there—push-ups, sprints, quarter-mile sprints, running stadium stairs, doing weight circuits, whatever. By the time we got to practice, it was easy.

By the time I was a sophomore, I'd developed a relationship with the quarterbacks. After every play we ran, we had to make the right blocks and then sprint down the field for 25 yards. I played part of the time as a linebacker and part of the time as an offensive guard. After every play, I'd ask Alan Lowry or the running backs to throw me the ball. We were playing catch. By the time I was a senior, the coaches had noticed that I could catch the ball, plus I was in shape, so they moved me to tight end.

When I was a senior, in 1972, I caught all the touchdown passes that year. Every single one. And I caught it in the A&M game. We had one touchdown pass the entire year. I was the leading receiver that season in touchdown receptions.

They were all decent people. It was not really a difficult time for me. When I went there, I told myself, as long as I get to play based on my skills, then I'm fine. Nobody gave me a hard time in the dorm or in the dining hall. In fact, I believe I was the only one on the team who had a personal relationship with the cook. Of course, he was black, and I'd come in through the kitchen when everybody else was out front, waiting at the door.

Kids those days were active in everything: ecology, civil rights, Vietnam, the draft, segregation versus integration, divestment of UT's investments in South Africa—that was the fun thing about UT. It seemed to be a real university. Many different viewpoints were tolerated. If there were racists on that campus, I didn't know it. They didn't find me, anyway. I remember walking on the west mall, with all the different booths students had set up to recruit and promote their various interests. That was one thing that made me understand how small San Antonio was. When I got to Texas, it seemed like the whole horizon got pushed back 5,000 miles. It told me San Antonio wasn't the only town on the earth.

137

That was a great time to be in college, not only because we were kicking butt in football but because the kids on that campus were genuinely and sincerely involved in more than just partying and sex and drugs.

The most memorable thing for me is not even football-related. My academic experience at UT was more than just getting the grades to graduate. It was waking up and appreciating the opportunity to go to a school like Texas and thinking, *How much is there that I don't know and don't understand?* That was the most amazing feeling.

Had I not gone to UT, I don't believe I'd be able to converse with as many different people as I am able to today. There's so much here—if you just let yourself experience it—that opens you up to many other realms of life that can be hidden from you if you have no clue how to act. UT is like a key; it opens doors.

The University is part of a state that was its own country at one point. There's no other state in the union like it. Texans are a lot like the institutions they created—for instance, the Texas Rangers. Texans are forthright—those who are true to it—they know what to stand up for, how to stand up, and when it's time to stand up. The University, aspiring to be a university of the first class, is a symbol of that spirit. Even though we come from a racist past, we should be proud that we have created this University that attempts to collect all of what is known about us, our lives, and the world we live in and to preserve the thought and reflection of it for future generations. I'm proud of that. I'm proud to have gone to The University.

To be a starting athlete on one of the best teams in the country—there's just no comparison. Football was my vehicle to become a Longhorn. Being a Longhorn is not simply about playing sports, it's about being part of The University life. There's far more to that in my life than just being a football player. I enjoyed pleasing my coach, and I enjoyed playing football. But the bigger thing is that Coach Royal turned me on to a quality University in my own state. When that group of men declared our independence in 1836, it was done with guys—whatever their thoughts on race—who had big ideas about the real world and the future. I'm proud of that.

Julius Whittier was the first African American letterman in Texas Longhorn football history. He began his career as an offensive guard and then switched to tight end his senior season. He serves as an assistant district attorney for Dallas County.

JAY ARNOLD

DEFENSIVE BACK

1971–1973

URING THE LONG RECRUITING RITUAL in 1970, I was fortunate to visit with, among others, Coach Royal and his assistant, Fred Akers; SMU's Hayden Fry; University of Houston's Coach Bill Yeoman; and the legendary Gil Steinke, who had been my dad's teammate at Texas A&I in the '30s and '40s. I had no special ties to UT, except that Tim Doerr, an assistant under Coach Royal, had coached at Liberty High School during my junior year. After several visits from Coach Akers, my mother asked him where he had gone to college. He replied, "To the University of Arkansas." My mom then stated, "Well, you seem to be such a nice young man, maybe that's where my son needs to go!" Coach Akers spent the rest of his time that night explaining to her why going to UT would be better than going to Arkansas.

I remember one coach who stood up during a recruiting trip and said, "In four or five years, we'll win the Southwest Conference." I sat there and counted, "Let's see…one, two, three, four…That's great. I'll be sitting in the stands by then."

One theme became prevalent: "If you come to '*our*' university, you will start as a sophomore. If you go to Texas, you will sit on the bench." Even as an 18-year-old, it seemed pretty obvious that if I could play as a sophomore at one school but never would get the chance to play at Texas, guess who's going to win that game? That strategy backfired with me. The recruiting propaganda the others put out made me want to go to Texas. It made me feel

Jay Arnold passed up a possible NFL career to return to Texas, becoming a successful attorney.

140

that if I went to their school, I was taking second-best. Another line they used against Texas was, "You'll just be a number, you won't ever get off the bench." So I was just very lucky to get to start as a sophomore.

Going from Liberty, Texas, a town of less than 6,000 to a university of 38,000 wasn't overwhelming, although I was probably intimidated from a standpoint of playing football. They were coming off back-to-back national championships. Everybody up there was good; everybody up there had been all-state. They had so many great players from everywhere. I don't know why I thought I could do it—I guess I just didn't know any better.

I visited Austin after the Longhorns had had an undefeated national championship season in 1969 and had just defeated Notre Dame in the Cotton Bowl. The atmosphere around the campus was full of excitement. You could feel the electricity in the air.

I chose Texas because I wanted to win a championship, and I knew Texas was going to win one. It had everything to do with winning. I liked the fact that Coach Royal recruited a lot of small-town athletes. It didn't appear to matter where they came from.

Coach Akers set up a time on the February signing date and told me he'd have Coach Royal come to Liberty for the signing. I told Coach Akers I was sure Coach Royal had other places to be that day with the big-name recruits. I said I didn't want to seem disrespectful, but it wasn't necessary for Coach Royal to be there, that he had done all the work. In typical fashion, Coach Royal called a couple of days before the national signing date and said, "Well, I understand from Coach Akers that y'all don't need me on Tuesday." I thought he was serious and stammered, "No, Coach, it's just that I thought you had better—" He stopped me, laughed, and said, "Jay, I know how you meant it. I'm just calling to tell you I appreciate you, and I look forward to having you as a player. But if you want me to come to Liberty, I want you to know I will."

141

Our freshman team was undefeated, 5–0. The freshmen had to sing before dinner until they won their first game. They couldn't come into the dining hall until all the upperclassmen were seated. Before they could eat, they had to march around the dining hall with both Horns up, singing "The Eyes of Texas," followed by "Texas Fight." If someone had a real bad voice or had a real bad high school song, they had to sing. As upperclassmen, we would always, always hope that someone came from Thomas Jefferson in Port Arthur or Austin High. I don't remember all of the words to the Austin High song, but *everybody* knew the last few words. The whole dining hall used to join in, "…forever Austin High." It was kind of the highlight of the dining hall.

Some players killed a deer one night and decided to skin it in the community bath. Our astute campus policemen thought they were carrying a body up to the dorm. They followed the blood trail up the elevator and when they came down the hall, everyone could hear their radios go off. "Are they carrying a body? Do not go any closer…." It was midnight, and you can imagine how loud those big old radios were. "How many of them are there? I think there are three of them. Wait…we'll close off the third floor and put men at every exit. Do not go. Do not go." So the guys quickly put this deer on the potty. Somebody lit a cigarette and put it in the deer's mouth, and put toilet paper on the deer's hoof. So this deer's sitting there, cigarette in its mouth with that tongue hanging out, toilet paper on one hoof, sitting on that commode. These cops were following the blood trail, and they all converged at the same time. They kicked the door open—you could hear it. We were all behind locked doors, but you could hear everything over the radio. Oh, those policemen were hot. That was my freshman year. I forgot the names of those involved, but they made them skin that deer and take the meat down to the Austin State School. Seems as if somebody had to run dummies as punishment for that one.

The only conference game we lost when I was there was against Arkansas, and we had critical breakdowns at the defensive end positions. We didn't usually suit out on Mondays, we just went in shells. But that next Monday, I saw about five or six guys' names on the board—"full pads." Normally full pads on a Monday was reserved for guys who had done something wrong. But these guys who were supposed to go in full pads hadn't had a bad game against Arkansas. My name was on the board—"full pads." I just went, "Oh, man." I asked Coach Campbell what that was about, and he said, "We're going to try to find somebody to play defensive end." We went out and basically went through tryouts. Malcolm Minnick and I started the next game. I played defensive end the rest of that year and the next year. I moved to corner at the beginning of my senior year.

Coach Royal didn't give many rah-rah pep talks, but one of the greatest speeches he gave was in 1973, after Miami beat us in the opening game and after Oklahoma just beat the dog out of us.

Coach Royal huddled us all up in the middle of the field at the stadium right before practice.

He told us that he had gone home and realized that he wasn't having any fun. He told us that from that day forward he was going to have fun and he wanted us to go back out, play with enthusiasm, and "have some fun." He took the blame for our lackluster play against Oklahoma, and said that if we wanted to finish the year with a winning record, he would do his part. Well, we went undefeated the rest of the regular season and played Nebraska in the Cotton Bowl, and we did have fun. Coach Royal put some excitement back into practice and the game without blaming us as players.

The whole atmosphere for game time was special: the Longhorn Band, the All-American cheerleaders, the greatest fans in college football, the Texas-sized flag, Big Bertha, Bevo, the Texas Cowboys, and the Spurs.

I was fortunate enough to play with some tremendous players—Jerry Sisemore, Rosey Leaks, Glen Gaspard, Doug English, Jim Bertelsen, Randy Braband, and Bill Wyman. The overriding things in my memory are being a part of such a great team of young men who defined the concept of "team," and being coached by men who were dedicated to winning but who never lost sight of the fact that we were going to make some mistakes. As long as we made them at full speed and didn't make it a habit, they could work out the rest. I relied upon the word of our defensive genius, Coach Mike Campbell, when he told me, "If you'll keep going until the glass breaks, I will find you a place to play on our team." As far as I am concerned, he kept his word. If you wanted to play, you definitely had an opportunity.

143

Jay Arnold handled the unusual combination of playing both defensive end and defensive halfback as a three-year letterman. He played on three Southwest Conference championship teams and was All–Southwest Conference in 1973.

PAT KELLY

OFFENSIVE END

1971–1973

I GREW UP IN LUBBOCK, and like many other kids I grew up with, I just assumed I'd go to Texas Tech.

I'd broken my arm in the third game of my junior year in high school. As starting quarterback, I had a couple of good games and had some success, but then my season was over, so I didn't have any kind of recruiting connection. I decided I hadn't had enough football, so I applied for and got an appointment to the Air Force Academy. Then, I had a pretty good senior year, and my head coach, Tommy Stone, was well-connected, so I got a little bit of notoriety and started getting recruited. I thought, *Well, I'll go play football at Texas Tech.*

After the last game of my senior year, Coach Stone came to me and said, "You've got a long-distance phone call," and it was Emory Bellard. He said, with that Mississippi accent, "Patrick Kelly, this Emory Bellard, University of Texas. I'd like to offer you a four-year scholarship to The University." I said, "Well, I'd like to think about it." It came as a total surprise. That was the first contact I'd had with any UT coaches.

After the season, coaches would swing through town and take me to dinner. "Come to Rice and get a ring from Rice Institute and it will open doors." "Come to A&M"—that was Gene Stallings—"be a part of the fellowship of Aggies throughout the state." SMU had attractive things, Steve Owens had just won the Heisman Trophy at OU, Arkansas was on a roll with

Pat Kelly, a three-year starter, earned postgraduate scholarship awards from the NCAA and the National Football Foundation.

Frank Broyles, as was University of Houston with Bill Yeoman. So I thought, *I'll be very organized and deliberate about this.* I took notes and had a list of pros and cons, advantages and disadvantages, for each school. I even visited Texas Tech across town. I told myself, *I'll just go through all these schools, sit down under a tree with my list, take my time, and decide logically which would be the best fit.* Texas was a big school, almost too big, and I didn't know if I was good enough to play there. They had just won the national championship.

In my three years there, my high school team won four games; one game each my sophomore and junior years, and two games my senior year. I was so tired of losing that I thought if I went to Texas, even if I never played a down, at least I'd be part of a winning program. Coach Bellard called again and said, "Patrick, I know you want to sit down, take your time, and think this through, but to tell you the truth, we're running out of scholarships. I'm trying to hold a spot for you, but we're having a fantastic recruiting class. If you want to go to Texas, I need to know pretty soon." So I said, "Coach, let me think about it…okay, I'm coming."

That's how it happened, over the telephone with Emory Bellard. My dad had died my junior year, the night before a game. My mother was supportive but was not too involved. My older brother, Dan, helped me with some advice, but I was pretty much on my own.

So I drove to school in my dad's '64 Chevrolet Impala, a four-door, old, beat-up car. It was the family car, and my mother didn't drive, so I took it. I packed up the family car and drove by myself. It took me about eight or nine hours because I kept getting lost. I had never driven the freeways before, so I'd take "Business Abilene" and "Business Brownwood" instead of taking the loops around town.

The guy I was supposed to room with changed his mind at the last minute and decided not to come to Texas. I showed up at Jester Dorm, and Coach Ellington said, "Well, Patrick, your roommate decided he was not going to make the trip, so we've put you with a boy from Travis High School named Mark Halfmann." Talk about fate and good things happening. We were roommates for the next nine or ten years. I had a ready-made family here with Mark's parents, and Mark and I ended up being lifelong friends.

They listed the depth chart every day, and I was seventh at left or right defensive halfback. I was way down there. I was with the Birds—the scout team—and a lot of those guys were fourth- or fifth-year seniors. They were never going to play. One day at the end of two-a-days, the defensive backs were lollygagging around, loafing. It was a hot day. Coach Royal was up in the tower, and our little group was on the 40-yard line. I remember working hard on all these crummy drills. The old guys would say, "Take it easy, you're making us look bad. Slow down." But I was going 100 percent. Sure enough, at the end of practice, Coach Royal called everyone together and said, "This is one of the sorriest practices I've ever seen. I know it's hot and you're tired of two-a-days, but you've got this kid over here, Pat Kelly, who's on seventh team, working hard." He obviously noticed a little bit. On the next day's depth chart, I wasn't listed with the defensive backs, and I thought, *Aw, heck. Where am I?* They'd moved me over to receiver.

We didn't have a lot of depth at receiver, and then Jimmy Moore injured his knee against Texas Tech. So, suddenly, by default, I was in. I started three years, but a lot of it was just dumb luck, being at the right place at the right time.

I told everybody I was the "play-carrier-inner." Jim came back the next year and, basically, he and I would alternate. I must have started the first game, because all the programs were printed listing me as the starter. But Jimmy and I would just say, "Who started last game? Well, you take the play in first this game." It was a diplomatic relationship.

One of my best memories is beating Texas Tech all three years. As a team, it was satisfying to beat Tech, and I had good games against them. I remember my junior year when we beat Alabama in the Cotton Bowl, where Alan Lowry "almost" stepped out of bounds, but not quite.

Coaches always say you remember the losses more than you do the wins. I remember some of those passes I dropped, and I wish I could go back and have another chance to make those catches. We only lost one conference game while I was there, to Arkansas in Little Rock. I remember the loss we had in Miami my junior year. We'd been picked a preseason No. 1, and the *Sports Illustrated* cover had a picture of a hand making the Hook 'em Horns sign. We had a good team—as it turned out, not a great team. We went to Miami, and everything that could go wrong did go wrong. Miami had a good team with Chuck Foreman, but that was a tough loss, to lose the season opener against a lesser opponent. We lost to Oklahoma three years during that reign. My junior year they blocked a quick kick. Of course, they'd been spying on our practices, and when we broke the huddle, their linebacker was saying, "Here comes the quick kick, here comes the quick kick!" They blocked the kick, scored, and went on to win that game. Those were some bitter times.

We lost to a Penn State team in the Cotton Bowl my sophomore year. Coach Campbell told us, "Well, I've been watching some film, and that Lydell Mitchell is pretty good. But they've got this other back who's pretty good, too, and his name is Franco Harris." My senior year we lost to Nebraska, which was just coming off a national championship. So every team that beat us was a very good team, except for Miami.

Coach Royal was 52 when he retired—younger than I am today—but when I played for him, I thought he was so much older. When you're 18, 48 seems old; my gosh, he was young. Fortunately, he's been around for another 30-something years. I appreciate him more every year. He was a great coach.

The most valuable thing I got from playing at Texas was just knowing I was part of the Texas tradition and spirit, which was there long before I showed up and will be there forever. I'll always know and cherish the fact that I contributed some small part to that tradition and to that very special program.

Pat Kelly was a three-year letterman and starter for Darrell Royal's Longhorns in the early 1970s. He was an honor student, earning awards for the National Football Foundation's postgraduate scholarship and the NCAA Postgraduate Scholarship.

DOUG ENGLISH

DEFENSIVE TACKLE

1972–1974

M Y SOPHOMORE YEAR IN HIGH SCHOOL, I was third string on the B team. We had a B team, a JV, and a varsity, and I was third string on the B team. I played some on the varsity as a junior but didn't start. I got my first start in a football game my senior year.

Bryan Adams High School [in Dallas] was a great school full of good, caring teachers and coaches. The principal was one of the finest men you'll ever meet. I had great mentors and great coaches from the get-go, and that environment helped me stick with it. And, although my dad didn't push me, he was a tremendous example. He is the poster boy for setting an example with his actions, not his words. That's what he does; that's what he is. He instilled in me the desire to succeed, to just hammer it until you succeed.

Despite my relative lack of success on the football field, I kept feeling that I wasn't through yet; I needed to finish this thing. Looking back, down deep I felt, *I can do this. I really can do this*. Plus, I continued growing. Everyone else just kind of leveled off, but I kept growing. I finally quit growing when I was 25.

I was surprised with each recruiting letter I got. I wasn't even that highly recruited, but I do remember a couple of schools—the more notorious ones— that made some pretty blatant offers to get me to sign with them. I thought, *If they're willing to do that for me, what would they do for the stars?* I wasn't sure where I wanted to go, but I do remember Texas A&M calling and my just

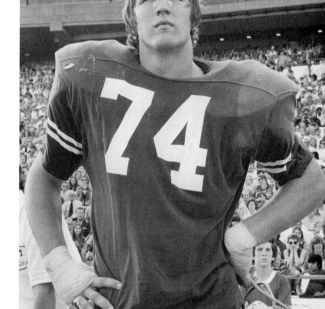

Doug English went on to be an All-Pro defensive tackle for the Detroit Lions.

saying, "No. I'm just not interested at all." I'd visited Baylor, TCU, Okla-homa, and a lot of schools, but I just had no desire to go to Texas A&M.

There were people who cared about me in high school who, in their own ways, discouraged me from coming to Texas. I remember one girl saying, "You know, Doug, a lot of really good players get lost down there." Our high school had had a few all-state players who came to Texas and didn't meet with success. These people's perception of my ability was built over the years, not just three months of football my senior year. So they were justified in advis-ing me to pick a smaller school somewhere.

I visited TCU, and that campus is drop-dead gorgeous. The people were all nice, and it was fairly handy to where I grew up. It was a place where someone with my record should probably have gone. Their locker room was really snazzy. They'd beaten a close rival that day—I think it was SMU—and they were celebrating. It was a big day at TCU, and as the players filed out of the locker room, at the end of the rows of lockers, there were boxes filled with apples. The players would grab an apple on the way out the door to meet their families and I thought, *Man, that is really cool! Free apples!*

The next weekend I came to Texas. I got a load of their facilities, and Texas beat the crap out of somebody. As the players left the locker room, they passed the cage where Mr. Jim, the old equipment manager, was sitting. He was passing out these apples, two at a time, that were as big as pumpkins. The players were grabbing these apples, and they could barely get their hands around them. They'd grab one and toss the other to their date and, believe it or not, those apples were to me a metaphor of why I needed to come to Texas.

Coach Pat Patterson recruited me. He is a fantastic mentor, a great man, and was perfect for me. I still have lunch with him once a month. He was exactly what I needed. He and Coach Royal knew how to deal with players exactly where they were. All they required was that you work hard. If you came out there and were just content to wear the jersey and not work hard, then maybe you needed to go somewhere else. You know, there were 150 players on the team then. But if you were willing to work hard, they'd give you a chance.

They took a chance on me. There were probably some coaches who said, "There's no record on this guy. He's had one good year. Why do we want him?" And, if they had had the scholarship restraints then that they have today, I wouldn't have been able to come here. I wouldn't have been in their top 20 or 30.

Pat Patterson was also my position coach. He was the master of knowing just what to do and say at just the right time. My first start on the varsity was in the Oklahoma game. I was a sophomore and I remember walking out of the locker room, down the tunnel and onto the field, into that wall of sound that everyone talks about. Maybe I hesitated or looked nervous, and maybe Coach Pat was watching for it, knowing that this was my first start. But I'd stopped and was looking around, a little stunned. He walked up next to me, looked all around the Cotton Bowl, and said, "No place for a timid man, is it?" I thought to myself, *Nope, it's not. Let's go.* And it worked. I think I had 16 tackles that day. But that was Pat. He knew what he wanted you to do and was going to give you the tools to do it.

I scored the one and only touchdown of my collegiate career against Arkansas on a punt that Earl Campbell blocked. That was the first year freshmen were eligible, and Coach Royal was trying to find a way to work Earl

151

into the lineup, so he put him on the punt-block team just to get his feet wet. Coach Royal lined Earl up on the center and said, "You follow the ball." It was a tight game, and we had Arkansas backed up to punt. We called the block, and Earl not only followed the ball, he almost outran the ball to the punter. I was lined up next to Earl and we just popped through the gap. I was a step or five behind Earl, and when he blocked the punt, it popped up and landed right into my hands. I ran it all the way into the end zone—about three steps, if that. I scored six points in college and eight points in the NFL. I just did it the hard way in the NFL with four safeties. Believe it or not, that's an NFL record.

I remember a goal-line stand against Alabama in the Cotton Bowl my sophomore year. It was first-and-two on the goal. We stopped them and won the game. That's back when defense was defense; it wasn't a chess game. You had to whip the guy over you. A well-coached defense was set up that way and certainly, under Mike Campbell, we had well-coached defenses.

When I think about what it means to be a Longhorn, I take my cue from Coach Pat. It means doing the right thing at the right time. It's getting in the end zone and acting like you've been there before. It's making a good, driving face tackle and not acting like that's the first good tackle you ever made; that's just how you do it. It's studying when it's time to study, it's preparing when it's time to prepare, and it's playing hard when it's time to play. Those qualities don't stop when you hang your cleats up, either. It's a way of living with integrity and a strong work ethic that most definitely was initiated by Coach Royal and his coaching staff. I'm really glad I went there.

Doug English was one of most respected defensive linemen both at Texas and during a 10-year career with the Detroit Lions. At UT, he was All–Southwest Conference and All-American and was a four-time All-Pro selection in the NFL. He is a member of the Detroit Lions' all-time team and a member of the Longhorn Hall of Honor.

ROOSEVELT LEAKS

FULLBACK

1972–1974

I CAME TO TEXAS AS AN AFTERTHOUGHT. I had no direction as to what college I'd go to. I was recruited by the University of Houston, and it was my intention to go there, but they signed several running backs, so they did not recruit me anymore. Coach David McWilliams was visiting me every week or so. A&M was on the doorstep every day, as close as they were to Brenham. Oklahoma State, Stanford, and some other schools recruited me, too. I decided to stay in the state because it was close to home and my folks could come see me.

I hadn't been out of Brenham much. Then I came up here and was going to school with 40,000 students, and I'd see that huge stadium every day. There was a learning curve in sports, but more than anything else, as a student-athlete. My first two years were tough, academically. I was borderline a few semesters, especially in the fall. That was probably the toughest part, but by my junior year, I'd learned how to learn, and that was exciting. I didn't have a problem with school after that.

Being one of a small number of African American students on campus, there were issues that happened on and off the field, but they were some of the same issues I'd faced in high school. Nothing was really different at UT. Brenham had integrated my freshman year in high school, so I'd been through it all, and people are still people. It was just a matter of whether or not you could tolerate it.

I won't say it wasn't tough; there were a few black athletes in basketball, and with Fred Perry, my roommate, there were four of us on the football team. Julius Whittier and Lonnie Bennett both had white roommates, so we got along with everyone. Most of the blacks hung out together. We'd go to Huston-Tillotson and go to parties over there. There were other students on campus we hung out with. Some folks thought it was a big thing, but it wasn't.

During spring training my freshman year, I thought I was the number-one fullback and that I should start my sophomore year. Rumors got around that they were not going to start me, so the question became, "Was I going to come back for my sophomore year?" It became an issue with me. I was working in Houston that summer. I guess Coach Royal got wind that I wasn't coming back, so somebody—one of the tutors—came down to talk to me. "Man, this is the best place for you. You need to come on back here." I hadn't really decided on where else I might go. I didn't really want to go anywhere else.

I had played in two freshman games when I got hit and stretched my Achilles, so I was through with that. When I came here, I weighed about 200–205. By the time the first semester ended, I was about 225. Of course, after I finished spring training with Mr. Frank Medina, I was back to 205.

Frank got us in shape. He did do that. When you talk about doing whatever it takes to get it done—not just in football—Frank had a lot to do with that. When times get hard today, most of us keep going, and that attitude is because of Frank. You learned little things that didn't make a big impression then, but today you're still doing those things and you wonder why. It's because we were taught how to get things done. Work smart about it, and just work, work, work at it.

The Ministry of Challenge's honoree one year was Coach Royal, and James Street was speaking at the banquet. James, talking about Coach Royal, commented, "Every day I file my fingernails and make sure they're clean." I thought, *Man, is that why I keep a fingernail file with me all the time?* When I played pro ball, I'd always have two fingernail files and my playbook in my bag. Coach Royal taught us to do that. There were many things Coach Royal taught us.

When my sophomore season began, I was the starter. There was still some friction with other players over whether I should start, but Jerry Sisemore and Travis Roach told me, "You're our running back, so the other guys had just better get with the program. Don't worry about it."

Roosevelt Leaks, an All-American who finished third in the 1973 Heisman voting, rushed for a school-record 342 yards against SMU.

A lot of folks talk about my junior year when we played SMU, but I tell them that if I hadn't fumbled two or three times, I wouldn't have stayed in the game long enough to reach 342. I would have been out of the game early. That was just one of those freak things.

Those days were probably the most fun days of my life. College is the time a kid has the opportunity to really enjoy himself. The first time he can get away from home, have the time of his life. I met folks from all over the country, and that was exciting to me.

I got hurt my junior year in the A&M game, stretched the ligaments in my left knee. When it happened, the kid who hit me jumped up and down, danced around. A lot of folks were mad about that, but he wasn't excited that he hurt me; he was just excited that he'd stopped me. He called me later that night and said, "It wasn't anything personal. I was just excited." I told him, "I don't have a problem with that. I understand the game."

I'd finished third in the Heisman and made All-American and had to go to all these different functions. I was on the *Bob Hope Show* in New York. Bob said, "And here are the running backs." I came limping out there with a cast on my leg.

156

So I missed the first week or two of spring, and some NFL scouts were going to visit practice the next week. My coaches said, "You probably need to get out here and show them a little something." We weren't even going full speed when a freak accident happened. I got hit on my knee, and it popped. I rolled up in the air, and when I hit the ground, my knee buckled—nothing held. Dr. Julian operated on me the next morning and told me everything was all torn up. The doctor said it would take six to nine months to rehab it, but six months came right at the first day of fall practice. The coaches asked if I wanted to go or not. I went out there to practice like everybody else. Of course, I had to tape it every day, you know—tape on skin. That was the fun part; had to shave my legs so they could put the tape right to the skin. And every day you had to pull it off. That was tough.

I wondered if those injuries happened to me to reign me back in. Was I getting too wild? Those things cross your mind. It made me concentrate on what I had to get done. Being voted third in the Heisman with the two guys in front of me being seniors, yeah, you could say I had a shot of winning it the next year. It was a tough break, but Coach Royal said, "There will be some tough days ahead. I hate to see this happen now, but you can always move forward." I made the decision to keep going forward.

Regardless of where I go, people say, "You're a Longhorn? Man, I used to watch you." Young people would say, "I'm gonna be Roosevelt Leaks," because they watched The University of Texas. I believe a whole lot of bright kids went to The University because of what Roosevelt Leaks did here. That is the thing I'm most proud of, that I might have opened doors for other young people to get an education and to make a better life for themselves and their communities. That means more to me than anything else.

There are folks who have animosity about The University, who don't like it. They think it's too big, that they're racist. I tell them, "I was there. All you know is what you heard. I was there." It's no different from anywhere else. That's just part of life, and once you learn to get past that, you'll see what you want to get done and just keep going down that road.

The most valuable things I got from being here were the discipline and the desire to win. That, and learning how to play with other players, using your talents to the best of your ability, and using your mentality or thought patterns. You learn how to mix with other players and make sure you all mesh. The team is always bigger than you. Look at some of those pictures when we were running the wishbone. You can see our offensive line, everybody coming off the line on the same step. That's what a team is about.

There's a great pride in anyone who ever played at The University. We all have the expectation that we're going to be winners. You can say what you want to about The University, but we know who we are, and we will always stand tall. You can feel proud of yourself that you've accomplished something. And regardless of how other folks think it was, they see that I'm still standing.

157

Roosevelt Leaks became the first African American All-American at Texas and finished third in the Heisman Trophy voting in 1973. He set a single-game NCAA rushing record with 342 yards against SMU in 1973. He was a two-time all-conference selection and was named to the National Football Foundation's College Hall of Fame in 2005. He is also a member of the Longhorn Hall of Honor.

KEITH MORELAND

DEFENSIVE BACK

1973

MY INFATUATION WITH THE UNIVERSITY OF TEXAS started when I went to the 1964 Cotton Bowl game, which was then the national championship game against Roger Staubach and Navy. I was nine years old and was in awe watching those players. I listened to Kern Tips on the old Southwest Conference network and became a huge Longhorn fan.

I was getting recruited by everybody—LSU, Arizona State, OU, all the SWC schools, Nebraska—and the deadline was closing in. I played at the high school where Bill Montgomery played, so I had Montgomery and Frank Broyles wearing me out, trying to get me to go to Arkansas. My parents said, "You've got to make a decision." Schools started calling, saying, "You've got to accept now, or we're going to withdraw our offer."

On the day before Christmas break my senior year, Coach Pat Patterson showed up at my high school, and I got a call to come down to the office. He reached out, shook my hand, and said, "My name is Coach Patterson from The University of Texas." My eyes lit up and I said, "Are y'all gonna offer me a scholarship, or is this just a visit?" He told me he wouldn't be there if they weren't going to give me an offer. I said, "Then, my recruiting days are over." That was the first and only time I'd heard from Texas.

I had the good fortune to have another part of my life in baseball, but at that time, football was king to me. I wanted to be Roger Staubach. I had all

Two-sport star Keith Moreland later became an outstanding major league baseball player.

159

the dreams that many kids have…I wanted to play in the NFL. Baseball was just something I did in the spring.

My baseball team went to the Connie Mack World Series. We won the national championship back-to-back, and I was the two-time series MVP. Coach Cliff Gustafson asked me what I was going to do in the fall. I laughed and said, "I'm gonna be on your campus." Coach Gus said, "Well, I need to talk to Coach Royal." That's how I got a shot to play baseball at Texas.

I played a lot my sophomore football season, and then I had a good sophomore baseball season. I was talking to every scout in the world, and they were telling me that I could make some money in baseball. By that point I was pretty sure, after trying to tackle Rosey Leaks and Earl Campbell, that my dream of playing on Sundays was not going to happen. That's a tough realization for a kid. Some kids realize that in high school, some in junior high. It hit me after two years of playing football at a school that was in the hunt for a national championship every year. *I'm not going to play on Sundays.*

We got beat by Nebraska in the Cotton Bowl, and I got to play quite a bit. I felt I'd be involved my junior year, but I kept thinking, *I'm going to be drafted in June. I'm going to sign and go out.* At that time you couldn't be a professional athlete in one sport and play another in college. I could play one more season, but if I got hurt, I would always regret it because I wouldn't get drafted. It wasn't because of a lack of love of football.

It was a hard decision to come back that summer before my junior year. I was getting anxious for football to start. I went through two-a-days, and one day I just said, "What if I get out here and tear up a knee?" I saw what Rosey had gone through—getting hurt, trying to get through practice. He was a great player, and this injury had hurt his chance to play. That says a lot about Roosevelt and his intestinal fortitude to get through that, to come back, and to go on to have a career in the NFL.

I called my dad and said, "I don't want to play the game and be afraid to get hurt, and I don't want to get hurt and lose a chance to play baseball." That was a hard 24 hours. Football had been a dream and a love of mine my whole life. I played Pop Warner football long before I ever played Little League baseball.

I remember that day, stopping Coach Royal as he was jogging. I probably should have gone more through the chain of command, but I said, "Coach, you're the one who brought me here and gave me this opportunity. I wanted to tell you that I feel I'll be better off—for my future—if I don't play football because I think I have a chance to play baseball." He told me, "I respect your decision and I understand."

I came back and got my degree. You can't imagine what it meant to me to get my "T" ring after playing 17 years professionally. I was fortunate to make some money playing the game, but to get my degree at age 38? The first thing I did after I received my sheepskin was to go straight to the athletic department and say, "I want my 'T' ring now." That's an integral part of the experience, knowing that you played football for Darrell Royal, graduated, got a degree, and have that ring. I've got a national championship ring for baseball and a World Series ring, and that "T" ring is just as important to me as those other rings.

There was an unwritten rule that freshmen football players had to find a way to "gather some equipment" from A&M's Corps of Cadets when the Aggies played basketball at Gregory Gym. That night we beat the Aggies, and all of us were right behind the bench. We knew some of the Corps guys were going to come by, but I was a sophomore, so I backed off to watch from the side. One of our freshmen grabbed a hat and took off running toward the dorm as fast as he could. About six or seven Corps guys came by, and I took off running, body-blocked three of them, and knocked them into the fountain. I jumped up and hollered, "You guys just ran over me!" They hadn't seen me, so they didn't know what had happened, but that allowed the freshman to get into the dorm with the hat.

We were wrong to be involved in that. But it sure was fun to watch those freshmen march into the dining hall the next day wearing those hats. It was great.

Those are the things you remember. Because when you're in two-a-days and the AstroTurf gets to 115–120 degrees, you really get to know the courage that human beings have; to be able to put up with all that and go through what you have to go through. In those days, Frank Medina gave no water breaks. The only thing you had was a frozen sliced orange. Boy, that orange looked pretty good most days.

161

Until I got into broadcasting, I never knew we had that big of a bulls-eye on our chest. Texas has one of the largest athletic endowments in the country, the best facilities in the country, and the best coaching in the country year after year. People are going to give us their best shot in every sport we play. At The University of Texas, especially in football, you're going to get the opposing team's best every time the ball is kicked off. I'm proud to be involved in a program like that.

I'm proud of the fact that when somebody mentions my name—they don't always say, "He's an ex-Cub"—you always hear them say, "He's a Longhorn." To be introduced as a graduate of The University of Texas means more to me—aside from God or my family—than anything else. To have had the opportunity that the Good Lord and Coach Royal gave me is something that will always be with me.

Is there any other hand sign that is more recognizable than the Hook 'em Horns sign? I don't think so. I've had the good fortune to travel, and it's mind-boggling to think that you could hail a cab in Milan, Italy, with your Horns up and have the cab driver say, "Texas!" It happened to me.

Maybe the reason we have the bulls-eye on our chest is that we are all—from the president of The University on down—extremely proud of Texas. We understand that we are supposed to show excellence in our lives. From the fans who never played a sport here to Earl Campbell and Ricky Williams—who walked away with the highest prize in college sports—we're all in that same category. That's the thing that sets me apart from any of those guys who end up in the National Baseball Hall of Fame...they didn't go to Texas. It will always be a major part of my life.

Keith Moreland was a two-sport star at Texas who followed his college days with an outstanding career in professional baseball. He set a Texas freshman record with seven pass interceptions in the five-game season and lettered in football in 1973. He was a three-time all-conference and All-American player in baseball and enjoyed a 12-year major league career. He is a member of the Longhorn Hall of Honor.

EARL CAMPBELL

RUNNING BACK

1974–1977

I WENT TO JOHN TYLER HIGH SCHOOL in Tyler, Texas. I was a middle line-backer because Dick Butkus was my hero, and I wanted to be the next Dick Butkus. One day our coach, Corky Nelson, said, "We don't have a running back, so you're gonna be our running back." I went up to the line of scrimmage and dropped the ball because I didn't want to be a running back. I wanted to be a middle linebacker.

I started seeing this guy from Texas around our school. I thought, "Texas? That's pretty big." I didn't know anything about Texas. He started coming to our high school when I was a sophomore, and I thought he was coming to look at those other guys, not me. That's how Ken Dabbs started recruiting me my sophomore—maybe my freshman—year. One time I asked him, "What are you talking about, 'Texas?'" And he said, "The University of Texas."

I said, "Oh, yeah…I remember seeing them on TV." I never will forget it. We had a black-and-white TV, and this guy named Roosevelt Leaks had on a white uniform with a Longhorn on the side of his helmet. My older sister said to me, "You think you can play football, huh?" And I said, "Yeah." She said, "Well, you need to watch this black guy…he's fixin' to break a record." That was my senior year in high school, and Roosevelt Leaks rushed for something like 342 yards against SMU that day.

Then, this guy Dabbs says, "Listen, we'd like to ask you about coming to our college." I said, "You a college coach?"

He said, "No, I'm a recruiter."

I said, "You run that school?"

And he said, "No, I just recruit for Coach Royal."

I said, "Well, where's he?"

"He's got to coach the team, so I go out and find players for him. I'll tell you what, Friday he's gonna come up here, and he'll come to your house."

"Who, Coach Royal?"

He said "Yeah. You don't sound excited."

I said, "Well, he's a guy, and I'm a guy, so...."

So this guy showed up and said, "I'm the head coach at The University of Texas."

We were kind of ashamed of our house. We lived in this...I'm not going to call it a shack, but it was the best my mom and dad could afford. Coach Royal got back there and was talking to my mom. She was sick, and she said she was feeling embarrassed about our house. He said, "No, don't be embarrassed. This is a lot better than what I grew up in." So they hit it off.

The next thing I knew, Coach Dabbs had talked me into coming down one Friday to visit Texas. I asked, "How we gonna get there?" He said a plane was going to pick us up, and Coach Royal would be on that plane. I thought, *An airplane?* When I worked in the rose fields, I'd look up in the sky and dream about being in one of those planes. I didn't show it, but when I got on that plane, I was nervous as hell. In order to calm down I asked, "Do y'all mind if I have a dip?" Coach Dabbs said, "Nah, because I have a chew." Coach Royal just sat there and went along with it. When the plane hit the ground, Coach Royal let me go up in his office and visit with him and Coach Dabbs. Then Raymond Clayborn came and met me, and Coach Royal said, "This is who's going to show you around." I said, "Show me around? What does that mean?" "Oh, he's gonna tell you about UT and how good it is."

I thought, *Man, that's a school.* Bigger than the ranch I used to work on. Raymond told me, "I guarantee you, man, if you come to this school, you'll win the Heisman Trophy." I had a good time. That Sunday, when it was time to leave, I got back in to talk to Coach Royal. About that time, this guy was coming up the hall, and he was red. He was bald-headed, but he was real red. He was a white guy. I didn't think about it then, but Coach Campbell was trying to get him away from me.

Earl Campbell, "the Tyler Rose," was the Longhorns' first Heisman Trophy winner.

He was saying, "Wally, come on over here." The guy was Wally Scott, who was one of the greatest Longhorns ever, and had one of the biggest hearts. Wally came from my home town. Wally said, "I want to tell that boy something. I want him to know he ain't the first SOB from Tyler, Texas, who is famous. You're the second, because I'm the first guy from Tyler that went to this school." I looked in that cup he was carrying, and I thought it was orange juice. Later, I understood why Coach Campbell was trying to get Wally away from me. But there wasn't a better person or a better friend in the world than Wally Scott. That's just how he was. He never did anything halfway.

Coach Royal got me in his office and said, "What do you think about our school?" I said, "I think it's great. I'll come to school here." He said, "That's great…that means you don't have to go visit Oklahoma." I said, "Nah, I'm going to Oklahoma to visit." He said, "If you are coming here, why are you going to Oklahoma?" I said, "Because I told that man Barry Switzer I would come up there, and I'm a man of my word."

My freshman year, Roosevelt Leaks asked me if I wanted to take an easy course, and he said, "Get in the speech department." I said, "Okay." The first day of class the lady says, "Everybody whose name begins with the letter *C*, I want them to get in front of the class on Wednesday. Give me a 10-minute speech on what y'all think about The University and what you are doing here." I tried my best to get up there and tell her what it meant to be a fullback. She was red-headed. I don't know why that lady took a liking to me, but she said, "Are you real serious about this?" I lied and said, "Yeah." She said, "After you get out of practice, come over here and I'll teach you how to get up in front of people and give a speech." She said, "When you get up to give a speech, look at everybody and move left to right with your head, and everybody is going to swear you are looking right at them." That's something I will never forget. Roosevelt Leaks tricked me, and it was a good trick, as it turned out, because I ended up majoring in speech. I had to do a lot of talking in pro football, and that's how I learned to do it.

The summer before my senior year, they were building a performing arts building on campus. Coach Dabbs got my twin brothers and me a job over there for the summer. It's where the old baseball field was. He said, "You see that plywood down there? It's got to be brought up here. Every day, go get that plywood." I had to jump the water because they had that little creek down there, and every day I had to tote that plywood because that was my job.

This guy named Tony Dorsett was playing in Dallas. He was raising all kinds of hell, and he hadn't played a down of football. He was doing everything—fighting people up there, dating women, but he hadn't played a down. They had an article in the paper that said if you win the Heisman, you could make a million dollars. One day at lunch, there was a guy on the job and we were reading the newspaper about Tony. He told me, "You are good enough to win that Heisman."

So I found our trainer, Frank Medina. I said, "You see this piece of paper right here, Frank? I want to win that award next year." He said, "If you want to win that award, come here every day after you get off that job." That's how I won the Heisman, because of Frank Medina. He had more to do with it than anybody.

I didn't realize what it meant to be a Longhorn until I got into pro football, and I'll never forget this. We were playing in Cleveland, Ohio. Looking back, I wish I had met these people. They sat behind our bench on the second level, upper deck. They had a sign that said "Hook 'em Horns. We Love Earl Campbell." When I came out for warm-ups, I would give them a Hook 'em. Win or lose, I would always give them a Hook 'em, and they would always stand up. What I am trying to say is, anywhere you go in this country, there are always Longhorns. I don't think you can say that about any other college. It's a tight group; once you go to Texas, you are always known as a Longhorn. My name changed from "Earl Campbell, the Tyler Rose," to "Earl Campbell, UT Main Man," and that's the way it will always be for me.

167

Earl Campbell was known as "the Tyler Rose" when he came out of Tyler, Texas, to become one of the most famous football players of his era. He was the Longhorns' first Heisman Trophy winner in 1977, was a two-time All-American and three-time all-conference player. He is a member of the Longhorn Hall of Honor and both the College Football and Pro Football Halls of Fame.

ALFRED JACKSON

OFFENSIVE END

1974–1977

ICAME TO THE UNIVERSITY OF TEXAS because my mom was crazy about David McWilliams. Coach McWilliams recruited me, so she really didn't want to talk to any recruiters other than David. Everyone told me that The University was not a good place for me because Texas hadn't recruited many African Americans and that it would be a hostile place for me to go. My mom never believed that; she just believed in David McWilliams.

I just wanted to get out of Caldwell, Texas, and in 18 years, I never had been to Austin. I was recruited by Baylor, Oklahoma, and other schools, but I always knew it was going to be between Texas and Texas A&M. They were my only interests. The deciding piece was David McWilliams and how genuine he came across, not only to my mom but to me. David told me, "Alfred, you should forgo the short-term bonuses that you could have because the relationships that you'll build here over a long period of time will be the relationships that will sustain you." I didn't really know what that meant then, but today I understand. Coming to The University has opened a lot of doors to me in multiple ways.

I remember to this day my most frightening moment at Texas. When I first came to UT, there were about 500 people in my first class, a history class. I was absolutely terrified. I came from a very small town—100 people in my graduating class—so I had all this luggage from the standpoint of my insecurities and not really knowing what The University would bring to me.

Alfred Jackson had 1,441 receiving yards in his Texas career and went on to a professional career with the Atlanta Falcons.

All I knew was that I wanted to be there. Quite honestly, when I looked around and saw all those Anglos who were in the auditorium, it literally scared me because I was the only African American in the class, and I thought they were all looking at me and noticing me. Of course, that wasn't the case at all, but it took me seven or eight months to get adjusted to not only how big The University was but to interacting with all the people who were very different from me.

My first UT game was also frightening, but it was a great moment. The band came out on the field and played the UT fight song, and that feeling took me to another level. I realized that this is what The University is all about and this is what my four years would be about—playing in front of this huge crowd of 80,000 screaming fans and the UT band and the entire spirit of the game. That moment was something that changed me forever. When I hear the fight song now, I think about my years there and about the deep tradition The University has had throughout the years.

My senior year, we won the Southwest Conference and lost to Notre Dame in the Cotton Bowl. My favorite memory—one of my all-time favorite memories—is when we were playing Oklahoma in the Cotton Bowl. Mark McBath [the starting quarterback] got injured, but we were all still hyped up. Jon Aune then came into the game, and on his first play he dropped back and ended up blowing out his knee. The offensive players looked at each other and said, "Who's gonna be our quarterback? Who's gonna take us down the field? What are we gonna do? What are we gonna do?" Suddenly, Randy McEachern came jogging onto the field, and we all went, "Okaaaaaaay. But what are we gonna do?" Randy was a little nervous his first two or three plays and wasn't into the flow of the game. But as the game progressed, you could see him grow in confidence. If you ask any player on that team, especially the offense, about the intensity of the game and what happened there, they'd agree it was the most memorable occasion. Randy came into his own in that game. As the game progressed, he got stronger and stronger and stronger, and by the end of the game, he started believing all of it, which was really funny.

After we finally knew we were going to win the game, Randy came back to the huddle and we were all jumping around, celebrating. Randy hollered, "Hey, hold on! Everybody shut up. Just shut up and listen." We were like, "Hey, you're still Randy McEachern, okay? Don't forget that." We ended up winning the Southwest Championship with him.

My last year at UT seemed like it went so fast. It was my senior year, and we played A&M at College Station. My dad and mom were there, as well as my favorite uncle and aunt. Randy tied a record for throwing four touchdown passes, and I was on the receiving end for two or three of them. What a moment…my last game, we were beating our biggest rival, my family was there. There is just something about the finality of playing your last game for The University and realizing how much you love it. It was over, and I'd never play on a college field again. The finality of it really hit me. It's an awesome thing to think about being on the field and competing at the highest level and having people watch you perform. You never forget that. I think about it when I go to games today…I used to be down there. I used to play here. It's an awesome feeling, and it seems like it was only yesterday.

After I got to UT, I don't remember a time that I ever wanted to do anything but play football for The University of Texas, and this is coming from a person who was scared to death his entire first year. I do remember, however—I think it was my junior year—when I thought I would be academically ineligible. I had one or two classes I wasn't doing well in. I loved going to The University and I didn't want to embarrass myself by failing. A man named Dick Jones helped me more than anyone. He was so supportive, not only of The University but of individual players. Mr. Jones always told me, "Son, you have the ability to make it. But you have to do whatever is necessary—go to the teacher, ask if you can do extra work…." All through that semester, I literally cried to him. He ended up "taking in" a lot of players, and he was a big part of my life, a second dad. When I think about people who helped me and helped build my character—he made a really deep impact on my life. Fortunately, I made the grades, so I didn't have to quit.

When you walked on the Texas campus and you played football for Coach Royal, you expected to win because you were at The University of Texas. It was never a question of losing, it was, "We're going to win; how far do we go?" It's feeling that you really are No. 1 and knowing there are people out there who would love to play at The University and to compete at this level. It's feeling that "I am here because this is the best school, we have the best players, the best coach, and we are about winning. It's not something we do on Saturday, it's something we do all the time." You expect to win, and it transcends your life in football. Everyone else aspires to be like us, even though they may not admit it.

171

I look at where I am today, and I appreciate Coach Royal so much because he instilled so much more in us than just football. In many ways, we didn't realize we were learning discipline, and we didn't know that we were getting lifelong lessons. Ultimately, we'll all have things happen to us that we're not happy with, but the main thing is, "Do I get up? Do I get up and go and fight another day?"

My first year in Atlanta, the Falcons had four receivers already on the team, then they drafted four receivers, and I was the fifth. There were six guys competing for one position. But there was never a time when I thought I wouldn't have an opportunity to play, or that I didn't have the ability to be out there. Where did I get that attitude? It was instilled in all of us at The University. You expected to win and you believed that you had the ability to get it done. That tells you everything about excellence at The University.

Alfred Jackson became a dependable receiver whose career endured from his final year at Texas in 1977 through a seven-year career with the Atlanta Falcons. He played in the 1978 Senior Bowl. He made the fifth-longest reception in UT history—an 88-yard touchdown—in 1977.

BRAD SHEARER

DEFENSIVE TACKLE

1974–1977

I WAS ACTUALLY RAISED AN AGGIE. My dad, who died when I was 10, was an Aggie, but my mother went to Texas, so I was in a very screwed up family—an Aggie on one side and a Longhorn on the other. When I moved to Austin from Houston and got to see the Horns in action in 1969 and 1970, it was a different deal for me.

It's crazy, but I almost ended up not playing football at all. We moved back to Houston before my 10th-grade year, and I was starting both ways at Lee High School in spring training. One day the coach called me in and told me that I'd been declared ineligible; the UIL got me on the transfer rule. At Reagan High in Austin, they wouldn't let ninth-graders play varsity, so I hadn't played for another high school, but I still had to sit out my 10th-grade year. At that time, my mom had been in Austin so much, she decided she was going to move back there permanently. I ended up at Westlake High School, which was an AA school—very small compared to the school I came from in Houston.

That's where I met Ken Dabbs. Coach Dabbs was head coach my junior year at Westlake, and Ebbie Neptune was the line coach. When I showed up for the first day of school, Coach Dabbs found me in the hallway between first and second periods. Toody Byrd [the school counselor] had called him and said, "There's some 6'3", 240-pound kid who checked into school this morning." Coach Dabbs found me and said, "Boy, you want to play football,

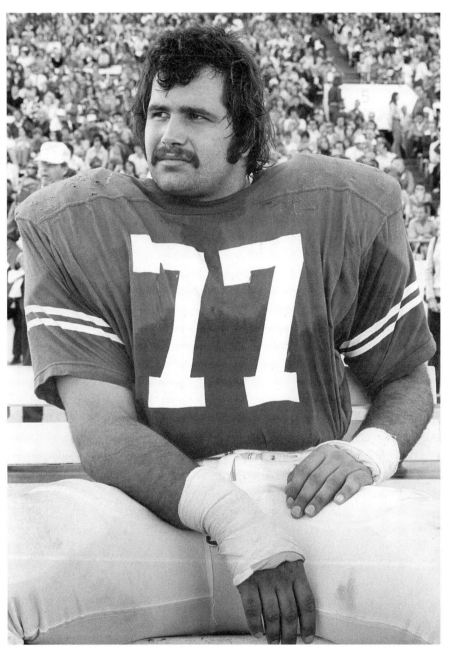

Brad Shearer was named the Outland Trophy winner as the nation's top lineman in 1977.

right?" I said, "Yeah, I want to play." He told me to come on out to football at sixth period. When I told him I had another class that period, he said, "No, you have football now."

I showed up that afternoon in his office, but they didn't have any pants, shoes, shoulder pads—anything—that would fit me. Coach Dabbs called Rooster Andrews [Sporting Goods]. Bunny Andrews, Rooster's brother, showed up with boxes of stuff, and they suited me up. I hadn't worked out much over the past year, and I'd torn up my ankle in a motorcycle wreck, so I was pretty gimpy. By the time we got the equipment and got out to practice, they were starting to run. They were running 220 gassers. I took off running, and all the other guys had already made it back to the line by the time I'd turned at the goal post. I ran a couple of those, and practice was over. Coach said, "I'll see you tomorrow." And I said, "Coach, I don't know if this is gonna work out. I'm not really a long-distance runner, and this seems to be a little long-distance for football." After that, we started running 50s.

Coach Dabbs is the reason I ended up at The University of Texas. He left my junior year and ended up being the recruiting guy at Texas. It took a phone call, basically, for him to recruit me. They didn't have to wine and dine me much for me to make a commitment. I'd decided about four or five years before that that's where I wanted to go to school. I didn't know that it would be on a football scholarship, but that was where I intended to go to college. Coach Royal gave me a call and offered me a scholarship, and I accepted.

175

I had a couple of buddies from Reagan High who played at Oklahoma, so I went on a recruiting trip to visit OU and to see my buddies. [Oklahoma assistant coach] Jerry Pettibone came to my house and told my mom, "We're going to make Brad go to study hall every day and make him go to class." My mother looked at him and said, "I really don't care what you do. I want him to go to The University of Texas." Coach Pettibone looked at me and said, "This wasn't a very good idea to meet with your mom, was it?"

When I got to Texas, one of the offensive linemen who was in my class decided to go home. Well, I came to Texas to play defense. That's why I came here, that's what they told me I could play, and that's what I wanted to play. I'd have played anywhere, but I was not as good an offensive lineman as I was a defensive lineman. I wasn't as disciplined as I needed to be to be an offensive lineman, although guys like Rick Ingraham played it, so maybe that's not a requirement.

After this other guy left, Willie Zapalac, the offensive line coach, called me in and gave me jersey No. 77. He pulled it out of a dryer, handed it to me, and said, "Here's your jersey. There have been some great players who've worn this jersey." Well, the last great guy who'd worn it before me was Bill Atessis, and I was pretty sure he'd played defense. I told Coach Zapalac right then, "I don't want to play offense." He said to me, "Well, you're left offensive tackle right now, and that's what you're playing." If there was anyone who could ever intimidate you, it was Willie Zapalac. He was tough. Fair, but tough. Today I'm shocked that I would even say that to him. So I lined up there, but I wasn't very good at it. I don't know if my heart wasn't in it or what.

The guy who'd left eventually came back. There were three seniors playing defensive tackle. Doug English was the starting right defensive tackle and Fred Currin was starting left defensive tackle. Fred went down with a season-ending knee injury. Coach Campbell didn't want to play any of us who were left. They kept shifting people around, and eventually, they threw me in the mix. So, five games into my freshman season, I was playing football for the Longhorns. It was pretty exciting.

The first time I ran onto the field, Doug English grabbed me up around my collar and hollered in my face, "Do you know what the hell you're doing?!" I hollered back, "I don't have a clue!" The first or second play, I tackled the guy three yards in the backfield, and English came over and said, "Hey, that's what you do, right there."

We played the "bend, don't break" defense. You're supposed to play more of a technique football, but I was always just running around the blocks, running around the backfield making tackles. Finally, Coach Pat Patterson, my position coach, said, "Hell, just do that." I started mid-season my freshman year and never gave it up. I loved it. I played next to some incredibly good football players.

We had such a poor junior year. Earl was hurt, and the offense didn't click. So our senior year we were picked to finish eighth in our conference. We weren't touted to do much, but the first three games of the season, we won by an average of about 70–0. That defense was incredible. It was all sophomores except for myself, Morgan Copeland, Bill Acker, and Glenn Blackwood. When you think about the age of that defense—we didn't give up a rushing touchdown until we played the University of Houston, which was the eighth game of the season. We beat Oklahoma and then beat Arkansas at Fayetteville. Those two games were the obvious turning point of the season. When Randy McEachern came into the Oklahoma game and we won, from there on, he caught fire and everybody else on the team did, too. It was a hell of a ride. That whole season was a highlight.

Everywhere I go, everyone I meet, I tell them I'm a Longhorn. Being a Longhorn is about the guys who came before me, the whole Texas tradition. Hopefully, our teams continued to build on that tradition. I say we did. To be a Longhorn was to hope to come close to achieving the level of the guys before you, to keep that tradition intact. All you could do was add to it.

I had the opportunity to play with some great guys: Randy McEachern, Earl Campbell, Rick Ingraham, Alfred Jackson. All these guys are lifelong friends, and more than anything, what I got out of it were the friendships. No matter when or how often you see them, they're still your buddies, your best friends.

I'm crippled now and don't get around worth a darn, but I would do it again no matter what. Of course, the coolest thing ever is when you marry your wife and have your kids. But other than that, the greatest years I've ever had were those four years. I'm as proud as I can be to be a Longhorn.

Brad Shearer became the third Longhorn to win the Outland Trophy as the nation's top interior lineman in 1977. He was both All-SWC and All-American, and was named to the Southwest Conference's all-decade team of the 1970s. He played in the 1978 Hula Bowl, and three years with the Chicago Bears before injuries ended his career. He is a member of the Longhorn Hall of Honor.

RANDY McEACHERN

QUARTERBACK

1974–1978

I F YOU EVER WONDER ABOUT DREAMS coming true, this is my story.

We had a good year my senior year at Pasadena Dobie High School, and when spring came, a lot of us were hoping to get a chance to play college ball. I wasn't highly recruited. In fact, nobody wanted me, really. They didn't think I was big enough to play at that level.

Five of us went to visit Blinn Junior College in Brenham. That was my only official visit to any school. As we sat in the coach's office, he looked at the three linemen and said, "You three can play here." Then he looked at the other guy and me and said, "You two guys are too small. You just can't play here."

My dad had played at TCU, and TCU wanted me to go to a junior college for two years. Then they'd consider picking me up. So I was headed to Navarro Junior College. That year, 1974, was the first year of the 30-scholarship limit.

Dad [an assistant coach at Houston's Madison High School] was in Austin for a coaching seminar, and either Coach Fred Akers, who was an assistant coach, or Coach Royal asked him, "What's Randy gonna do?" He said I was thinking about Navarro. The Texas coaches said, "Let us have your number, maybe we can get some tape on him." The next thing I know, they asked me to visit. Texas was already in spring practice, and they had two scholarships left. I came up, visited with Coach Akers, and he showed me around. I'll

178

Randy McEachern came off the bench as a third-string quarterback to lead the Longhorns to an unbeaten regular season in 1977.

never forget sitting in the stands with my dad, watching them go through practice. Marty Akins, Mike Presley—all those guys were out there. Dad said, "What do you think?" I said, "I think I can play here." So when Coach Akers called me and said, "What do you think about being a Longhorn?" I said, "Absolutely."

How could I not want to come here? I was tickled to death that they'd offer me a scholarship. I was recruit number 29, and my friend Ronnie Miksch was number 30. We argue about that today—who was offered last? Coach Akers sent the papers in the mail, there were no big press conferences. I'd been a Dobie Longhorn, and I was about to become a Texas Longhorn.

That fall, we checked in at Jester Center, where the athletes lived. My dad and I were early, waiting for them to open the doors. I was standing near the front steps of Jester, and I saw this little bitty car pull up. Two small people get out of the front, and then this guy gets out of the back. You could see the tail end of the car rise up when he got out, and he walked like John Wayne. It was George James, who would letter four years as a lineman. He introduced himself, and our parents introduced themselves. Then he looked at me and said, "What are you, the manager?" I said, "No…I'm your quarterback." I thought he was going to faint. And that was my start. That's how I got to Texas.

My first years, Marty Akins was the quarterback. Despite the new scholarship limits, there were a lot of us competing for a chance to get on the field. That's part of all that you go through. The work. The pain. The wondering…*Am I ever gonna play?*

In two-a-days, going into my junior year, 1976, I tore up my knee. Coach Royal came to the hospital and said, "It doesn't look good, Randy, but you've got a full scholarship, you'll be taken care of. We want you to concentrate on school." So, in what turned out to be Coach Royal's last season, I was in with Charlie Craven, our rehabilitation specialist.

As far as a chance to play, it didn't look good. I thought if I could just hang on and come back the next spring, I might have a chance. After Coach Royal left and Coach Akers came in, they moved me to defense. I'd never played defense in my life, and I hated it. I didn't have a chance over there; I was lost. I was sick to my stomach because I knew I needed to be at quarterback. That's what I loved, what I knew. I finally decided I didn't have anything to lose; I talked to Coach Akers after spring and said, "I think I'm as good as any of the quarterbacks you have. All I want is a shot." He told me I needed to get a stronger arm, so I worked all summer, and when we came back for two-a-days, they at least had me down as fourth-string quarterback. Mark McBath was our starter, Jon Aune was pressing him, and Ted Constanzo, who'd been highly regarded out of high school, was third. Then Ted hurt his knee, and I was third-team.

And this is where the dream comes in. The week before the Oklahoma game, we had an off-week. We had averaged over 60 points in our first three games against Boston College, Virginia, and Rice. Earl Campbell was our running back, and people were beginning to mention him for the Heisman Trophy.

I was home that weekend, watching the Ohio State–Oklahoma game. Oklahoma kicked a last-minute field goal to win the game. That night, I had a dream that I got to play against Oklahoma. I didn't remember how I got in, but I told my family about it at breakfast the next morning, and we all hooted and laughed.

The next Saturday was a dreary day in Dallas. My parents didn't go, because they were sure I wasn't going to play. The game wasn't on TV, so my parents were listening to it on the radio. They never expected me to play, and I didn't, either. We hadn't beaten Oklahoma since 1970. Even though we had a good start to the season, they were ranked No. 2, and we were as high as No. 4.

181

Early in the game, Mark McBath went down with a leg injury. I hated to see it, but I still didn't think I'd get in. On the next series, Jon Aune tore up his knee. It happened so fast. All of sudden, I'm hearing my name being called, and I'm standing beside the head coach. Fred looked at me and said, "Well, this is what you've been waiting for." And I said, "You're right, Coach."

Going out to the huddle, George James came out and met me halfway. He grabbed me and said, "We can do this." I got in the huddle, and there were all the guys I had come in with. Things happen so fast in that game—more so than in others, it seems—you don't have time to think about it. Earl scored on a good run behind Steve Hall's block. Alfred Jackson made two great catches. We kicked two field goals and made a late defensive stop to win 13–6. The game went by so fast, and at the end, I remember thinking, *What just happened?*

It changed my life. That game will always be special to me. My parents heard it all on the radio and were getting calls right and left. People wrote letters and notes from all over the country, and there was a write-up in *Sports Illustrated*. But the bigger game for me actually came the next week at Arkansas. Against Oklahoma, I had nothing to lose and everything to gain. But as far as a vote of confidence as the Texas quarterback, the following week would be the measure. Now, I was expected to perform. I was no longer an unknown. The OU game was my first chance, but the Arkansas game gave me the confidence I needed to finish the season. We were No. 2, they were No. 8, and we won 13–9. It was a great feeling then, and it still is today.

We went on to an unbeaten regular season; Earl won the Heisman Trophy, and Brad Shearer won the Outland. Had we won our bowl game with Notre Dame, it would have been a perfect dream. Even so, it did change my life forever. I played with some unbelievable talent, some unbelievable guys. Those guys are still my closest friends today. That unique little piece of history is ours forever. It reinforces what it means to be a Longhorn—the pride and tradition and the class of The University. It's like the state of Texas; it's big and it's grand.

Every day that I wear this "T" ring, it means so much to me. Different people see it differently, but it's the blood, the sweat, the hard work on the field and in the classroom. To be a Longhorn is to realize that all these guys you've heard about—some of whom you've never met—feel like big brothers. They have passed on a tradition of excellence and a feeling of pride.

Wally Scott, who played in the 1940s and was a huge supporter his whole life, would talk to the team and would break down crying, and we just knew that it meant so much. Former players talked about running onto the field and how the other teams would just stop and watch. I never thought about that until I got to run out there. I'd watch these other teams, and they'd just stop in their tracks and watch us. I get goose bumps thinking about it years later. That's what it means to be a Longhorn.

Randy McEachern became a Longhorn legend one afternoon in Dallas, when, as the third-team quarterback, he replaced two injured players and led Texas to a 13–6 victory in the annual Texas-Oklahoma rivalry in the Cotton Bowl Stadium at the State Fair of Texas. He later threw four touchdown passes to blast the Longhorns by Texas A&M and finish the 1977 regular season ranked No. 1 in the country with a perfect 11–0 record.

GLENN BLACKWOOD

DEFENSIVE BACK

1976–1978

M Y HIGH SCHOOL, SAN ANTONIO CHURCHILL, had a very good football team, and Ted Constanzo, our quarterback, was a *Parade* All-American that year. Everyone wanted Ted. Darrell Royal and Mike Campbell were recruiting Ted and another teammate named Larry Martin, who ended up at Texas Tech.

One day my mom stopped in to see Larry's folks, and the Texas coaches were there. My family knew the Royals and the Campbells years ago when we lived in Austin. My mom told Coach Royal, "Y'all are making a mistake not giving my last son, Glenn, a scholarship. He's gonna be better than Lyle was." My brother, Lyle, had been All-SWC at TCU and was in the NFL.

Up to that point, I had had zero contact from Texas. They came to watch those other guys, so they had seen me play. I only weighed 155 pounds, so it wasn't like I was some blue-chip athlete. Other than a few letters from Howard Payne and Texas Lutheran, Blinn Junior College was going to give me a scholarship because that's where Lyle had played before he went to TCU. I was pretty much resigned to going there.

I had no recruiting trips whatsoever, other than driving myself to Blinn Junior College and TLC. My friends—Ted, Larry, all these other guys—had told me about their recruiting trips, and I was just sitting there, twiddling my thumbs.

184

Glenn Blackwood followed his Texas career with a great run with the Miami Dolphins.

About a week after national signing day, I got called down to the coaches' office. My head coach was Marvin Gustafson, the brother of Cliff Gustafson, the former baseball coach at UT. I went to the office, and my defensive coordinator, Coach Jerry Comalander, said, "Coach Campbell from Texas wants you to call him. And call collect." I'll never forget that; I got to call collect. I called the number, and Coach Campbell came on the line and said, "Glenn, do you still want to come to school here at Texas?" I said, "Yes, sir, I'd love to." He said, "All right. We'll send the scholarship up in the mail." That was my recruiting trip to Texas. They sent the scholarship up, and I signed.

Bubba Simpson posted the depth chart every day on the glass window of the equipment room. Texas had signed about four or five defensive backs, and I was the least on their radar screen of who they thought would play. I looked on the depth chart, and they had me at corner—I played safety in high school—and I was ninth-string. I found my name at the very bottom of the list. As I was standing there, I felt someone looking over my shoulder, and it was Darrell Royal. That was the first time I had met him, and he said, "Where are you, son?" I pointed to my name at ninth-string at left corner. He said, "Just remember, the cream always rises to the top. If you're good enough, you'll move up that depth chart." Well, by the first game, I was backing up Raymond Clayborn at corner. I've never forgotten those words— here was the head coach at The University of Texas, and he gave me hope.

I got the Frank Medina off-season experience. You know what he was like? Darrell Royal was Obi-Wan Kenobi and Frank Medina was Yoda. This little guy was a piece of work. "Mr. Man. Come on, Mr. Man." He couldn't remember our names, so he just called us all "Mr. Man." One time he had us run the "religious relays." "I want the Baptists over here, the Methodists here…" I've never seen anything like him.

My daddy had instilled in me a work ethic and a perspective that, once you started something, you finished it; that character was built out of finishing the job, whether you came in first or 10th. So, although it was tough at the beginning, I never wanted to quit. My asset as a player was my ability to think and pick up things quickly and learn what the coaches were trying to do. Coach Campbell picked up on that, and it helped me to move up pretty rapidly.

When I walked out to my very first practice, all the freshmen were huddled together like a covey of quail, kind of scared, looking around. After we filtered down the sideline, somebody walked up beside me. I was on my knee and turned to look, and there was Earl Campbell. Everyone knew who Earl was. I looked at his thighs, and I'd never seen anything that big in my life. My jeans back then were a 32-inch waist, and Earl had 34-inch thighs. His thigh was bigger than my torso. I thought, *I am so thankful that he's on this team and that I'm not playing against him. If there are others out there like him, I'm gonna get killed.*

My freshman year, we were playing A&M at College Station. ABC was broadcasting the game for TV. It was a pretty good battle; I think they were up 17–10. Bubba Bean busted a 78-yard run down to the 1-yard line. Ray Clay [Clayborn] caught him from behind at at the 1. The play was to the left of our bench, and my roommate, Joe Bob Bizzell, and I were on the right side of the bench by one of those big dishes that picks up sound for TV. We were yelling into the dish, trying to get our names on TV. "Way to go, Blackwood. Way to go, Bizzell." We figured that was the only way we were going to get our names on TV.

A&M ran George Woodard into the line, and our defense stuffed him. I heard, "Blackwood!" and I thought, *Who's calling my name?* It was Coach Campbell. So I jumped up from yelling my name into the dish and ran down there. Coach Campbell said, "Go in for Clayborn. They won't throw the football. Oh, never mind." It was too late for me to go in. They ran Woodard one more time, we stopped him, and it was third and one. Coach Campbell said, "Go in for Clayborn. Don't worry about the receiver, just play the run." I ran in there, all 165 pounds of me, and the whole defense looked at me like, *What in the world are you doing out here?* Brad Shearer, Bill Hamilton, all those big guys. I said, "Clayborn. Get out." He said, "You're kidding me!"

So I lined up on their receiver, Carl Roaches. Coach Campbell had said to play the run and not worry about covering Roaches, so I lined up like I was covering him man-to-man. Right at the snap of the ball, I turned and bee-lined it like I was blitzing from the outside corner, and sure enough, they ran the option toward me and pitched it to Bubba Bean, who weighed about 225. He was looking inside, thinking he had it made. I drilled him on about the 2-yard line, knocked him for a loop, and knocked myself out. Both of us left the game. All I remember is lying on the ground and Frank Medina coming up and saying, "Mr. Man! Mr. Man! Are you okay, son? That was a great play, son. Just lay there, son."

The joy of it was that I did exactly what Coach Campbell said, and I kept them from getting in the end zone. There's nothing better than keeping Aggies out of the end zone.

There's a thread in my life that God has blessed me with, and that is character and quality of coaches. My privilege has been to play for men who get it right. They taught the game with integrity and they weren't looking for ways to bend the rules. They taught me to play the game with character. I am so blessed to have had every one of my coaches be men of that caliber. Those coaches at Texas made me a better football player, yes, but also a better man.

I was a little bitty kid when Nobis was playing, but I'll never forget watching No. 60 play. I remember Cotton Speyrer catching that pass against UCLA on the last play of the game. And who could forget the '69 season? This is the history that I'm privileged to have been a part of. For me, the culmination was to walk out as a captain representing our team my senior year. I'll carry that with me the rest of my life.

It creates immense pride in me to have been part of that program. To walk down the Cotton Bowl tunnel when we played OU and see all crimson on one side and all orange on the other in what I believe is the greatest college game there is, and to stand on that field, victorious, with your Horns up in the air listening to "The Eyes of Texas"—I'll remember it forever.

Glenn Blackwood played in two Super Bowls and spent 9 years in the NFL with the Miami Dolphins. He was a captain of the Longhorns team in 1978 and a three-year starter in the Texas secondary.

DWIGHT JEFFERSON
DEFENSIVE END
1976–1978

I DID HAVE SOMEWHAT OF A FAMILY HISTORY with The University of Texas. I had a grandmother who lived on Comal Street in East Austin, and who worked for 20 years in the Varsity Cafeteria. When we stayed with her, my cousins and I would play in the park that used to be where Disch-Falk Field, the Longhorn baseball field, is now. We'd cross the interstate and go hang around Memorial Stadium and Clark Field, the old baseball field.

I played football at Fox Tech in San Antonio, and it did not have a strong football tradition. I was being recruited by several schools—SMU, TCU, Tulane, and a few others. I never heard from Texas, until the last game of my senior year. We were playing San Antonio Churchill, with Ted Constanzo, a highly touted quarterback, and Glenn Blackwood, who ended up being a co-captain with me in 1978. The day before that game, I got called out of class. I went to the office, and Coach Mike Campbell was there. He told me that he'd be at the game that night, and he wished me good luck. So that night I had a pretty good game, but my team got spanked. Nevertheless, the next day I got a call at my home from Coach Campbell, and he asked me if I'd like to play football at The University of Texas. I didn't let them know right away. In fact, I held off for a while. I waited right up until signing day. I'm a Libra—I guess it was just indecision, although my wife would say it's being passive-aggressive. I could not decide, but I talked with one of my

Dwight Jefferson received a law degree and became a district judge.

friends, who said, "The University of Texas? The University of Texas? Man, they play on TV!" So I suppose that helped make up my mind for me.

The SMU coach came to see me, and I told him that I'd decided to play for The University of Texas. He was not happy with me. But I guess SMU knew where I was going before Texas did.

My most memorable moment was my entire first semester, when I realized just how ill-equipped I was, academically. I was not prepared for the rigors of college. My high school had a somewhat limited curriculum; I don't believe they even offered economics.

David McWilliams was my position coach, and I started out fifth on the depth chart, but by the time the season started, I had moved up to second-string. I broke my wrist in the third game, so my season was over. And when you're injured, there's a separation from the rest of the team. You're just not involved with what your teammates are doing every day. So one day as I was walking past the Littlefield Fountain, it kind of all came together, and it really hit me that I had better get serious about school. I understood at that moment what Frank Medina was so fond of saying: "You have an opportunity to get an education at The University of Texas through your athletic ability."

190

The coaches got me a summer job working construction in Austin. This was during the time when alums were allowed to play a part in recruiting. One day Coach Campbell took me to meet this attorney, and if he wasn't the first lawyer I'd ever met, it was certainly the first time I'd ever been in a law office. The next summer I decided I'd rather work inside, so they arranged for me to work at the law office, where I was basically just a gofer. But I was working inside. Looking back, I realize I'm probably the only attorney who ever helped build the Texas Bar Association Building.

Later, I worked as a law clerk for Pat Maloney. He was a very sweet man. Then I worked with another attorney, and much of the time we'd sit in the law library and talk football while he drank Tab. I truly believe that that's when I started thinking about becoming an attorney. I said, "Well, shoot. If he can be an attorney…I mean, I can sit around, talk football, and drink Tab all day, too." And he did more than that, of course, but that is what made me realize it could be attainable.

My mother benefited greatly from the opportunities afforded her by the programs of the Great Society. She started out as a cook in the cafeteria of the Friedrich Air Conditioning plant. We lived down the street from that plant. She took advantage of a program that helped her become an assistant librarian, and she became an assistant librarian at the city libraries. She worked there for a while and then entered another program that enabled her to become a nurse's assistant. While she worked during the day as a nurse's assistant, she took classes at night. The Great Society legislation presented these opportunities to my mother, and she took advantage of them. She ended up being an LVN and worked for 20 years as a nurse. During that time, my brothers and I learned how to make a really mean Hamburger Helper. Man, we ate so much Hamburger Helper during those years, I won't ever eat it again.

Here's what The University of Texas represents to me: it represents an opportunity. Because of my athletic ability, I received the opportunity to receive an excellent education. I had the opportunity to learn the valuable lessons you gain from being a part of a team. And, when I was injured, I had the opportunity to realign my thoughts on why I was at The University to begin with. And, of course, I met my wife, Elaine, while studying at The University of Texas law library. When you're a Longhorn, there is a network of alums who are willing to give you an opportunity to succeed. No one hands you anything, of course. But my coaches and those alums opened doors which might have remained closed to me had I not been at Texas.

I wear my "T" ring proudly. It means a great deal to me because it signifies that I have taken advantage of the opportunities offered me through my athletic ability. It means that I finished the task.

191

Dwight Jefferson was team captain of the 1978 Longhorn team and the Most Valuable Lineman in the 1978 Sun Bowl victory over Maryland. He entered law school after his graduation and became the first African American civil state district judge ever elected in Harris County.

JOHNNIE JOHNSON

DEFENSIVE BACK

1976–1979

I WAS A FOUR-SPORT ATHLETE at La Grange High School, in La Grange, Texas, and I had a number of tough decisions to make. Would I go to college to play football, run track, play baseball, or would I play basketball, my favorite sport? And the biggest question of all was, where would I go college?

No one in my family or in La Grange had experienced what I was about to venture into. Being heavily recruited in four different sports by colleges from around the country became overwhelming. Every time I turned around, there was another recruiter speaking about how great it would be to attend their school.

I played running back on offense and free safety on defense for the La Grange Leopards.

Most schools that recruited me in football did so with the thought of my playing running back. So, not only did I have to decide what sport I would play and which university I would attend, but if I chose football, would I play running back or defensive back, which was my favorite position?

I had taken several visits to other colleges, but it was on my trip to The University that I found answers to my questions. The thought of meeting Darrell Royal made me nervous. To me, Coach Royal was bigger than life.

I was a shy and bashful kid, and when I met Coach Royal for the first time, I shook his hand in a timid and shy manner, as if I did not belong in the same

Johnnie Johnson was an All-American and an All-Pro defensive back who became a motivational speaker and author.

room with him. I further demonstrated my nervousness by not looking him in the eyes when I introduced myself.

What took place next had a lifelong impact on me. Coach Royal, sensing my discomfort, introduced himself and welcomed me by putting his arm around my shoulders. He walked me over to a corner of the room where no one could hear what he was saying.

He asked me to look into his eyes, and, as he extended his hand to demonstrate a firm handshake, he stated, "Johnnie, you are a gifted and talented young man. You have every reason to be proud. From now on, when you greet someone, no matter who they are, look them right in the eyes, extend your hand, shake theirs firmly, and say, 'Hi, I'm Johnnie Johnson, pleased to meet you.'" He went on to say, "Each and every time you meet someone, greet them with more and more confidence." He then led me back over to mix with the rest of the crowd, as if nothing had ever happened.

That was so different from other recruiting activities I'd experienced. I recall saying to myself, *The University of Texas is the place for me. They care about me as a person here.* I ended up a Longhorn because I felt the coaches cared about the player as a person, as well as an athlete.

Representing Texas as a defensive back and punt-return specialist meant great opportunities. Coach Akers often said, "Great opportunities, being accountable, and making plays will enable you to continue that great Longhorn tradition."

The first opportunity came when I earned a starting position at free safety as a freshman against North Texas. I had my first interception as a Longhorn, which I nearly returned for a touchdown. It was also the first game I played in Memorial Stadium.

The opportunities as a Longhorn kept coming. My sophomore year, we went into the annual Texas-Oklahoma game in Dallas with UT ranked fifth and OU ranked second in the nation. Both teams had high-powered offenses and stingy defenses.

Although Texas went into the game averaging more than 61 points an outing, and OU had just beaten Ohio State in Columbus two weeks earlier, the game quickly demonstrated it was going to be a defensive struggle. If you were a fan, you held your breath on every play because you knew either team could strike at any moment. And if they did, you had the feeling the other team might not get an opportunity to answer because of how well the defenses were playing that day. You could feel the tension in the air.

OU had been winning the battle of field position when, early in the first quarter, our defense held them around midfield and forced them to punt for the first time. I recall saying to myself, "This is a chance to change the field position in Texas's favor."

I went into the OU game as one of the nation's leading punt-return men, so I wasn't sure if they'd kick the ball to me. They did. Although they kicked it to me, the punt was angled to the right corner of the field near our goal line. From the Longhorns' perspective, this wasn't the best punt for the play we'd called. We had a left return called, which meant my teammates were on the other side of the field.

As the punt traveled toward me, I first thought about protecting the ball because that was my first responsibility to the team. As I settled under the kick, I could see a Sooner defender barreling down on me. He arrived about the same time I fielded the kick.

I fielded the ball cleanly while sidestepping the defender. I started working my way across the field toward the left return, but six members of the OU coverage team were taking angles to cut me off and prevent me from getting to the wall. They were between me and my teammates, who had aligned themselves beautifully along the sideline to my left.

I changed directions by making a quick cut, first up the field and then back to my right. The move enabled me to avoid all six defenders and to break free, running full speed toward the right sideline and away from the wall.

As I exited the pack and ran upfield, I angled toward the right sideline. I could see just two OU defenders standing between me and a 91-yard punt return for a touchdown.

One of the defenders was waiting at the 50-yard line near that side of the field, while the other was moving at about a 45-degree angle to my left. Between the two, they had me boxed in with few options for running room.

I made a quick move toward the sideline, went around him right in front of the OU bench, and broke into the open, running along the sideline and toward the goal line.

The Longhorn fans roared as I made that move to avoid the last OU defender, and I broke into the open and into the end zone for an apparent touchdown.

After turning to celebrate with my teammates, I noticed that the cheering on the Longhorn side of the field had subsided, and the Sooner fans had begun cheering because the officials had ruled that I stepped out of bounds around the 50. I told myself, *That's okay, it changed the field position to our favor.* We continued to play a game of field position until OU received the ball late in the fourth quarter.

Our defense had held OU to two field goals. With UT leading 13–6 and four minutes left in the game, OU got the ball and began a drive that stalled on fourth down at the Longhorn 6-yard line. Down by seven points late in the game, with the Texas defense playing well, the Sooners decided to go for the first down or the touchdown.

They ran a down-the-line option to the Longhorn defensive right side. My responsibility as safety was to cover the quarterback through to the pitchman on the option play.

Thomas Lott, the OU quarterback, started down the line, saw what he thought was an opening, and turned the ball upfield. I met him right in the hole he was trying to run through and stopped him short of the first down. We took over at that spot and went on to win the game.

When I think of what it means to be a Longhorn, I think of games like that Sooner game. I think of being ranked No. 2 and traveling to Arkansas the week after that tough OU game to face the No. 8–ranked Razorbacks.

Again our defense was outstanding, limiting Arkansas to three field goals during the game. Just like in the OU game the week before, I returned a punt for 57 yards late in the game to change the field position in UT's favor. In the end, the Longhorn offense scored late to win the game 13–9.

When I think of what it means to be a Longhorn, I think of playing the University of Missouri on the road as a senior before the largest crowd to ever watch a football game in the state of Missouri at that time. I think of playing Arkansas on the road that same year before the largest crowd to ever watch a football game in the state of Arkansas at that time.

When I think of what it means to be a Longhorn, I not only think of the Texas-OU rivalry, or the Texas–Texas A&M rivalry, I realize the Longhorns are looked at as a rivalry game by every team on its schedule. I have been blessed to have had the opportunity to carry on the rich Texas tradition and to have had all the relationships I continue to enjoy today. I am a Longhorn for life.

Johnnie Johnson was chosen the nation's best defensive back by the Heisman committee in 1978. He was a two-time consensus All-American and a three-time All-SWC choice. He played 10 seasons in the NFL and, following his pro career, became a motivational speaker and author. He is a member of the Longhorn Hall of Honor.

JOHNNY "LAM" JONES
WIDE RECEIVER
1976–1979

As a junior in high school I started thinking about the possibility of getting a scholarship to college. Back then, I was a big Oklahoma fan because they had Joe Washington and Greg Pruitt and those high-powered running backs. I was a running back at Lampasas High School. We ran the wishbone, and OU ran the wishbone, so I leaned more toward Oklahoma from a football standpoint.

My grandparents had worked for 20 years for a family there in Lampasas, a banker who was a Texas alum. They'd never really talked to me about going to school there, but when my senior year came around, people started noticing some of my success on the field and in track, and where I was going to school became more of a question. I was getting letters and phone calls from all the schools. I started leaning more toward Texas because Austin was only 60 miles down the road, my grandparents worked for a Texas alum, and my high school coach, Scott Boyd, had played at Texas.

I was recruited by Kenneth Dabbs and Coach Royal. I was raised by my grandparents, and they were so proud to have Coach Royal eat dinner at their house. If you've been around Coach Dabbs, you know that he never meets a stranger. He was at the house one time, and my grandmother happened to mention her maiden name and that she was from Bastrop. Coach Dabbs recognized the name, and, apparently, when he was growing up in Freer, his family owned a café. The cook at their café was my grandmother's brother, and he helped raise Coach Dabbs all those years. When Coach Dabbs was learning how to hunt and fish and drive a car, my grandmother's brother was there to teach him. Now Coach Dabbs was coming back around and was going to watch out for me when I went off to Texas. Once that was revealed, there was no question where I was going.

Before I came to Texas, I'd qualified for the Olympic team, gone to the Olympic trials, gone to Montreal for the Olympics, and won a gold medal. It was pretty much like a haze for an 18-year-old kid to be going through. It was a blur for me, but someone else may have handled it a lot better.

Once you decide where you're going to school, even if you're still in high school, people view you as being part of that new family. Even though I was at Lampasas running in the Olympics, I was representing The University of Texas. At the state track meet we won the state AAA championship for Lampasas High, but a part of me was still representing The University of Texas. I've been very fortunate in sports; I don't have a single most memorable moment. I have been very blessed that I've had a number of moments.

People ask me, "Hey, what was it like to win a gold medal in the Olympics?" They look at me like I'm crazy when I say, "It's almost as exciting as running in the state meet in Texas." Winning our team championship was probably my most special moment.

It wasn't the race, the mile relay, that made it so special, but that winning the state championship was our goal. People talk about "the Race," but the special part about that was that a lot of people were involved. We were in that position all the time; we were behind like that every week, but that's the way we ran. Those guys didn't have to run as fast as I did, they just had to run as fast as they could. As long as everybody did his best, we'd have a chance to win. All those people saw it at the state meet, but that's what we did every week.

Lampasas High had the track records posted on a banner in the gym. I had the record for the 440 and for the 220, so I'd been pestering the coach to let me run the 100. I wanted that record, too. He got tired of my pestering him, so on Wednesday before the Brownwood track meet, he let me run the 100, a practice race. He marked off 100 yards on the old dirt track, and I ran the race. He had a little smile on his face as he looked at his clock, but he wouldn't let me see the time. He said, "Don't worry about it. You did pretty good. Run another one." He made me wait while he marked off the track again. He stepped it off all over again. I didn't think about what he was doing at the time, but he was double-checking the distance. So I ran another one. This time he

Johnny "Lam" Jones won an Olympic gold medal as a sprinter before he ever came to Texas.

had a bigger smile on his face, but he still wouldn't let me see my time. On Saturday, Coach said, "I'll let you run the 100, but you still have to run your other races." So that day I ran the 440, the 220, the mile relay, and in the 100 I ran a 9.2 in the finals. That's what I had run that day on the high school track.

So that was the beginning of "the Race." When I came into Coach's office that next Monday, he had newspapers spread out all over his desk. The papers used to publish all the best times across the state. He had figured out that, if he took me out of the quarter, if Mike Perkins, our other quarter-miler, could make it to state, if I won the 100 and 200, if we could win the mile relay, and if we picked up some points with the long jump or with Perkins, then we could win the state meet by two or four points. The state championship came down to that last race. It was between us and two other teams, and whoever won the mile relay was going to win the state meet. That special moment wasn't about me. The joy came from our winning. I had gone to state my junior year by myself and had won state in the quarter. It wasn't as much fun; it wasn't half the joy of those other guys' getting to come along.

As a player in high school, you felt so honored that Coach Royal would even consider you to play at his school. You might be thinking about going to some other school, but when you found out that UT wanted you, it was a done deal. That's how it was for me, anyway.

Texas recruited me as a running back. I came through with Coach Royal's last class; then he retired, and Coach Akers switched offenses. With Earl back there, we didn't throw the ball that much. But when we did throw it, we were pretty good at it.

I might have gotten closer to my coaches had I done things differently, had I not been so dysfunctional in some areas. I didn't take advantage of having someone older to help guide me and keep me on the right path. When I think of how I spent my time and how disorganized I was, I see that I didn't allow myself the opportunity to develop special relationships with coaches. There were guys who were more mature than I was who were close to their coaches. It was like having a homing beacon, somebody to keep you close to the ground. And back then, my feet were planted firmly in mid-air.

But when you're a Longhorn, you're part of a special family, a special group. You get the feeling that other people feel it's special, too. They might be an alum of another school, but deep down inside they wish they could say there were a Longhorn. Some might admit it and some might not, but it's like if they went somewhere else, they settled. Some people will tell me, "I went to such and such school, but I wish I could have gone to UT."

This school impacts your life because you're placed in an environment where you always want to do your best. That's the kind of people you're around at Texas. It helps guide you and mold you and puts you in a conscious awareness about what The University is about, the pride and the traditions.

I wouldn't change anything, not for a minute, not for a second. A person couldn't ask for a better roller coaster ride than what I've been on—still standing and fortunate to be able to sit here and talk about it. You know that poem "Footprints in the Sand"? I'm the reason they wrote that…I'm the one He's been carrying all this time.

Johnny "Lam" Jones won a gold medal in the 1976 Olympics the summer before he entered Texas and was known as the fastest football player in the country. He was a two-time all-conference and All-American in football and held the world record in the 100-meter dash. He was a first-round draft choice of the New York Jets and played five seasons of pro ball. He was inducted into the Longhorn Hall of Honor in 1994.

The EIGHTIES

MIKE BAAB

CENTER

1978–1981

IT WAS VERY SIMPLE. I was fortunate to be a high school All-American, and I could have gone to any school I wanted to, but I knew my parents couldn't afford to fly out to Penn State or USC or places like that. I grew up in Euless, a little town right between Fort Worth and Dallas. I never was one of those little boys who grew up wanting to be a football player; I always wanted to be a doctor. The whole way, I was just good at football. It was easy for me to do, and it was fun. I found out about halfway through high school that I might be good enough to get a scholarship. We'd had several good players who went off to college and came back and said, "You could do this! Get free college!" I decided to take it a little more seriously, and I actually turned into a pretty good football player.

I liked Texas. I thought they were a classy bunch, and that was important to me. The only schools that didn't offer me suitcases of money were The University of Texas and Rice. That's it. One coach stacked hundreds in front of me. Well, money's nice, but that's not how I'm going to pick my school. I sat down with my granddad and my mom one night and said, "I've got all these letters. What am I going to do?" Granddad said, "Michael, I'd never tell you what to do, but don't you dare go to Notre Dammit. In Texas there ain't but one school to go to…Texas." My mom said that when she was a little girl, her dream, if she could have possibly afforded it, was to go to Texas. They didn't push the issue, but they sure laid it out there for me.

Mike Baab was one of the best centers in Texas history.

It was a combination of things; I was premed, and they had the best medical school in the state. Earl had won the Heisman. I came down for my recruiting trip, and a guy named Lance Taylor, a consensus All-American, recruited me. The atmosphere was just wild. They were 11–0, and this place was just bubbling. They were playing Notre Dame for the national championship. Once I went to Texas and saw that attitude of winning, I said, "This is really easy." I canceled all the rest of my recruiting trips.

Back then, Texas was nothing like it is now. Today it's a showplace. It was not like that when we went to school. You were not induced to go to Texas by the great facilities; you went to Texas because you wanted to go to Texas. If a little boy could go to Texas, he did, unless he was born into an Aggie family, and then he was cursed to be an Aggie for the rest of his life.

Out of 22 starters at the Texas High School All-Star Game my senior year, 14 of us went to Texas. My freshman year, we had seven freshmen starting on that football team. That was the kind of talent we had. It was just amazing. Four years later, 12 of us went to the pros.

One thing that I really enjoyed—I played in the late '70s—there was no racial tension on our team in any way, shape, or form. It was the disco era, remember? Everyone went to the same clubs, and we all danced like idiots and had fun. It didn't matter what color you were or if you were from East Texas or West Texas. We never had any of that undercurrent ugliness. We were teammates, we were Horns, and that's the way it was.

My best memory would have to be the last game of my senior year. We played Alabama in the Cotton Bowl. We were No. 4 or 5, and they were No. 2 or 3 in the country. We ended up beating them in the last seconds of the game. We had a kid named Robert Brewer, a little, short white guy who couldn't run that fast but was smart and made very good decisions. He was our quarterback, and he'd taken us to the Cotton Bowl. We called a play called "zero," which was just a quarterback draw. We ran it all the time with Donnie Little, who was the quarterback before. Donnie had tremendous scrambling skills. Robert had no scrambling skills. Alabama had been blitzing us from the outside all day long when we called "zero." We all said, "What?" in the huddle. Robert looked at us and said, "Y'all, please block." I was playing this All-American nose guard, and I got a real good block on him. Robert burst up the middle for 30 yards, untouched, and we won the Cotton Bowl. Roger Staubach said on TV, "Mike Baab made a good block." It doesn't get any better than that. I've got goosebumps right now just talking about it. We went out in such style. We went out on top and finished No. 2 in the country.

Other than that, I remember my welcome to the Southwest Conference. Back then, it was all about the SWC. I came out for my very first practice, and I was used to running over high school linebackers. I'd just run right over them and go get a safety. I thought I'd just go bust up Lance Taylor and show him what I could get. I came off the ball to hit him, and the next thing I knew, I was lying flat on my back. Lance had his forearm imbedded firmly in my throat, and I couldn't breathe. My brains had been knocked out, and he leaned over and said, "Mike, welcome to the Southwest Conference." He picked me up off the ground, and I walked back to the huddle. I couldn't breathe and I couldn't talk, and the next play I was a whole lot lower and a whole lot more respectful.

I started as a freshman. Jim Yarbrough is a great man. He hurt his neck about game four or five, so I started the rest of the year, playing right guard for Jim. When I signed with Texas, Wes Hubert [center] was a junior. The coaches told me, "Look, you may be a high school All-American, but this is the Southwest Conference, this is Texas. You're going to sit on the bench for a few years behind Wes Hubert, and you're going to learn to play." In a weird, ugly football way, I just got lucky when Jim got hurt. If he hadn't gotten hurt, I definitely wouldn't have started that year. Then, in game nine or 10 of my sophomore year, I blew my knee out. So I started four years, but it was actually three years' worth of games.

When you're a Horn, you actually carry a burden. You're supposed to behave, not cause problems, stay out of trouble. You're supposed to put your nose to the grindstone, get your education, and turn out to be something. For me, the biggest thing was hitching onto something that had 100 years of pride behind it. I was fortunate enough to be elected captain my senior year. In our little world of the Horns, I can tell someone I played at Cleveland, I can tell them about my career, but when I tell them I was team captain in '81, they'll go, "Oh, you were a team captain for the Horns?" That means more than anything else in my life, except for keeping a successful marriage together and raising beautiful children. I love my kids and my family, but other than that, being a Longhorn team captain is right on top of the list of things I'm most proud of because of the men who went before me. I mean, Tommy Nobis was a captain, for God's sake. And I got to do it, too.

It comes down to that sign they've got on the wall of the weight room: "The Pride and Tradition of the Texas Longhorns Will Not Be Entrusted to the Weak or the Timid." For macho guys like us, that's pretty cool. It hits you right in the heart. You're always going to be a Horn. If anyone ever says anything about it, we're going to fight. If I'm 85 years old, I'll hit you with my crutch.

205

Mike Baab was an All–Southwest Conference center in 1981 and was a captain on the 1982 Cotton Bowl champions. He played 11 years in the NFL with the Cleveland Browns, New England Patriots, and Kansas City Chiefs.

DONNIE LITTLE

QUARTERBACK/
WIDE RECEIVER
1978–1981

KEN DABBS AND CHARLIE LEE recruited me to The University of Texas. Fred Akers was the coach. They did an excellent job selling The University. When I took my visit, I was here with a lot of the top players. We all got together—A.J. "Jam" Jones, Rodney Tate, and some of the rest of us—and said, "I think this is the place we ought to come and start our dynasty."

I had some reservations, though, and they were obviously that there hadn't been an African American quarterback at Texas. The year before there had been a player who had basically left Texas at the altar. He had said he was coming and then changed his mind. So Coach Akers's request of me was that I be honest. I hadn't committed at that point. I told him I was strongly considering coming, and if I had to make up my mind today, I would sign. But I wanted to go back and talk it over with my parents, and I said I had a few questions for him. He said that was fair.

The only thing I promised at that point was that, if I told him I was coming, I wouldn't leave him hanging like the other guy did. He answered all the questions, at least those that he could answer. Some things he didn't have the answers to. I asked him if I would be given the opportunity to play quarterback. He assured me that that was what they were recruiting me as, regardless of what some of the other schools were saying to me. He assured me they weren't going to move me to receiver or defensive back or running back. The part we never talked about was that, as long as the team accepted it, and we were playing well and winning, he would stick with me, regardless of what the alumni and fans thought. When you get here and you play, that is just something you're exposed to. You learn on the go.

But I liked what I saw and decided to come.

It didn't take long for reality to set in for us freshmen. One of the best memories of my career came early in my freshman season at the Rice game in Houston. It was the first game of the year, and I was excited that my family from Dickinson was going to have a chance to see me. We came out in pregame, and there might have been three or four thousand people in the stands. We went back in, and when we came out to start the game, the stands were full. That was the first time my freshman teammates and I had seen 60,000 people in the stands. As we ran out onto the field, we knew we weren't starting, and we doubted that we would even get in the game. But it was our first chance to grasp the atmosphere of college football.

I remember running with Jam Jones. Here's a guy who grew up in Youngstown, Ohio. He went to an all-black primary school, an all-black junior high, and an all-black high school. When he ran out on the field, he was horrified. He was like, "Man, we better be good, or those people are gonna get us. Look at all these white people in the stands." It blew him away. Of course, my feeling was, *Wow, I hope I get to play, because my family is here, and it's the first game of the season.*

207

I knew the chances were not good, but I hoped that the first team would score some touchdowns and give some of us other guys a chance to play. I was the third-team quarterback, and sure enough, I got in the game. I was as excited as I could be. I remember walking to the line of scrimmage, and the Rice public address announcer said, "The University of Texas is about to make history. This is the first black quarterback to take a snap at The University of Texas." I was in the middle of my cadence, and I was hearing this. I forgot what I'd called and just went through the progression and ran the play.

It was tough early. I'd only played two years of football in high school, so I had been pretty sheltered. Coming to Texas, where they are so used to winning, was eye-opening. I'd never had so much criticism in my life. You do your best, but sometimes you are going to screw up, and in big games if you screw up, they'll let you hear about it. They want the next guy. Everybody

Donnie Little, the Longhorns' first African American quarterback, led the team in passing in 1979 and 1980, and in receiving in 1981.

loves the number-two quarterback until he becomes the number-one quarterback, and then they like the other guy again. At first, I thought it was a color thing, but I realized they booed the white quarterbacks, too. It made me mature at a very early age. Not every person in the stands was against you. There were a lot more people for you. I'm not bitter at all, and I wouldn't trade that experience for anything. It has allowed me to reach out to other African American quarterbacks like James Brown and Vince Young.

Of course, the irony of my career at Texas was that I did wind up moving to receiver for my senior year, but it was my choice. It was all up to me. Coach Akers did not come to me and say, "We're moving you." In the spring before my senior year, I told him I'd like to experiment at wide receiver. Rick McIvor was the back-up quarterback, and Rick's strength was his arm. And Coach Akers had said that we'd probably open up the offense more. Looking at it from a realistic standpoint, if I was going to play football in the pros, it was going to have to be at wide receiver. So I thought if it would help the team and it would help me, then we should go for it. Everything went fine in the spring. Rick grasped the offense, but we didn't throw the ball any more than we had. We had the same offense. That's not a knock. We were winning, but we didn't throw the ball.

We came to a crossroads in the Houston game when Rick got hurt in the first half. Coach Akers was talking about switching me back to quarterback. It was the same offense, and I knew it. Charlie Lee and Coach Dabbs were totally against it. They said, "Let's give the next guy a chance." Well, the "next guy" was Robert Brewer, and in the second half of that game, the Robert Brewer era began.

I tried pro ball after college, and I had a good experience at Atlanta. But I was just too inexperienced at receiver. So I went to Canada to get a chance to play. That's when I blew out my knee, and football was over for me after that. I came back to The University to work in the athletics department, and that has opened a whole new world to me.

When James Brown came to Texas, he was shy at first, so I had to seek him out and tell him who I was, and that I was there for him if he needed to talk. Then, when Vince came, James and I took him to lunch, and Vince and I spent time together, just talking. I wanted Vince to hear from the old school, the middle school, and now we had the young school coming. It was good for him and James to have a dialogue, and then he and I had a dialogue, and we became friends. I remember the time he came in after the Missouri

209

game, just before he took off on the streak. He had heard some boos, and he was really down and mentioned to me that he really thought about switching to receiver. I said, "Naw, you don't want to do that." Thank God he didn't.

I guess I have a different view of what it means to be a Longhorn. Because of all that has happened in the last 30 years, so much has changed. When you go back to your community, you see young kids, whether they are in the projects or just in the community, and they are wearing Texas colors. That didn't happen when I was growing up, especially in the inner city. You saw Michigan, Notre Dame, whatever. Now you see the Longhorn and that burnt orange.

A lot of doors have opened since then. Mack Brown has seen to it that there are no differences in people, with his staff and his team. We have more and more African American kids who come here, and there is a network that doesn't want to see a person fail. They are going to give you every opportunity. I try every day to give something back to kids. My door is open, and they know I'm there for them. James Brown remembered the image. For me, it matters if we can walk in the stadium and say, because of these kids, a lot of streaks were broken and a lot has changed.

Donnie Little was one of the state's most heralded high school players and became the first African American quarterback in Texas history. After playing three years at quarterback, he moved to wide receiver his senior season of 1981 and helped lead Texas to a No. 2 national ranking. After a pro career that was shortened by injury, he returned to The University of Texas, where he serves as an assistant athletics director for development.

KENNETH SIMS

DEFENSIVE TACKLE

1978–1981

I GREW UP IN BAYLOR COUNTRY and Aggie country. I was almost an Aggie, but they fired my buddy, Emory Bellard. I was very fond of him. He was like a father—he's still like a father to me. A very nice guy.

I grew up in Kosse, Texas, and I rode the bus to Groesbeck to school for 12 years. I hurt my neck my junior year and didn't get to play that much, so I didn't make a lot of folks' blue-chip lists. I was only getting recruited by small-time schools until word got out. Groesbeck had a great defense, and supposedly Ken Dabbs was riding to the airport with a coach from Rice, Ray Alborn. Coach Alborn was bragging to him about, "Man, have you seen that kid at Groesbeck? He can really run." Dabbs, being a poker player, said, "Yeah, I've seen him. He's really something else." Dabbs got to the Dallas airport—this was before cell phones—and he called The University and said, "Mike Parker, do you know where Groesbeck is? No? Well, you'd better find it because there's a player over there."

My high school football coach was always fond of UT. He said, "Son, I think you need to go down there and look around." This was during the time when Earl Campbell, Randy McEachern, and that '77 bunch were undefeated. I'd never been to Austin, but that was the time to come. When I came down, this city was much like it was when Vince Young and the team were winning. It was wild! So I came down here for a visit. I spent the whole day at the mall with Steve and Tim Campbell, and I've been in Austin ever

Kenneth Sims won the Lombardi Award and was an All-American.

212

since. Every time I see Emory Bellard, he always laughs and asks me, "What happened, podnah?"

I'd made up my mind I was coming to Texas. It was cold that weekend, bitter cold, and I didn't own a coat back then. I asked Coach Akers if I could get No. 77, and he said, "I think we can arrange that. You're easy."

Everybody asked me, "Man, you didn't get anything?" I always say I got an opportunity and I got my number. When I came in I was sixth on the depth chart. I remember looking up at that wall, and I was number six.

When you're a high school kid, you pick a school primarily because of the coach. I came here because of Parker. My mother thinks he's the salt of the earth, which he is. I'm friends with his family today. He's a Marine, Purple Heart. He's a real tough guy, and that's why we were all tough.

My whole career at UT, we were trying to get to the Cotton Bowl. We were No. 1 at one point, and when that happens, some people tend to relax. Now that I look back on it, when they put that "No. 1" on your back, you've got to kick it up a notch. Everybody's gunning for you, and when you get labeled No. 1, you have a tendency to relax mentally, and that's not the time to relax. You start "acting like" instead of "being like," and we got knocked off by Arkansas.

I tried to be shortsighted. I didn't really want to know who we were playing next week. It didn't matter. It's who we're playing this week.

If we'd had the offense these guys have today, we'd have won a couple of national championships, but we had a very conservative approach to things. Of course, had we been allowed to run with the fumble back then like they are today, who knows?

Coach Campbell said we would have been 10–1 my senior year had we just punted the ball back to the other team and put our defense back on the field. Everybody chuckled, but he was serious. You know Coach Campbell; that's probably the finest compliment I've received, that and Bear Bryant's saying that, had I played in the Cotton Bowl, Alabama probably wouldn't have scored. I'll always remember that and discussing the game with Bear afterward. That was the highest compliment, next to Coach Campbell saying that about our defense.

213

Our quarterback was Rick McIvor, who had that strong arm, but he got hurt against Houston. It was a blessed day for us when they sent Robert in, in his place. Robert was the quintessential quarterback when it came to running and throwing, all of it. He was just a heady guy. I remember when he walked out on the field. We're still friends today. He was just a winner. So when they sent him in there—it didn't hurt that he was wearing No. 16—it started coming together. We ended up tying Houston that game, and I think that game kept us in the running for a shot at a national championship. Of course, we had to go up to Dallas and beat an SMU team that was favored to beat us. I didn't know they were picked to beat us—they said they were supposed to whip our butts. We went up to Texas Stadium and put the

Pony Express—Mr. Eric Dickerson and Mr. Craig James—out of business that day.

The game at Texas Stadium against SMU was a sellout. The guys from SMU had been talking lots of trash that week. Their receiver, Perry Hartnett—I'll never forget his name—had my picture pinned up in his locker. At one point in the game, Mark Weber decided he wanted to switch sides with me—"Let me get some of him." Out of sheer tenacity, he wanted to get a little piece of that guy. That next play, after Weber had switched over, SMU ran a reverse back to my side that would have beat us, because we only won the game 9–7. They ran it into the right side, where Weber should have been. Sometimes the Good Lord puts you in the right spot. I stuffed him. I was the last guy.

I don't know if I would have been able to make the play if Weber hadn't wanted to switch. They ran the reverse, and a half-step into chasing it, I figured out it was a reverse. I think that five yards made a difference, because if I'd been five yards farther away, I don't think I'd have been catching any wide receivers. But they say it's a game of inches, and that day it was.

We beat them 9–7 and kept our season on track. Then we had to beat Baylor here and go to College Station and beat A&M to clinch the Cotton Bowl. But it all fell into place. My senior year both Mark Weber and I got hurt. I broke my leg, and he tore up his knee, so we had two real pups in John Haines and Ralph Darnell playing defensive tackle. They did a yeoman's job, because our defense really played well.

I played scared all the time. I did not want to go back to Groesbeck as a failure. My brothers went to college and are proud graduates. I said, "I need to go handle this." Along the way I found out I was really blessed. The Good Lord just blessed me immensely. I could do things other guys couldn't do, and I was fortunate enough to come to a place that perpetuated greatness. I played with some great guys and learned a lot from one of the best defensive tackles ever to play the game, Steve McMichael. He should be in the NFL Hall of Fame. Between Steve and Coach Parker, the Pup learned how to play. "Bam-Bam" [McMichael] nicknamed me "the Pup."

The game hasn't changed that much. I've been telling those guys ever since Tony Brackens was here, the first chance you have of winning is to really get off on the ball. If you come off and play the game on the offensive side of the ball, your team's going to be better off. We call it "the money step." If you can get off that ball and play on the other side, it's going to cause problems for the other team. Back when I played, everyone was running the veer and the option, doing a lot of ball handling in the backfield. I think I still have the all-time record for career fumbles caused at UT. I really focused on causing fumbles.

When I broke my leg, my mother came down. Adam Schreiber's family was in town, and they all came by the dorm to see me. My mother told me, "Son, you couldn't have made a better decision than to come here. These folks love you." It couldn't have worked out any better for me because, ultimately, being here propelled me to No. 1 in the draft, even with a broken leg my senior year.

The ride was great. I'm very proud to be associated with such a great school. Every April in the NFL draft, they mention my name, "Kenneth Sims from the University of Texas," and it will always be on that board. I feel blessed that I got to play here. I'm a Longhorn for life.

> Kenneth Sims was a consensus All–Southwest Conference and All-American selection and the winner of the Lombardi Award as the nation's best lineman in his senior season of 1981. He was the first overall pick in the 1982 NFL draft and played eight seasons with the New England Patriots. He was enshrined in the Longhorn Hall of Honor in 1997.

WILLIAM GRAHAM

DEFENSIVE BACK

1979–1981

I WAS A TWO-WAY STARTER on the Silsbee High football team—running back and defensive back. We had some very talented athletes, but most weren't thinking about college. For some of my teammates, getting a job on the railroad or getting a job at Temple-Eastex was the goal. But I had to get out. I could not stand the racial divide and the segregation. It was just killing me. In that area—Beaumont, Jasper, Vidor—you weren't referred to by your name, but by "boy." My parents stressed education because they knew the standard of living we'd have if we didn't have an education. My mom's only wish was, "Don't go too far, baby."

The letters started coming in my junior year, but during my senior year, things started heating up. All the college coaches started to come to town. One coach from A&M actually moved into town for a week. I mean, the recruiters would wake you up in the morning and put you to bed at night with their phone calls.

Doug Shankle was my teammate at Silsbee, and we were both being recruited by Texas. The Silsbee football program was rich in tradition and had produced a number of great football players who received scholarships to smaller colleges, but to my knowledge, no one from Silsbee had ever been recruited to play football for the Longhorns.

We had one coach who wanted us to go to the University of Houston. I said, "I don't want to go there. I want to play for the best." They thought I

William Graham followed his Texas days with an outstanding pro career at Detroit.

was a little arrogant, but I said, "I've got to find out for myself how good I am. If I don't, I'll always wonder if I could have competed with the best." I was not content just being comfortable. It would have tormented me the rest of my life. I had only one factor that would influence my decision: they had to be the best team in college football. And the team that stood out was Texas. The Longhorns were on their way to an undefeated season, and Earl Campbell was a human highlight reel each week.

I was getting pressure from everyone—my mom, my preacher, folks in town—to go to A&M, and everything A&M was throwing in the mix was really inviting. I told Coach Bellard that I'd leave the door open for the last game of the season. I had narrowed my decision down to the two Texas teams. If the Aggies had defeated the Longhorns, I would have chosen the Aggies.

Well, Earl killed them. The Longhorns rolled over the Aggies, and my decision was made. I was going to Texas to play with the best. Not everyone was happy about my decision, but I knew in my heart that I had made the right decision.

When I came up for my recruiting trip, before I went in to see Coach Akers, I got a chance to meet Earl Campbell. He was the first superstar athlete I'd ever met. I knew he was leaving for the pros, and I thought I'd be the next Earl Campbell.

I played behind Johnnie Johnson. Coach Leon Fuller said, "Just watch him, okay? Just watch that guy, and when you get a chance, do what he does." So I watched Johnnie until my junior year. I had to wait two years, and it was awful, but it was good for me. I got stronger and smarter, and I gave it to God. I finally said, "Lord, please. You know this means a lot to me. I'm used to playing. I'll be patient, but if you'll give me a chance to play here at Texas, I'll give you all the glory for it."

God started to transform me. I had always gone to church, but then I started going to Bible studies, trying to understand the Word. And it was all about faith. Even though I wasn't playing, I was at peace. The guys could sense it, too. Going into my junior year, I started a Bible study in my dorm room. A few guys showed up at first, and I told them, "I'm not here to try to convert you. I just want to share this Word with you because it's changed me. I now know where to put my faith; not in UT, not in football, but in God." A few guys said, "Man, I need some of that in my life." It started to grow, and more guys came. There were rebels, guys who got in trouble, coming to Bible study. It was as if I were watching all of this, and God just took over my life. I don't care who you are or what you're doing, God will use you and there's nothing you can do about it. That's the God I believe in.

My junior year rolled around, and I got my first start as a Longhorn in the season opener against the Arkansas Razorbacks. It was the largest-attended game in University history at that point, and the game was nationally televised. After the game, I was named the defensive player of the game, and I recall being surrounded by the press. My prayers had been answered; I knew then that I could compete with the best. I also recall the headlines in the paper the next day: "Graham Gives the Glory to God."

During my senior year, against the Aggies in my last regular season game, I tied a 41-year-old record for most interceptions in a single season. I joined Noble Doss and Jack Crain in the record book by intercepting seven passes. Noble Doss would later become a dear friend and an important person in my life. In 1993, under the loving care of his son, Dr. Noble Doss Jr., my wife Lisa gave birth to our son, Hayden. Three years later, Dr. Doss delivered our second son, Gavin. I was destined to become a Longhorn long before I realized it.

My senior season, we played the Crimson Tide in the Cotton Bowl. With less than two minutes to play, the Alabama quarterback went deep with a pass to try and win the game. I intercepted the pass on the goal line to secure the victory for the Longhorns—my eighth interception of the season. I think the record still stands some 26 years later. The Longhorns finished 10–1–1 that season with a No. 2 ranking. It was truly a dream season for me and for the Longhorns.

Coach Fuller and Coach Alan Lowry taught us how to study the game. Those guys were geniuses as coaches. Coach Fuller knew how to reach us. He could take a player wherever he was and help him understand so that when he walked on that field he had no doubt about what he needed to do or his ability to do it. That was the beautiful thing that they did with every player.

The commitment, the dedication, the sacrifices—it wasn't all rosy, God knows, but it was worth it. It's a privilege to be a Longhorn. It means you're associated with the best. It means excellence…class. Other schools are competitive and good, but people around the country look up to Texas. Maybe that's one of our downfalls. Folks tell me, "You guys carry yourselves with a certain amount of arrogance." Well, I don't know if it's arrogance, but it is pride, that's true. Anyone who played here respects every former and current Longhorn. No matter the level of athletic achievement, you respect everyone who ever put on the burnt orange because you know the price they paid and what it made them feel like. To me, anyone who ever wore a Longhorn jersey is equal.

219

I am honored to represent one of the most respected programs in the nation and to be part of a family that spans the world. Playing for Texas, I was privileged to touch the lives of thousands of individuals who support the Longhorns. Being a Longhorn means that the blood that flows through my heart is burnt orange.

William Graham is one of several players holding the team's single-season interception record, and he was the defensive player of the game in the 1982 Cotton Bowl following the 1981 season. He was a six-year starter for the Detroit Lions following his Texas career.

MIKE HATCHETT

DEFENSIVE BACK

1979–1981

I HAVE AN OLDER BROTHER, DERRICK, who preceded me at The University, so my de facto recruitment to The University of Texas began when I was 16 years old. That's when my brother was being recruited.

We are only 18 months apart, and our relationship was somewhat contentious, not very giving. It was a relationship based on competition and on outdoing one another. So we would often fight.

He was being recruited in 1976, and I was aware of rumors and allegations concerning The University and concerning Coach Royal, that he was a racist and didn't want to or could not coach African American athletes. When my brother decided to go to The University, I had a major problem with it.

Coach Royal and Coach Mike Campbell came to my parents' home to recruit my brother. I was not in the room during that process, but whatever Coach Royal said to my parents, it was enough to convince them that Texas was going to be a good place for their son.

During the '70s, the Southwest Conference was plagued by recruiting scandals and illegal inducements, things of that nature. There were innuendoes about these other guys from our neighborhood who'd gone to play Division I football and what factored into their choices. I don't know the truth of those rumors, but I do know that's not something my parents would allow. We were not raised that way. We did not believe that you should sell yourself or allow yourself to be bought. That had a lot to do with my

As a defensive back, Mike Hatchett helped lead the Horns to a dramatic Cotton Bowl victory over Alabama.

brother's choice. Coach Campbell said that if my brother went to The University of Texas, he would be competing among and against the very best in the country. He said that Texas played for national championships, and if Derrick were not afraid to compete, he would be given an opportunity to play. That's all they offered.

When it was time for my recruitment, it was a foregone conclusion that I would choose The University. It speaks to your makeup, what you're all about. I said, "Texas is the standard, and I want to see how I'll measure up." Plus, there was no way that I would play for any school that would pit me against my brother.

One of the most valuable things about attending The University was being able to be around my brother and to build a closer relationship with him. During his senior season, we roomed together for away games. The years at The University I spent with him, discussing football and girls and life were the most fulfilling years. Before UT, the closest bond that my brother and I had was sports.

The first game that I started was against the University of Arkansas in 1980. It was Monday night football, and as far as I know, it was the only time ABC ever televised a collegiate game on Monday night. It was the first game of my junior season, and I made my first interception. For all of us juniors—William Graham, Lawrence Sampleton, Kenneth Sims, A.J. Jones, Rodney Tate, Mike Baab, Mark Weber, Doug Shankle, Joe Shearin, Donnie Little, Bobby Johnson, John Goodson—we were all classmates, and this was our coming-out party. Some of us had played before our junior year, but this was the first time we had taken the field as a class, and the entire nation was watching. That's one of the reasons you go to The University of Texas, for those opportunities.

The interception that I made was toward the end of the game, but it should have been William's. The ball was thrown in the middle of the field. William was in the middle of the field, and I was coming from the corner. As the ball went up, I saw it, and I broke on the ball. I didn't see William at all, and I cut in front of him and got the interception. In the film study afterward, everybody was giving me the business. "You stole William's interception. That should have been William's." William and I were suite-mates, so we lived together. He was my boy, he's my guy. So I said, "Hey. I didn't see you. I'll get it back for you. I'll get you one."

The OU game my junior year was memorable because it was finally our turn. We were no longer special teamers; we were starters. We went into that game as underdogs. OU was ranked No. 2 in the nation, and we were both undefeated. They had a senior team, we had a junior squad. We had defeated them the year before, and this year was supposed to be payback for OU. We won the game, and what made it even more memorable was that's where I got William his interception back. We were running a combination coverage, and on this route, the receiver ran straight downfield about 12 yards, stopped, and turned around—a hook or a curl. I broke when I saw the ball in the air. I came over the receiver's outside shoulder with my left arm and tipped the ball up in the air. I was falling to the ground on my back as the ball was going back over the receiver's shoulder. He had the awareness to spin and try to catch the ball as it was coming back down. I saw this guy spinning, trying to make the catch, so I reached up and grabbed him by the back of his jersey and shoulder pads and pulled him down with me. William was coming from the inside and made a diving catch to intercept. As we were running off the field, I said, "There you go. That's yours."

The last game of my collegiate career was the 1982 Cotton Bowl. We played against Bear Bryant and the Alabama Crimson Tide. Coach Bryant had just established the all-time wins record, and they were looking to extend that record. Of course, they didn't. It was a dramatic comeback victory because they were kicking our butt for three quarters, but the game is played for 60 minutes. We won the fourth quarter and won the game.

I could not have scripted that game any better. When I speak to players today, I tell them the way you go out is the way you're remembered, so you'd better make it count. We went out victorious and were ranked in one poll as No. 2 in the nation.

Best of all are the lifetime friendships I made there. The guys that I met are just the absolute best. That bond with your teammates—it's based on sacrifice, it's based on commitment to your team and to your goals, and it transcends football. It may have been years since I've talked to a guy, but I'll get a phone call from him and it's as if the time never passed. You're godparents to each other's children, and you're present at one another's parents' funerals. Those are the things you carry with you.

One thing I am proud of is the number of football players from northwest San Antonio that have gone to The University. I like to think that my brother and I might have had a little something to do with that. People's memories aren't that long, but I take ownership of, "Here's a kid who's from where we're from, and he's playing high school football on the same field we played on, and he's making the same choice—the right choice—that we made."

223

Being a Longhorn means you make a choice, a decision that you will live by a certain standard. My decision had to do with how I viewed myself and what was important to my family and how we wanted to be viewed. I spoke earlier about my parents telling us never to sell ourselves or allow ourselves to be bought. So to me, being a Longhorn is choosing to live by a standard, and that standard is excellence. We all truly believe that The University of Texas is a great university. After all, it's The University.

One of my favorite quotes, and one that I choose to live by, comes from Martin Luther King Jr.: "We can't all be famous, but we can all be great, as greatness is defined in your service to others."

My father played Texas high school football and, by all accounts, was a good football player. But because of segregation, he didn't have an opportunity to attend a flagship university in the state of Texas. He went to a smaller school on a football scholarship, but soon after he arrived, the Korean War broke out. My father, out of a sense of duty and service, joined the United States Air Force. He made a career out of the Air Force, staying in for 20-plus years. He played Air Force football, but he sacrificed his opportunity to play in college.

This, the greatest university, means so much to the state and to our country in its contributions. So, once having attended The University, for the rest of your life, you'll be measured by that standard. Some people live up to it and some people don't. I relish it because of the sacrifices that my parents, my grandparents, and my great-grandparents made.

Mike Hatchett led the Longhorns in passes broken up and in interceptions in 1979 and 1980, during an era of great Texas defensive backs. He played in the 1982 Olympia Gold Bowl All-Star Game following his senior season.

BRYAN MILLARD

OFFENSIVE TACKLE

1980–1982

I DID NOT HAVE ANY INTENTIONS of going to college. No one in my family had ever gone. We just didn't have the means for college. I grew up in Dumas, north of Amarillo, and going into my senior year in high school, I started to get a bunch of letters about football. That's when college became an option. My high school coach, Don Barton, was a great influence, and he helped my family and me weed out the schools he didn't think would be the best fit. We had to trust what this guy had done successfully for other student-athletes. He was influential in leading me to schools where I would benefit. I took a handful of recruiting trips, but once I went to Austin, there was no decision to be made.

Back then, a school could only be on TV a handful of times each year, excluding bowl games. Well, Texas was always going to go to bowl games. Texas was always going to play for championships. Everybody knew what a Texas Longhorn was, everybody knew what that helmet looked like, everybody wanted to go to The University of Texas. I had told all the other coaches, "I want to talk to my mom and dad first." But when Fred Akers and John Mize gave me that opportunity—when they actually said, "We'd like to offer you a scholarship to The University of Texas"—I said, "Okay." I went into the living room to inform my mom and dad, and I just said, "I'm going to Texas."

Bryan Millard was part of an outstanding group of offensive linemen in the early 1980s.

As a defensive tackle, Mike Parker was my position coach. Then Leon Manley, in his wisdom, said, "You know what? He's just not a very good defensive tackle, but he might be an offensive lineman one of these days." Coach Manley was the only voice the offensive linemen could hear when the place was packed on a Saturday. He had that deep baritone voice, and he knew what everybody had done on each play. The guy was magical. You played as hard as you could because of him. He was a big, tough, bruiser guy. I can think of only one other guy from Oklahoma who's been so loved around here. Anyway, I became an offensive lineman because I was a bad defensive lineman.

The first time I got to play in a game, I was a rookie, and I was sent in to hit the center on field goals and extra points. That was my job, to attempt to knock the center out of the way so Steve McMichael and Bill Acker and those guys could block the kick. That first game of the year, we were playing Iowa State, and all I could think was, *Just don't fall down when you're running out on the field*. It was a giant thrill to run out there.

The big highlight was our Cotton Bowl victory over Alabama and Coach Bear Bryant. Donnie Little had a heck of a catch, and Robert Brewer had a heck of a run. That was a great deal, beating a tremendous school like that with a legendary coach. Robert made a career-defining play in that game. Unfortunately, we ended up being No. 2 in the country.

I cannot tell you how valuable Dana LeDuc was because of his strength training. I played with some very good offensive linemen who played not only at Texas but went on to have extended careers in the NFL, and a lot of it had to do with Dana. The guys were so tight and so close, I think that we pushed and pushed and pushed based on the leadership that we had—Spanky Stephens and Eddie Day, Coach Manley, and specifically Dana. He could make you get one more, jump an inch higher, do five more pounds. That's why he's had such a great career beyond The University. He knew how to get those guys ready. When we got to Texas, we were boys, and when we left, we were men.

227

The University of Texas has always and will always give you all the options, all the unique tools to compete and to succeed. If you can't have that at the school you go to, well, you're going to lag behind a school like Texas. How you plan to compete with them is one thing, but how do you plan to beat them?

A coach from Texas Tech sat in my living room with my mom, my dad, and me. Tech was big on getting the West Texas guys to go to Lubbock. He held this little piece of paper, and he said, "We've got a good stadium, we've got a good program....What does Texas have that we don't have?" I just said, "Coach, it's The University of Texas. They play for championships all the time. Texas Tech doesn't." My dad and mom backed me up. As red as his hair was, his face was even redder. Thank you, but no.

A 17-year-old kid is in a tough bind with everyone saying, "Come to my school, come to my school." You're flattered that these guys are giving you a chance to leave the packing house in Dumas, Texas. It was tough to say no. I wasn't a world-beater recruit by any stretch, but listen…Texas called, I said yes. Pretty simple.

I keep in close contact with many of my teammates. Mike Baab, Bruce Scholtz, Adam Schreiber, Rob Moerschell. We had a neat group of people. College football, far more than pro football, is where relationships are built. When you go to the pros, you're there to make a living; but in college, you're there for a reason. You're there for the love of the school, for the school song, for the love of Saturday afternoons—all the things that are great about college football. And it doesn't hurt when you win. The more you win, the prettier the girls are. That's the way it is, and at Texas you're going to win.

The only time I was frightened was a brief homesick period when I was a rookie. I was a week into it, I was getting beat up every day in practice, I was 500 miles away from home. I'd only been to Austin twice, once for the state track meet and once for my recruiting. So when I left Dumas for Austin, I took out a map, and I asked Coach John Mize, "Coach, how do I get there?" He said, "Drive to Austin, and when you see a big stadium on your right-hand side, stop." That's exactly what he said, and that's what I did.

It's not what *we* did, it's what's been done before us. What we did is just an extension of what will be done after we've gone. That's what makes Texas: the people who started the tradition, the people who did all this. This University can get the players, the students, the faculty—everybody who will help keep that focus on excellence. We are going to be the leader no matter what it is, be it the Blanton Museum of Art, the Bass Concert Hall, the biggest JumboTron. It doesn't matter. We get the people who are worthy of things like this. It starts with the chancellor, the president, the athletics director; they get the right guys in here to carry on the legacy and to add to it.

At Texas, they ask you to be the best there is. No matter what happens, the rest of your life, you can hold up those two fingers and everybody knows what you're saying. It's a language in itself. There are some out there who don't like it, but the only reason they don't like it is because they didn't come here.

Bryan Millard was an excellent offensive lineman for the Longhorns in the early 1980s. He was a team captain of the 1982 team and followed his Texas career by playing nine years in the NFL with the Seattle Seahawks.

ROBERT BREWER

QUARTERBACK
1981–1982

THE FIRST MEMORIES I HAVE were the big parties at our house the night before the Texas-OU game. My cousins came into town, and I got to stay up late. We'd go to the game and the state fair the next day. It was huge. My dad's older brother, George, played running back at Oklahoma in the same backfield with Darrell Royal. My dad broke tradition and became quarterback at Texas. My dad was a good football player, and he started at Texas during '53, '54, and '55. So there was an interesting family dynamic that weekend every year. It was fun the night before and fun going to the game, but somebody was always upset after the game.

Texas played TCU, SMU, and Oklahoma, and since we lived in Dallas, we always went to those games. That's when my blood turned burnt orange. As I got older, I started to dream about how great it would be to play at Texas. I didn't know if it was attainable, but it became my dream. I remember sitting in the Cotton Bowl when a guy named Randy McEachern came running out—an underdog, a forgotten third-team quarterback—and helped Texas beat OU. That made an impression on me. I said, "I can do that." Somewhere along the way, I started believing I could do it.

Signing day came and went my senior year, and there were no offers from major colleges, just a few from small colleges. That just didn't wet my whistle. I was fortunate because my dad had some relationships at The University, and he said, "I'll take you down there." So Dad and Ken Dabbs set up a time

for me to visit during spring training. I got to go down on the field for practice. I met Coach Akers and I asked him if he'd give me a shot. He looked me
in the eye and said he'd give me a shot, but it might take a while. That was all
I needed to hear. So I got to walk on. I was so focused on being a walk-on
that once, when flying on Southwest Airlines, they asked me if I had a reser-
vation and instead of saying, "I'm on standby," I said, "No, I'm a walk-on."

To be honest, walk-ons were treated a little bit differently. As you walked
into the locker room, if you went left, you went to the varsity locker room.
If you went right, you went into the room where the washers and dryers were,
along with about 25 lockers for the graduate assistant coaches, ex-athletes, and
the walk-ons. I can remember being in there with the washer and dryer,
thinking, *What am I doing here?* But that was just for that first fall. In the spring
I got lucky.

When I first got to Texas, there were seven quarterbacks. They posted the
depth chart, and I was seventh. I was scout team quarterback and then, in the
spring, it's as if everyone left. They moved Herkie Walls to receiver, they
moved Jon Aune to defense, Ted Constanzo graduated. Then it was Donnie
Little, Rick McIvor, and me. I got some stats, being third-string. Then someone got hurt, and I ended up that first spring getting a lot of snaps in scrim-
mages. It went well, so that fall going into my sophomore year I had a chance
to play. I didn't do very well. I finished third out of three in that competition.
Coach Akers was trying to give me a little bit of a chance, and I just didn't get
it done. The following spring, I was up to second-string after Donnie moved
to wide receiver. Thank goodness they didn't have a bunch more good quarterbacks. That had a lot to do with my getting to play.

My junior year, we were halfway through the season when Rick got hurt
right before halftime of the Houston game in the Astrodome. Coach came
up to me right before we went out and said, "All right, you're going in."
Herkie said, "You're not the second-string quarterback anymore, so don't play
like it." It was fun, and it went well. We were down 14–0, and the only bad
part was that we didn't win, we tied. I got to play the rest of that year.

My big moment was at the 1982 Cotton Bowl. We played Bear Bryant and
Alabama. We won, and thanks to my teammates, I was elected MVP of that
game. That was January 1, 1982. We won 14–12 in the Cotton Bowl Stadium.
Afterward, we came back to my parents' house, and my dad pulled out a
newspaper to show me that 30 years before, on January 1, 1952, his team had
won the state championship at the same stadium, and he was elected Most

Walk-on quarterback
Robert Brewer
led Texas to a
No. 2 national finish
in 1981.

231

Valuable Player. Guess what the score was? 14–12. It was like God's neat gift to me. We were so grateful.

It was so special to our family. Our faith is an important part of our lives, and football, as big as it is, doesn't come first. You have to learn that as a young person. Through my failure my sophomore year, I had taken an inventory, and that's where I figured it out on the priority scale. My relationship with God became the most important thing.

The funny thing is, earlier that year, after the OU game—two weeks before I got to play—I'd decided I was going to quit. We were No. 1 in the nation, and things were going really well without me. I wasn't getting to play, so I told my mom and dad the Sunday before I went back to school, "I'm behind a little in school, there are new guys coming in…." Of course, I wouldn't have quit in the middle of the season, but I decided that I was going to quit at the end of the year. And then two weeks after I said that, it all got crazy.

I was just on a great team. I am a student of UT football, and that offensive line we had that year was as good as any ever. Terry Tausch, Mike Baab, Joe Shearin, Doug Dawson, Bryan Millard—all of those guys had long careers in the NFL. They were really good, and if we'd had a really good quarterback, there's no telling what we could have done. I came in as a backup quarterback and got to come in and calm it down, make sure the ball got handed off and thrown to the right guy and just drive the train. I didn't have to be spectacular because everyone else was so good.

So that was my biggest moment, walking into the Cotton Bowl, and there's Coach Bear Bryant, leaning on the goal post. At a function before the game, he was sitting right there at the table next to me, with those big old creases in his neck. I dropped half my meal on the ground just watching him. That was my moment, no doubt.

What does it mean to be a Longhorn? I could answer that when I was in grade school. I was taught early what it meant: you give everything you've got all the time. Coach Royal brought teams down that tunnel at the Cotton Bowl Stadium, and maybe some weren't as talented as OU some years, but they would fight to the death. That's what it meant to be a Texas Longhorn.

It's the way you go about things, the ethics of what you do. There was always a question of how some schools were getting players. There was no question how The University of Texas did things. We wanted to win just as badly as other schools. At Texas, there's only one place—first place. That's always your goal. But that's worthless if there's no regard for how you get there. Being a Longhorn means conducting yourself in a first-class manner; it's excellence. The team is more important than individual players at Texas, and the team is stronger than the sum of its parts. That's Texas to me. Coach Royal gave that to all of us, even those who didn't play for him. These principles serve me well today.

I'll never stop giving thanks that I was blessed to get to be a Texas Longhorn. It was beyond my wildest dreams, and that is not lost on me. I will always treasure that.

Robert Brewer became perhaps the most famous walk-on in Longhorn history, leading the 1981 Texas team to a No. 2 national ranking and, as MVP of the game, a Cotton Bowl victory over Alabama. He was chosen as a team captain and the team MVP in 1982.

JERRY GRAY

DEFENSIVE BACK

1981–1984

ONE OF THE BIGGEST REASONS I came to The University of Texas was, when I was a sophomore in high school, I got a chance to run track at Memorial Stadium. That, of course, was long before the reconstruction, when the track was moved out and the stadium was renamed Darrell K Royal–Texas Memorial Stadium. I had made it to the state track meet. I was from Lubbock, and it was the first time I'd ever been to Austin in my life, and that was probably the best trip I ever had. I was just a sophomore, so I wasn't recruited by Texas or anything. But I made up my mind then that when the time came, that was the place I was going to go.

When my senior year came and it was time to get signed, I think I took one other recruiting trip, and that was to Colorado. But other than that, I turned everybody else down. I let them know I really didn't want to waste their time or anyone else's. And I never had a chance to look back.

I was a wide-eyed freshman when I got there in 1981, and I really didn't know anything about how to play on that level of football. We had veterans like William Graham, Bobby Johnson, Mike Hatchett, and Vance Bedford in the secondary as the starters. I remember thinking, *Man, these guys are good, because when they go out there to play, they really understand what they're supposed to do.* You could see how professional they were in the meetings and the way they went about their business. But we had fun. Those were the examples I had. So when those guys graduated after my freshman year, they

All-American Jerry Gray had a successful pro career, then coached in college and the NFL.

left it to us. The younger guys were Craig Curry, Mossy Cade, Fred Acorn, and me.

That was 1982. We lost to Oklahoma, and we lost to SMU. But even so, that was an eye-opening thing for me, because with a young secondary, we were competitive in both games. I knew then that if we could compete against those guys, we had a chance to win a lot of games. After that, we never lost a regular season game until midway through my senior year. That kind of says how good we were, even though we were young. We lost in the snowstorm in the 1982 Sun Bowl in El Paso, and then lost the Cotton Bowl game to Georgia 10–9 after the 1983 season.

To me, the 1983 team was one of the best teams I ever played on, college or pro. It wasn't that one side of the ball was better than the other side. There was a lot of camaraderie. Guys had been there for three years and some for four. I don't think it was an arrogant deal. We just knew that we could play. Even though people said our defense was pretty much dominating, we knew that our offense was really good, too. They did what they were supposed to do.

We played against top teams and top players. We played against Bo Jackson at Auburn twice, and we wound up winning both of those games. We played Penn State in the Meadowlands when they had D.J. Dozier, and we won that game. We played against Oklahoma when they had Marcus Dupree, and we won that game. That's what I think about at The University of Texas. It wasn't like we were playing teams that didn't have really good players on their side. Whenever you can go out and compete against those guys, week in and week out, then when you have a chance to go play in the NFL, you are ready to compete.

We were so dominant for 16 or 17 games in a row that we never thought about losing. And then one play changed all of that. The Cotton Bowl game against Georgia was painful. We went down there, and we had one of the better defenses in the country. Herschel Walker had just left Georgia. We went in as the No. 2 team in the nation, and we were dominating the game on the field, not just on the scoreboard. Then one play changed the whole outcome. We were leading 9–3 with less than three minutes left. We fumbled a punt, and they drove the short field, scored, and kicked the extra point.

235

But what I came to learn later is, that same thing happens in the NFL every week. You can be winning the game by the numbers, but if one side of the ball makes a mistake, it can cost the whole team. And those are the things that got me to really understand that you could be the best team and still not win every week.

We picked up the 1984 season where we left off before that bowl game, however. And the play people will always talk about was the tackle I made on Bo Jackson of Auburn in our game in Austin. It was a night game, a national TV game. It was one of those plays where I was playing center field. They basically ran a little easy sweep to our right—their left—and Bo cut back. Most of the time, I never over-pursue guys. But he cut back across the grain, so I had to cut back. All I could think about was just trying to run him down. In all the tapes I'd seen from the years before, nobody ever caught him. He's a great athlete. So my thinking was, if I couldn't catch him, nobody else on our team was going to. You don't go in and think, *I'm gonna run down Bo Jackson*. It was just one of those things that happens. When I tackled him, he fell the wrong way and hurt his shoulder. He should have won the Heisman that year, because he won it the next year. It was an opportunity for me that showed up in a good way, and an opportunity for him that caused him to finish in a bad way.

We went on to get to No. 1 that year after we beat Penn State, but then we tied Oklahoma, and we lost three of our last four games, and we shouldn't have. To me, it goes to show that the best team doesn't always win. Even though I thought we had better personnel, we didn't win those games that we should have won.

I guess when I think of my time at The University of Texas, I look at the people who made a difference for me and have become great friends. One of them is Larry Falk, who was our equipment manager and is now director of operations. Larry doesn't get a lot of notice, but he works every day to make that place better, and he takes pride in what he does. He's a great friend, and the kind of guy you know you can always count on. You won't see his name on the JumboTron, but he does his job well.

When I think about what it means to be Longhorn, I realize that it is about pride and the great tradition, but it's also about the feeling that you have that you were just a little bitty piece of that, and there are some kids who came before you and who will come after you.

I thought about that when, as an NFL coach, I spent some time at the combine before the NFL draft in 2007. There were three defensive backs from The University of Texas there, and just as I looked up to the Johnnie Johnsons, the Derrick Hatchetts, and the Ricky Churchmans, they were looking at me. Those guys put on the same pads I did, and they understand there is something special about putting on the uniform of The University of Texas. When you look at it like that, you appreciate why you went there.

Jerry Gray was a two time All-SWC and All-American in the Longhorn secondary in the mid-1980s. He was chosen the team MVP in both 1983 and 1984. He played in four Pro Bowls during his nine-year NFL career, earning MVP honors in the 1990 Pro Bowl. He is a member of the Longhorn Hall of Honor and has had an extensive coaching career both at the college and professional level.

TONY DEGRATE

DEFENSIVE TACKLE

1982–1984

I'D ALWAYS DREAMED OF PLAYING FOR The University of Texas. I think any kid from Texas who says he doesn't is not telling the truth. There are certain schools that you dream about playing for, and when I knew God was giving me that opportunity, when I knew the dream was going to become a reality, there was no question where I wanted to go. I was ready to leave West Texas, and what better place could you go than Austin?

I grew up in Snyder, a small West Texas town of about 12,000 people. It's a great community. I enjoyed being raised there, and I had great parents who guided me in the right direction. Of course, that's big Texas Tech country out there, but I had made it known where I wanted to go. When you're a little kid wearing all your Texas stuff, it's apparent where your heart is.

My position coach was Mike Parker. When I visited The University of Texas, he told me, "I'm gonna give you No. 99. Do you remember the last person to wear 99?"

I just looked at him. I knew Texas history, and I said, "Yes, sir, it was Steve McMichael."

He goes, "Do you know he was an All-American here?"

I told him I did. He said, "That's exactly what I'm telling you, Tony."

I was blown away that he thought that much of me. That made an impression on me, to be able to wear No. 99. I realized there was a lot of pressure on me, but I relished the opportunity to wear that number.

Tony Degrate won the Lombardi Award and was also an accomplished artist.

Another thing about my recruitment impressed me, although at the time I wasn't that excited about it. They had a group of girls called "Akers's Angels" to show you around campus. When I got there, everybody else had their "Angel," and I was sitting there by myself, thinking, *What's going on here?* Coach Fred Akers came over and said, "I'm going to show you around campus." I was a little disappointed; I didn't get an "Angel," I got the coach. He took me to the Fine Arts department, which is really impressive, and showed me around. Then I realized, *I'm an 18-year-old kid from a small town, and if the head coach takes time out to show me around, maybe The University of Texas does think something about me.* I knew then exactly where I was going, and I knew what my calling was—to be a Longhorn.

When I got home, every other coach who was recruiting me knew that, as well, because my phone was ringing off the wall. The hardest thing was telling people, "I'm a Longhorn." Some coaches were gracious, others started badmouthing Texas, saying, "You'll never play there, you'll get lost in the shuffle." It got a little nasty. Of course, my mom, protective mom that she is, asked them, "Why did you recruit him then, if you don't think he's good enough to play at a major college?"

I tell people in order to be the best you've got to go where the best is. Some may perceive that as being cocky, but anyone who knows me knows that's not what I'm saying. I'm saying if you're confident in the abilities God has given you, you want to showcase them at one of the best universities. The University of Texas, without a doubt, is one of the top five programs where you have that opportunity. I wanted to see how I stacked up against some of the other top recruits. It was a no-brainer.

I was blessed and fortunate to start as a sophomore. Back then, sophomores rarely got to play at Texas, much less start. My junior year was special, but at the same time it was a nightmare. We were one point away from winning the national championship. We were 11–0 and lost to Georgia in the Cotton Bowl. Our team holds the record for most kids drafted in one day, which was 18. It was an honor to play on a team with that much talent. We knew we were good. We knew we could be special, but at Texas, that's what people expected from us. Actually, our opponents expected it from us.

My junior year I had the opportunity to be an all-conference player. I think I led the nation in tackles behind the line. I realized that maybe I could do something on the national stage. One good thing about The University is that, because you're in the national spotlight, if you excel, people will recognize you really quickly. Of course, it can work against you if you don't excel, because people will recognize that, as well. It's a catch-22.

Coach Akers met with us individually, and he'd ask about our team goals and our personal goals. For my personal goals, I said I'd like to repeat as all-conference and perhaps make All-American and just be the best player that I could be. Coach Akers said, "You left one out…the Lombardi Award."

I told him that, until then, I'd never even thought about it.

He said, "That's what I'm trying to tell you…that's the type of player we expect you to be." When you have a coach who really believes in you—when I left that office, I was flying high. I just kind of took it in. I didn't tell a whole lot of people. But I was like, *With God's help, I hope to accomplish this.* And what better playing ground to have than The University of Texas? Texas opens so many doors and offers so many opportunities. It's up to you to take advantage of them.

Of course, I put the team goals first because, at Texas, the first thing you think of is winning the national championship. Then, of course, winning the conference and all those other things. But I did start thinking about the Lombardi Award. I did some research on it, and I was taken aback to think that my coaches thought I was one of the top linemen in the United States. But, once again, if you're at The University of Texas, you realize you are one of the top players. That's why you're there. That's why they recruited you.

Consequently, I worked even harder my senior year. The first game that year we played Bo Jackson and that group. Auburn was a preseason No. 1; we surprised them. It got us a lot of recognition. I had 16 tackles and started getting mentioned for the Lombardi Award. By the sixth or seventh game of the season, announcers started saying I should be the frontrunner.

The following week, we beat Penn State and Coach Joe Paterno in East Rutherford, New Jersey. That was a strange season because, after the third week, we were No. 1 in the nation. Then the wheels fell off the vehicle. We lost three games in a row and ended up with a dismal 7–4–1 year. That's why my senior year was bittersweet. From an individual standpoint, it was a dream season. But from a team aspect, which is the most important, it was very disappointing.

I established myself as a legitimate contender, not just to be nominated but to win the Lombardi Award at the TCU game. TCU was good, I think No. 9 in the nation, and we handled them pretty well. That particular game, if I'm not mistaken, I had 21 tackles. Being on national TV helps your cause quite a bit. Coach Akers came out and said, "If there's a better lineman in the country, I haven't seen him."

The night of winning the Lombardi Award was a special highlight. I was so proud to win in Houston, because I think 95 percent of the audience were Longhorns. I saw a lot of Hook 'em Horns out there. It represented all the hard work I put in at that great University, and it planted a seed that people would remember.

Evidently, I held the record for most tackles in one season. I didn't even realize that until Mr. Bill Little told me when I was inducted into the Hall of Honor back in 2005. I was extremely proud to be inducted into the Longhorn Hall of Honor.

It's hard to talk about myself. God taught me to be a humble person. But it was such a tremendous ride, and to be able to establish myself at Texas is gratifying. Sometimes I'll ask myself, *Did I really do those things at Texas?* To have an opportunity to play at The University and to achieve some success—it went beyond my wildest dreams as a kid.

When I used to get interviewed, I always spoke of what an honor it was to play for The University. I also liked to thank God because he gave me that opportunity. I love to point that out. Today it seems taboo; you're not supposed to mention anything like that. But it was God that opened all those doors for me.

I equate being a Longhorn with—I don't know if this is an accurate or fair analogy—once you're a Marine, you'll always be recognized as a Marine. It's something you're extremely proud of. The University of Texas is the same way. To say that you played in the burnt orange is something I will take to my grave. I tell my mama, "Make sure you bury me in burnt orange." I'm serious about that. When people speak about me, the first thing they mention is "Tony Degrate," and then they say, "from The University of Texas." It's a marriage that's going to be forever.

Tony Degrate won the 1984 Lombardi Award as the nation's top lineman, was a two-time All–Southwest Conference selection, and was All-American in 1984. He set a school record for solo tackles with 123 and was named to the Longhorn Hall of Honor in 2005.

TODD DODGE

QUARTERBACK
1982–1985

I WAS RECRUITED OUT OF PORT ARTHUR–Thomas Jefferson High School by Kenneth Dabbs. There were four who signed that year off of our state-finalist team—myself, Brent Duhon, Don Holloway, and Robert Smothers. All four of us were leaning toward different places as second options, but we all ended up at Texas. I took recruiting visits to A&M, Ohio State, Florida State, and to Missouri. In the big picture, in my 17-year-old mind, if The University of Texas was going to recruit me, there wasn't anywhere else.

I could remember the 1969 and 1970 national championship teams, and it was one of those deals that, if you were in the state of Texas and the Long-horns recruited you, that's where you were going to go. I loved watching Texas. Back then, there were three channels—ABC, NBC, and CBS. It seemed even to an ol' boy from Port Arthur, Texas, that the Longhorns played on TV an awful lot.

The first college football game I ever attended was the first one I suited up for. I'm not kidding. I don't even remember who we opened up with—maybe the University of Miami in Austin. I was 18 years old, standing on the sideline at the first college game I ever attended, and I actually got out there and ran three or four plays. I was probably like a deer in the headlights that first game. Being in a place with 80,000 people in it—it was everything I'd ever dreamed of. I'd seen it on TV but never experienced it. It's one of those moments you never will forget.

Todd Dodge became one of the most successful coaches in Texas High School football history.

In 1981 there was a rule in the Southwest Conference that you could not redshirt freshmen. I was the third-string quarterback behind Rick McIvor and Robert Brewer. I played about as much as you'd expect a third-string quarterback to play. Between my junior and senior year, the SWC went back and made a retroactive rule that any freshman who had played in 30 percent or less of the games in 1981 could now go back and take a redshirt. So, going into the football season of '84, instead of being a senior, I was going in as a junior. I played in five seasons, although I didn't play enough that first year to letter, so I ended up being a four-year letterman.

Going into my sophomore year—the season of '82—I was the solid number two to Robert Brewer all year. I played a lot that year, but Robert was a great player and was the established starter. I always tell people that during the football season of '82, I caddied for Robert. We roomed together on the road and got to know one another well.

We were getting ready to go to the Sun Bowl. About the day before we left, he hit his hand on a helmet as he was falling, and it just shattered his right thumb. I found out then and there what it was really like to be the starting quarterback at The University of Texas.

I went from being the second-string quarterback that a few people remembered from his high school career to giving a press conference at the airport when we landed in El Paso because now I was going to be starting in the Sun Bowl. I found out really quickly how things can change. When you're second- or third-string, you really don't realize what the starter's going through, with the media attention and the demands on his time. So we got to the Sun Bowl, and that whole week was fabulous. They always do a great job.

There's not a whole lot I remember from the game, but I had my first college start and my first and only white Christmas all in the same day. We played North Carolina on Christmas Day. It started snowing in El Paso about 5:00 in the morning, and it snowed the entire day. It was pretty miserable.

The next year, the '83 season, we had a fabulous year. That year I'd won the starting quarterback job throughout the spring and two-a-days, but I separated my shoulder 10 days before we played Auburn, and I was out about three weeks. That was the year that Rick McIvor, Rob Moerschell, and I were there and it was kind of "quarterback by committee." It was one of those years, offensively, where it was, "just don't screw things up." I think we had 18 players from that team get drafted, and a bunch of them were defensive players. We were undefeated going into the Cotton Bowl, where we got beat by Georgia. I'd had some big games; I came in off the bench and threw the winning touchdown against SMU. I started several games that year, but my most memorable times in that '83 season were the games I came in "in relief," so to speak, and led our team to win.

In the 1984 season I won the job and started the whole year. It was one of those years that molded me as a coach, because it was a year that gave me the opportunity to learn how to handle success and how to handle failure, big-time, all in the same four- or five-month window.

We started out the season ranked 10th or 12th in the nation. We opened up and beat Auburn at home; that was a tremendous game. Auburn was No. 1 in the nation, and they had Bo Jackson. It was a nationally televised Saturday night game on ESPN. Offensively, we just lit it up.

The next game, we traveled to New Jersey to play Penn State up in the Meadowlands. They were now the No. 1 team in the nation. We beat the No. 1 team in the nation two games in a row to open the season. Now, we were No. 1. We went from 12 to 1 in about three weeks. We rocked along, but at the end of the year the bottom fell out, for whatever reason. We'd had success, and I knew now what it felt like for everybody in Austin, Texas, to want to love you up and be around you, whether it was all your doing or not. Later in the year I found out what it was like to be the one who got a whole lot of the blame for losses. That was tough at the time, but anybody who's played quarterback for a big-time Division I program—I don't care whether they're going into coaching or whatever—they're prepared and they're pretty thick-skinned, whatever they choose to do.

When I took the job at Southlake Carroll, we lost our first three games. A lot of people don't remember that. People started talking to me about the pressure of the job, and I said, "Listen, I've been booed by 80,000, and I've been given a standing ovation by the same 80,000 the same afternoon, so this stuff doesn't affect me a whole lot." To have played quarterback at this place, I don't know that there could be a better internship in life for anybody, whatever profession they choose.

There is no better decision I could have made for myself. I couldn't have known when I was 17 years old that the decision I was making would affect my life so much, in the connections I'd have and the associations I always will have with the great University of Texas. When I told Coach Akers that I was committing to Texas, there was no way for me to know how that decision would be so beneficial, even now that I'm 43 years old.

No one else could ever understand what went into earning that "T" ring. If you stop to reflect on what it means and to reflect on the other people who are wearing it and what it means to them, you realize you're in a pretty special fraternity of athletes.

As I reflect back on my life, being a Longhorn is being a Texan. If you're going to live your life in the state of Texas, and you get the opportunity to go to school at The University, take it. You'll be doing yourself a great favor. That's what it means to me.

Todd Dodge came to Texas as one of the most heralded high school quarterbacks in state history. He helped lead the Longhorns to three bowl appearances. Following his career at Texas, he became one of the most successful high school coaches in state history during his tenure at South Lake Carroll, and he is now the head coach at the University of North Texas.

JOHN HAGY

DEFENSIVE BACK

1985–1987

THE TRUTH OF THE MATTER IS, I got to Texas by default. My entire life, I wanted nothing more badly than to go to The University of Texas. My room was painted orange, and my brother Bill was a walk-on in the late '70s. I followed Texas football from junior high on. David McWilliams was recruiting me at John Marshall High School in San Antonio. I got a few letters my junior year from Texas, TCU, and Southwest Texas [now Texas State]. David was recruiting me and saying they wanted me to come to Texas. He was very positive and seemed to be a fan of mine. So I came to UT on my official recruiting trip, and I went in to Coach Akers's office, where he told me that they didn't have a scholarship for me. I was devastated. I think Coach McWilliams was under the impression that I was being offered one, because he was standing there, basically waiting to congratulate me. I had to tell him, "Well, I didn't get an offer." It was getting close to signing date, and I didn't want to be left out in the cold. The only other school that had offered me was Southwest Texas, so I committed to them.

Then, the day before signing date, I got called off the field at baseball practice. David McWilliams was on the phone, and he said they'd had a kid who backed out, they had a scholarship available, and did I still want to come to Texas? The answer was obviously, "Yes," but without this kid backing out, I would never have been able to go there. That's how I ended up at The

University. I believe I was the seventh or the eighth defensive back that they took in that class.

Besides the many off-the-field experiences and the camaraderie with fellow players, my best and most vivid experience was in 1987. Understand that I am an extreme David McWilliams fan. He had gone to Tech in 1986, I guess, and was the head coach up there. When Fred Akers left, Texas hired David to be head coach. So, in 1987, Tech was coming to town. They had a good team, and they were going to stick it to David because he had "abandoned" them to come back to The University. Well, they came down here, and we whupped them pretty good. That '87 Tech game was my fondest memory of playing at UT, not only because I had a good game, and we won the game, but because we validated David's decision and his ability to coach by beating Tech pretty soundly. He's a wonderful guy. I've never run across one person at UT who's ever said anything negative about David McWilliams. You'd think you'd run across somebody who's bitter about something, but everybody likes the guy. He's honest. That's the thing I really liked about him. I mean, I got many butt-chewings from him, but I got an equal number of pats on the head. You always knew where you stood with him. Everything was above board, you knew the rules, and it's easy to follow that game plan.

We had some lean years. The on-field experiences were good at times, bad at times. But to be a Longhorn, to play for the state's university, the school that every kid going to Tech or A&M or SMU or Houston would go to if they had their druthers—some of them won't admit it, but I guarantee if they'd had the opportunity to play at Texas, they would have. Just like me. If I'd ended up at Southwest Texas, I would tell you today, "That's where I wanted be," when in fact, where I really wanted to be was Texas.

When you get here, they make you test. You know, how high you can jump, how fast you can run, how many times you can bench press a certain weight. When I got here as a freshman, I went up to the weight room and saw all these massive guys. I was a little high school kid saying, "Oh, man." They put a 45-pound weight on each end of the bar, which [with the bar] makes a total of 135 pounds, and they wanted to see how many times you could press that. There were guys pressing that weight 25–30 times. Our strength and conditioning coach, Dana LeDuc, put that thing on there, and they took it off the rack. It went down and, I kid you not, I could not get it

247

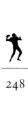

John Hagy was an outspoken redhead who backed up his talk with his play.

off my chest. One hundred thirty-five pounds. I remember the humiliation of Dana and all these guys looking at me, going, "You've got to be kidding me. Get that off your chest right now." And I was like, "I can't." I remember calling home and telling my parents, "I'm horrible. This is going to be horrible." I couldn't get the weight off my chest.

Dana pulled me aside and said, "Son, you're at The University of Texas, and until you can bench press 300 pounds, you will not smell that field." I was thinking, *135…300 pounds…that's a lot of work. How am I going to do that?*

Two weeks later, we played Auburn and Bo Jackson. They were ranked No. 1. And as a true freshman, I played at cornerback in that game.

When I finished playing for Buffalo, I'd train here during the off-season. I remember going to Dana's strength camps, and he'd tell all these kids the importance of strength training and conditioning. And that's true, and you need to have it, but it can also be overrated. I would always tell the story to those kids: Coach LeDuc explained to me that until I could bench press 300 pounds, I would never smell the field here. Of course, he was so right—because two weeks after he told me that, I was playing against Auburn.

I would always rib Dana about that. I'm sure if I had been stronger, I'd have been a better football player. Certain things will make you a better football player. But it doesn't mean you can't be a good football player just because there's this one condition you can't meet. How much I could bench press didn't have a whole lot of bearing on how good a football player I was. The question is, How good are you? I never lifted weights in high school. They didn't see that much value in it. Of course, those were the days they were shoving salt pills down your throat. And no water.

249

There's a lot that goes into being a good football player. Guys would come into the weight room, and we'd say, "Looks like Tarzan, plays like Jane." Who cares what you look like? You go into the weight room with all these fifth-year seniors; you do feel intimidated, and you either sink or swim. Some guys say, "I'm going to do whatever it takes," get mad, and make it. And some guys just shrivel up and fall by the wayside. That's why you see so many blue chips that are supposed to be the end-all to everything who don't ever play. They just get lost.

My drive was I wanted to see how I good I was compared to the best. You don't have a way to gauge yourself. If you're coming from a high school that didn't make the playoffs, and you hear about the kid from so and so whose team's in the state championship, that's good. The kid's probably a good player. But what about the outstanding player who played on an unsuccessful team? He's probably salivating to get to UT and say, "You've never heard of me, but you're gonna hear me now." That's hard for a guy like me, who had to prove himself over and over again, to see someone with all the talent in the world and you think, *Man, if I just had that talent with my drive, I could have been unstoppable.* So you look at someone with all the talent and think, *Why are you wasting that?*

You do appreciate it more after you're removed from it and you're gone. You don't understand the magnitude of it when you're playing. And I guess all of us wonder, Could I have put out any more effort? Did I leave it all out there? Did I conserve anything?

To strive for excellence, to strive to compete with the best athletes in the country, to be able to look at your academic career and know that you've walked among some of the brightest and smartest people in the world—to know that, from an athletic standpoint, you've competed against some world-class athletes. That is what it means to be a Longhorn.

John Hagy was the captain of David McWilliams's first Longhorn team in 1987. He was a four-year letterman and All–Southwest Conference selection his senior year. He played three years in the NFL.

ERIC METCALF

RUNNING BACK

1985–1988

I WAS A JUNIOR IN HIGH SCHOOL IN ARLINGTON, Virginia, and I was sitting in the stands at an indoor track meet in Preston, New Jersey, waiting to long jump. That's when I met Coach James Blackwood.

I didn't know who he was or where he was from, and he didn't know who I was. We were just talking. He ended up watching me long jump, and I jumped 25 feet, 8 or 9 inches, something like that. He was coaching track at the time [he later became football recruiting coordinator], so he went back to Texas and told everybody in the football office, "There's a guy you need to check out."

From that point, Coach Fred Akers and his staff started recruiting me. I eventually visited, and I liked it. I had committed to the University of Miami, but my mother and my father did not want me to go there. I had everybody and their mother calling me, trying to talk me out of it, even people who were alumni of Miami. They didn't feel it was a good situation, because Miami was getting in a lot of trouble. My folks wanted me to go to Notre Dame. So I said, "I'm not going to Notre Dame. I won't go to Miami, but I'm not going to Notre Dame."

I ended up signing with Texas, and I don't even know how that happened. I don't know how they had a scholarship left for me, because I waited a week to 10 days after the signing date before I signed. I don't know where the scholarship came from, but I was happy.

Eric Metcalf was a multi-threat star as a receiver, runner, and kick returner who led the team in all-purpose yards each season from 1985 to 1988.

To be honest, we didn't get the recruits that The University of Texas was accustomed to getting, so we weren't as good as we could have been or thought we were going to be. When I eventually decided to take a visit, I was thinking, *This is Texas football. This is as high as you can get, and there is no reason we can't win games and get recruits.* But we just never got the people who could win the big games. I came to Texas in 1985, just two years after they had been unbeaten through the regular season.

But it was a fun time, and I feel good about my decision in going to Texas. I know I'd do the same thing if I had it to do all over again. It was great for me, meeting people I would have never met and staying as close to those guys as I am today. We didn't win the conference or anything like that, but we had some moments, like the Bluebonnet Bowl in 1987, against Pittsburgh in a major setting. We had Craig "Ironhead" Heyward on the other side, and he had been a Heisman candidate. It was Coach McWilliams's first year at Texas, and that was one of the games where I thought that's how it would be my whole career at Texas—I'd catch a few balls and gain some yards as well as rushing for close to 100 yards. I felt like the more I could get those opportunities in receiving and running, the better I could be. That game sticks out because it was a national game, and I got to do the things I thought I would be able to do my whole career.

Unfortunately, we didn't win all the games that they're experiencing now, or even the games that they won before we got there. We ended up playing for two head coaches in four years, and I think I played with five quarterbacks in that time. Changing offenses like that, you are not going to be able to win too many games, regardless of who's around you.

Things looked positive before my senior year in 1988, like things were going to change. We had accomplished some things in 1987, beating Arkansas on the last play of the game and winning our bowl game. Going into the season, we were ranked in the top 20, and everybody had high hopes for the upcoming season.

That had been a pivotal summer for me because the Olympic trials were being conducted, and I had a strong chance to make the team in the long jump. But I knew if I did, I was going to have to miss the football season. It was the first time in my life that I didn't want to win, and that's hard to believe. Anybody who watches track and field knows that it is about going to the Olympics, and possibly being an Olympic champion. But all my life I had concerned myself with being a football player, and that's what I wanted to do. I wanted to be like my dad, Terry Metcalf, and play football.

At the time I faced the decision, I had one of the best jumps in the world. The Olympic trials were coming up, but at the same time, my senior season was coming up. It was the Olympics on one hand, or go for the Heisman Trophy on the other. For me—our family, my upbringing—I would rather have the Heisman than be on the Olympic team. So going into the trials, I kept telling people that it didn't matter what happened there, because if I made the team I wasn't going, anyway. I was going to play football and try to win the Heisman and win some games and possibly win the national championship. That was my focus. That's something I had been wanting to do all my life. So I got to the trials, and I wasn't jumping well. I got fifth place and didn't make the team. I wasn't really mad about it at the time. Being older and thinking about the fact that I could have made the Olympic team, it is a little different now. But it didn't bother me then because I wanted to play football.

Just before our first game with BYU, everything changed. I had been told to pick up money for summer school in June, but because of the trials, I didn't use the money to go to school. I paid the money back before school started but was ruled technically in violation because I didn't give it back when I decided not to go to summer school. The NCAA penalized us by making me miss that first game, which was on Labor Day night on national television. We didn't get a final ruling on our appeal until just before the team left for Provo, and Coach McWilliams had to tell the team on the plane that I wasn't coming with them.

We had such hopes, and then to receive a blow like that in the beginning of the season was a major setback. It wasn't that we weren't a good team, but mentally we just weren't able to overcome that. Things just didn't work out like we thought they would after that. We never caught a break. I knew all I could do was go out and play and play well, but missing that first game was too much to overcome. I'm not saying I would have won the Heisman, but that took me out of any shot I had. If I had really tried to win the long jump and make the Olympic team, things might have been different, but I don't know…things happen for a reason.

It didn't change how I feel about The University of Texas. I'm still happy about the time I had there and everything I was able to accomplish. Growing up, I never thought of Texas football. I never thought, *Wow, one day I'll play at Texas.* I just thought I'd play football and didn't have an idea where.

But to come there and be taken in like that, it was a great time and great feeling, knowing that people cared for me and still do. They gave me an opportunity to say, "I'm a Longhorn."

I spent 12 years in the NFL, but my loyalties will always be with Texas. My son thinks when he gets out of high school he can go to Texas, and he's six years old. He wants to go to Texas because of the love that I received there. I never thought that once I got out of school I would still feel this way about The University, but I can't help it. Granted, I didn't get to win like I wanted to, but I learned a lot there. I got a lot out of the school and I contributed to the school and its well-being, as well. The University was good to me and good for me, and I love everything about it.

When we won the national championship last year, I felt like I played in that game. I was so happy and proud of the guys who got to go out there and do it. But I felt like I had, because that's how connected I am to The University. That's how I feel every time we take the baseball field, basketball court, track—it doesn't matter. I expect we're going to win; I expect great things out of The University.

Eric Metcalf earned the distinction of being a three-time NCAA long-jump champion as well as a three-time All–Southwest Conference football player. He set records as a receiver and as a running back and punt returner. He played 12-plus years in the NFL, set the league record for kick returns for touchdown, and was named to the Pro Bowl three times. He was named to the Longhorn Hall of Honor in 2002.

OSCAR GILES
DEFENSIVE END
1987–1990

TEXAS WAS IN MY BLOOD. My mother has a family picture from when I was growing up in Palacios, Texas. I don't know why, but I had a Longhorn cap on. I was fortunate—I was heavily recruited. One day my mother said, "Look at this," and she showed me that picture. "That was your favorite cap, and that was your favorite team." I was nine or 10 years old. When it came down to it, Texas was in my blood.

When I took my official visit to Texas, it was my first plane ride. It was a small plane, just me and a couple of guys. It was neat and scary at the same time. David McWilliams was the head coach. He came to our school and said, "You know, I drove and flew through the fog to see you." He had on boots and was chewing on a cigar, just as country as all outdoors. I thought, *This guy's kinda like me*. I related well with him, and he's still the same person today as he was then.

When I first walked into Jester Center, somebody made a mistake and put me in a senior's room. There was a question as to whether Charles Hunter, a running back, was coming back, so I wound up in room 550, which was to have been his room. Usually, freshmen are on the third floor. My mother had raised four boys by herself. I'm the oldest, and she was helping me move in. The elevator was packed with everybody moving in, so we moved ourselves using the stairs. She'd have pillows, I'd have the stereo—we both had our

Oscar Giles, a four-year letterman, went on to become a Longhorn assistant coach.

hands on the TV. We did that for five floors. I was happy, and she was crying. You know…we'd made it.

The first thing I did was to write down the five things I wanted to accomplish at Texas. The number-one goal was to get my degree because I was told by a couple of guys who didn't do well at Palacios that I wouldn't make it. Number two was to help my team win a championship. Number three was to be all-conference or possibly All-American. Number four was to bench press 450 pounds. And number five was to make an NFL team. We had boxes everywhere, and I wrote that down and put it on the wall. Mama was crying, and she said, "Boy, we did it...you're here." I told Mama, "See that, right there? I want you to see it because it's going to happen."

By my senior year, that paper had some cuts on it, and it was all wadded up, but I carried it with me. Guys used to come in and say, "What's this old thing?" I'd say, "Those are my goals." As a freshman, they'd say, "No way." And I'd say, "I'm going to do all those things before I get out of here." I kept believing in those goals. And when each happened, I put the time, the date, the year it happened...I put it right there.

For a while, Charles kept trying to get his room back. I told him my mother and I moved that stuff in that room, and I wasn't giving it up. He started teasing me about my mother helping me, and I finally said, "Charles, you don't know me, and we are going to be teammates, but you've got to understand, my mother and I did that, and I'm not moving my stuff." He bothered me for about three days, and I finally said, "Enough is enough. Let's go down in the alley and settle this like men." He looked at me like I had 10 heads. I said, "Either you're going to beat my tail up, or I'm going to shut you up. Then we're going to get ready to play Auburn. Because this is bothering me. It's removing my focus from my goal—to help us win a championship." He said, "Okay, okay, it's okay." After that, we became the best of friends. But it taught me that if you want something, you have to stand up for it. Doing that gained me respect from the other freshmen, as well as the upperclassmen.

Our first game that year was at Auburn, and they had a great team. I planned on redshirting, but Coach said, "I'm taking you on the trip, but you're probably not going to play." So I went on the trip. I didn't have a tie—I mean, we were from Palacios. I didn't have a sports jacket. I barely had a sports bag. I had a little plastic bag that I got from the co-op. They gave you bags for your books, and I used that for my toothbrush and toothpaste. I didn't think anything about it, but I could see guys looking at me like, *Where's your luggage?* After that game, I found four or five bags outside my door. At first it bothered me because I have tremendous pride, and I thought, *I don't need your damn bags. I got a bag.* But it was neat to gain respect and have teammates who love you.

Auburn was the first game, and I was supposed to be the "rah-rah" guy. I had my towel going, and Auburn was unbelievable. They had more than 80,000 fans in the stands. We had 700 at homecoming back in Palacios, and that's a big night. The third series of the game, Bobby Duncum went down, and I went in the game. I was nervous, very excited. Auburn had a big tight end. He was a monster with a cut-off jersey, and all I could think was, *Hit him before he hits me. Hit him before he hits me…* So I hit him and drove him back about four yards, but the ball carrier went inside of me. I thought I'd messed up, but Britt Hager, our linebacker, made the tackle and said, "Hey, Oscar, good job." My mother was watching the game, and she told me she could see who I was because my leg kept on twitching…*Hit him before he hits me…*

Two years later, Oklahoma had a defensive lineman whom we could not block. He had about three sacks, and every time he got one, he'd make a motion like he was digging with a shovel. We hadn't beaten OU in several years, and late in the game Johnny Walker made a hell of a catch for a touchdown. But they had time to drive down the field. We had to find a way to stop them. I thought, *I've got to do my best. I've got to do something.* Their quarterback, Charles Thompson, was a good athlete. I tried a move that I had really worked on, a spin move inside, and I got him. There were 10 seconds left on the clock. Everybody started running on the field, and nobody noticed, but out of respect for our quarterback, Peter Gardere, I did the shovel motion. That sack was the last defensive play. That might have been my best moment as a Longhorn—that last sack, that last play—because that game started a streak of wins for us over Oklahoma.

The Houston game was a special night for Texas football. Houston had played so well, and they had beaten us badly the years before. The night before the game, Coach Leon Fuller, our defensive coordinator, said quietly, "I can't share anything else with you." He didn't talk loud, he just made you listen. He had the chairs lined up like a defensive set, made some calls, and everybody followed. Then he said, "That's enough. I'm not going to give you a rah-rah speech. I am not going to talk about the fact that they embarrassed you last year or that they don't respect you, because you have heard those things. I want you to take some time to feel how it's going to feel to beat these guys. Close your eyes. I want you to experience it in your head right now. Now, get some rest tonight and get ready for a war tomorrow."

I was ready to play. That night, I could look everybody in the eye, and there was no doubt. I don't care who they had. They were averaging almost 500 yards a game, but I could tell you this much, they weren't going to get it that night. We won 45–24. It was a special year.

When Coach Brown hired me as an assistant coach in 2005, the first person waiting for me was Coach McWilliams. "Ready to go to work?" he said. "Still sleeping in?" He was there to greet me, just as he was when I came from Palacios.

When I first sat in my new chair and closed my office door, I had tears in my eyes. I don't cry often, but it was the passion and emotion I feel for The University of Texas. I have that old piece of paper, with its cuts and faded ink, framed and hanging on the wall at home.

As I sat there on the first day, I made a new list of goals. Number one was to help Texas win a national championship. Number two was to help kids graduate from The University. Number three, I want kids to be better sons, better fathers. That's my duty: to teach kids the pride and tradition of this program, not only while they are here but once they leave.

It's all about the passion. I love being at this place. What does it mean to be a Longhorn? Sitting in this chair, in this office, getting a chance to see that Tower light burnt orange every time we win…I get goose bumps talking about it because it means the world to me.

Oscar Giles was a four-year starter at defensive end, including the stellar season of 1990, when the Longhorns' "Shock the Nation" tour propelled them to a No. 3 final regular-season ranking. He played for the Atlanta Falcons in the NFL and then began a coaching career that led him back to Texas as defensive ends coach for the Longhorns in 2005.

CHRIS SAMUELS

WINGBACK

1987–1990

EVERYTHING I KNEW ABOUT TEXAS FOOTBALL changed in the spring of 1990. I remember coming to Texas with an attitude of rebuilding the excellent tradition of the past. Coach McWilliams came into my home in San Antonio, and I was comfortable even though his personality was so different from mine.

I was a former city kid from New York who had moved to Texas, and I really didn't embrace "Southern hospitality." And here comes this Southern gentleman. Yet I was so at home and comfortable with him that making the decision to come to Texas, based on that chemistry and wanting to rebuild, was easy. In the first several years, we had some high moments, but for the most part, we hadn't gotten it done.

Going into the spring of our senior year in 1990, the coaching staff and, to some degree, the team said, "What are we going to do different?" And then it became "boot camp." We started getting up for 5:30 practice in the mornings, and that spring changed our whole season. It was so mental. Here we were, pretty much the same players. Nothing changed but our attitude and our belief. We went through such a rough off-season that we were much better players just from that.

In the spring, our trainer, Spanky Stephens, and Dana LeDuc, our strength coach, were up with us early in the morning. We were working out, hitting bags and running. We had gone 4–7 in 1988 and 5–6 in 1989. I remember

Chris Samuels was a leader on the 1990 Longhorn team, which took as its slogan, "Whatever It Takes."

somebody saying, "Didn't we all come from great programs in high school? Aren't we all just as accomplished as any big name playing college football? The difference is, our mental desire, drive, or toughness hasn't been there. Let's turn it on." And it changed everything. Of course we came from great programs. We were very good athletes, but we were playing mediocre football. So we said, "Let's change that." We didn't necessarily have any speeches or have to talk to any individuals because they weren't buying into it. No, we all bought into it, hook, line, and sinker, and it turned our program around. It made us tougher, it made us more driven. I remember our coming up with an expression and attitude for our team: "WIT—Whatever It Takes." Those things were birthed out of that off-season.

We looked at Spanky and said, "We always knew you were a tough trainer in terms of taking care of us when we were injured." He never babied us when we were injured, and he worked hard to get us back on the field, but we didn't know he was such a tough coach. That was one of the first things we noticed. Now, he was a strength and conditioning coach. My gosh, it was like, "Spanky, take it easy, can we rest this set?" Nah. There was no resting with him. He kept pushing and pushing. Spanky had never been a pushover by any means, he was just not involved in coaching outside his training room. Now, when you said, "Come on, man, give us a break," there was no break. He was like a Jekyll and Hyde.

263

We would go into the freshman locker room—there were 500-pound bags hanging from the ceiling—and we had to brush those like we were coming off the line. At first, it didn't move much. It wasn't like a punching bag, where you thought you were "the man" because it swung. These things barely moved. You'd shoot off the ground and explode into that bag and do so many reps. Then we punched it. It was humbling, but it showed us how far we really needed to go. Once everyone realized that, everyone stepped it up and got there. I remember Spanky mentioning the old trainer, Frank Medina, who had been such a part of Texas teams in the past. He said this was what had gotten us great in the past.

Everyone stepped up what they were doing—the coaches, the players, the staff. We all took a look at what our contribution had been and what extra we were going to do to make it better.

It was amazing to have played for Coach McWilliams because of his character, the type of individual that he was. He had made it a very easy decision for me to come to Texas. I enjoyed it from start to finish, but much more toward the finish. All of that hard work that off-season paid off, because we had the taste of success my senior year in 1990. The difference was incredible, not only with the electricity of the fans but the support of the community. It was nice to have gotten a taste of that, to start off humble, build our way to a good ranking, play some good football, and bring some pride back to Texas.

The game everyone will remember from that season of 1990 is the Houston game. Colorado had been good, in fact they went on and tied for the national championship. But it wasn't a cross-state rivalry like Houston was, not to mention that we had been embarrassed as a program by the Cougars in prior years. After the off-season work, the way we had played against Colorado helped us. They barely left our house with a win, and we said, "No one needs to tell us, but we're for real, and we know this." By the time we played the University of Houston, we were a good football team. They had David Klingler at quarterback, and everything was going great for them. We had an attitude of, *They are going to come into our house in a night game before a full stadium and a national television audience.* You couldn't have gotten us more motivated to get back some of what had been robbed from us, just taken in the years past against them.

The night games were cool. Young kids seem to like the night games. You're not getting up early, and most college students want to sleep all day, anyway. All in all, it was a great feeling. That was the loudest I'd ever heard our fans. We played well. Butch Hadnot, our running back, ran tough. It was smash-mouth football. Our defense? Wow! They stopped the "run and shoot." That game epitomized the hard work that we had put in, and it expressed where we were as a team in terms of energy. It was everybody coming together, being unselfish, and getting a win for not only ourselves but the program. That game was our finest moment. We went on to win the Southwest Conference and reached a No. 3 national ranking during the regular season.

Before our Cotton Bowl game with Miami, the Cash twins, Keith and Kerry, and I joked, "Man, if you ever get knocked out, don't jump up and just fall out and make a scene and let a team recognize that they've got you. Stay down, take some time." On the opening kickoff of the Miami game, I got hit, and I knew I was hurt, so I followed their advice. That's when I learned that kids will do anything for their teammates and their coaches. I mean anything. I sat out several series, but nothing was broken, and I wanted to play. I don't know if they'd let a kid play today. I did end up with a concussion and slept about 30 hours straight after the game. I got firsthand knowledge of the fact that, with these kids, these players, there is no limit to what they'll give or risk for the sake of winning for their team and their coach, of helping to create that history. It is an amazing bond. I haven't been to war, but I think football is the closest you will ever get to combat in that sense. We know that soldiers have a lifelong bond. When I came off the field, I remember the looks that were in my teammates' eyes. It wasn't like, *Aw, man, you really got popped*. It was like, *I hope you are all right*. I have never forgotten those looks, those stares of *Come on, you can do this, get up*.

I guess that's what it means to be a Longhorn. It is family. I love the fact that when I step on the surface of the field, I feel like I own a piece of it. I belong here; I'm at home. I bring my kids up there. It keeps me young. When I am up there in Austin, teammates see each other, and we goof around. We're not quite as young as we were when we were 19 or 20, but for a moment, we go back and hug each other and talk about things only we have experienced.

Chris Samuels was one of the leaders of the 1990 Longhorn team that finished ranked third in the nation at the end of the regular season. A four-year letterman, he doubled as a receiver and a running back on the SWC championship team of 1990.

The
NINETIES

PETER GARDERE

QUARTERBACK
1989–1992

I'M A THIRD-GENERATION LONGHORN. My grandfather played in the 1920s, my father played in the 1950s, and I came along in the late 1980s. But there was never any parental pressure to go to Texas. I grew up watching Texas, but my sisters were going to SMU, so I mainly watched SMU. My father broke his neck on the first play of his first game his sophomore year at Texas. He wasn't able to play, and he kind of lived the football experience through me. He wanted me to play, but he never pressured me to play any sport for that matter. It just came naturally.

When it came time to choose where to go to school, David McWilliams offered a scholarship my junior year at Robert E. Lee High School in Houston. Fortunately for me, we had started running the "run and shoot," which was the "West Coast" offense of the '80s. We threw the ball a lot, and I got a lot of records and a lot of attention. Thanks to David for giving me a scholarship early because, being 6′0″ and weighing 175, I probably wasn't the prototypical quarterback that you'd take these days. But he understood that I knew the traditions and knew what it would take to be a Longhorn. At first, I wasn't sure where I wanted to go, but my thought process was, *If injuries happened, such as my father's, where would I want to go to school?*

And it was, of course, The University of Texas. I had a lot of friends there, and not only could I get a great education, but if you choose to live and work in the state of Texas, there is only one logical choice, and that's The University of Texas. In athletics, there are a lot of things that can happen, and injuries are one of them, so you need to go where you'll be happy and get an education. You're a student first, and then an athlete, and that's why we're called "student-athletes."

My freshman year, I wound up playing against Rice, which is in my hometown, and I scored a late touchdown where I knocked over the pylon at the goal line. I had a really good game against Arkansas, but for me, the Oklahoma series has to be my biggest.

The Oklahoma series is, bar none, one of the best rivalry games in college football—in college sports, for that matter. Playing in it from my freshman year to my senior year, and actually winning every game, was incredible. It's the one thing I hear over and over again—"You're the only quarterback to beat OU four years in a row." Of course, I had nothing to do with it—just handing the ball off and throwing it. The defense and special teams won at least three of those games. But one memory I have is that senior season and beating OU handily for the first time in my four years. We played really well offensively, and it was just an overall great game.

After the game, I remember being on the sideline and hearing the OU fans chanting, "Graduate, Graduate, Graduate…" At first I didn't know what they were saying, but when I listened, I could make it out. It was pretty neat. I think they had had enough of getting beat by the Longhorns, and they'd probably had enough of me.

As far as memories, being known as "the Sooner Slayer" is the one I have to pick. But it is hard to pick one because there are so many people—players and coaches—who are still my friends today. You remember the rivalry games—the Texas A&M game in 1990, where the seniors had not beaten the Aggies. I felt like we won the game for them. That was one of the greatest moments, and, like I said, I had nothing to do with it. It was mostly the defense, but it was a fond memory.

The Arkansas game my freshman year was in Fayetteville, and that was a really neat place to play. They were ranked in the top 10. It was a packed house and one of those old Southwest Conference rivalries. That was one of my best games. I was 16-for-20, and we won 24–20. It was after that game that the media started calling me "Peter the Great." And on bad days, it became "Peter the Late." It changed a couple of times.

"Peter the Great" became the only player in the Texas-Oklahoma series to win four straight games as a starting quarterback.

There were a lot of changes in those four years. We had a lot of success my sophomore season. We won the Southwest Conference and went to the Cotton Bowl. Lynn Amadee was our offensive coordinator. He had his own personality and his own ego, which was pretty big, but I enjoyed Lynn. I had learned one offense coming in, and since I was having to learn another, he spent a lot of time with the quarterbacks because it was his first year. I learned a lot from him, going over every position and teaching the coaches and players his offense.

The next year, in 1991, I could sense that he was kind of coasting. We had had a great year in 1990, and we had lost a lot of talent with those seniors who left. We had eight or nine guys in the NFL draft, and it was tough for him. After that season—at Texas there is a lot of pressure to win—we had a losing season. Coach McWilliams had been told that certain people had to go, and I think David saw the writing on the wall and stepped aside.

I was actually on one of the committees to hire John Mackovic, and I think their choice was pretty well wrapped up before we got involved. John was a very smart coach. He lacked the personal skills, as far as being a player's coach. David was a person whom you really wanted to play for and someone who was very genuine. He knew a lot about the tradition of Texas. He'd played for Darrell Royal and knew everything that went on with Texas. Then we brought John in, and he had been in Dallas, but he really wasn't versed in the tradition that Texas had. He came in with an ego, himself. He was a very smart offensive coach. I learned a great deal from him, also. It was an interesting transition for me because it was my senior year, and this would be my third offense in four years. It was difficult, and it was a lot to learn. He put a lot of pressure on the quarterbacks. He told me that he selected his starters by how they performed in practice. So there was a lot of pressure as a senior, having been a three-year starter. He was very smart, but he didn't wrap his hands and arms around the traditions of Texas, everything that is Texas. When you're the Texas coach, you have to be multifaceted. You've got to be in position to go out and talk to high school coaches and deal with everything that is Texas. He didn't really want to do that. He had certain things set. He was a great football mind, but he wasn't a great fit for The University of Texas.

I have thought a lot about what it means to be a Longhorn. I thought about what Texas embodies, and that's tradition. The definition of *tradition* is: "the handing down of statements, beliefs, legends, customs, and information." I wasn't the prototypical quarterback, as I said, coming into Texas; I was smaller. I came in with Jason Burleson, who was 6'7". I was recruited probably more as a punter than as a quarterback, but I knew the traditions. You come in, as the definition says, and you look at the statements: UT's winning three national championships, multiple bowl appearances, and many conference championships. Beliefs: knowing you can win, providing the best facilities, coaches, and talent that you will find in the country. Legends: Darrell Royal, Earl Campbell, Tommy Nobis, and the list goes on and on. Customs: sold-out stadiums, Bevo, the cannon, "The Eyes of Texas," Hook 'em Horns, the band, wearing the orange and white, and the Longhorn on your helmet. Information: the best education, coaching, atmosphere, and experiences you can find anywhere in the country. All those words define *tradition*, and that's what it means to be a Longhorn. For me, the traditions went a little deeper than just a football field. I grew up in Texas, my parents met at The University of Texas, and my grandparents met at The University of Texas. So it goes a lot deeper for me. You are only given one last name, and you have only one chance to be a Longhorn, so you've got to represent those two the best you can because that's what defines you. I'm a Longhorn, and I'll be a Longhorn for life.

Peter Gardere became famous as the only quarterback from either side in the long history of the Texas-Oklahoma series to start and win all four games of his career. He was the team's Most Valuable Player selection in John Mackovic's first season of 1992, as well as a co-captain that season.

STONIE CLARK
DEFENSIVE LINEMAN
1992–1995

GLADEWATER IS A SMALL EAST TEXAS TOWN, and it was a happening place in the 1950s and 1960s, with the likes of Elvis Presley, Tina Turner, and James Brown coming to town to perform. I grew up hearing stories of packed nightclubs and bootlegging. But by the time I came along, Gladewater was just a good town with good schools, good people, and was a good place to raise a family.

My dad's sister, Virginia, lived in Austin with her husband and their daughter. Each Thanksgiving, my entire extended family would make the pilgrimage to visit them. As I got older and more interested in sports, my mom and dad, uncle, myself, and a few of my cousins would come to town for the UIL state track meet. We had a blast sitting in the stands at Memorial Stadium, watching the meet and battling the heat. I would tell my dad that one day I'd play on that field. He'd offer encouragement and advice as to how I could accomplish the goals I had set for myself. It was a time during the year for my family to get away for a weekend, but more importantly for me, it was an opportunity to dream and to see a world of possibilities that didn't exist where I lived and grew up.

I was MVP of some pretty good soccer teams growing up. There was Pop Warner in my hometown, but my dad discouraged me from playing. He told me later in life that he wanted me to work on my footwork by playing soccer.

He knew I'd be a football player in due time. I never watched much football on television, and when I started playing for the school in seventh grade, I really didn't know what I was doing. By the ninth grade, I had figured the game out and weighed in for freshman football at 6′1″ and 286 pounds. I was a terror on the field, playing guard on offense and nose guard on defense. No one was the same size as I was, and the years of soccer paid off in an ability to run and move well laterally. As a sophomore, I started 15 games at nose guard for the most successful team in Gladewater school history. The letters from universities started coming the following spring.

I was recruited by most of the schools in the country. I took enough recruiting visits to realize I wanted to be closer to home. One of the things I loved about football was the joy and fun my family had watching me play. A&M was the team to beat in the Southwest Conference at the time, and UT was in the middle of a coaching change. Baton Rouge is about the same distance from Gladewater as Austin, so I gave LSU a lot of consideration. My familiarity with Austin and having my aunt in town were big in my decision to become a Longhorn. The now-famous Austin nightlife definitely didn't hurt, either.

When I got to Psychology 101, and there were more people in the auditorium than in my entire high school, I knew college was for me. School and football helped broaden my horizons and satisfy my desire to be a part of something bigger and more important than myself. The guys I came to campus with quickly helped me learn what I consider to be the best part of sports, camaraderie. I also learned to be humble. There were some great athletes who came to campus that year. Mike Adams, Dan Neil, Priest Holmes, Shea Morenz, Lovell Pinkney, and Taje Allen, just to name a few. I had heard so much in high school about "the playing field evening out," and it had finally happened.

We were not bowl-eligible at the end of my freshman or sophomore years, and I had knee surgery after each of those seasons. I was beginning to worry about if I would be a part of a dark period in Longhorn football history and if I had chosen the right football program. Each of those years, we started out with ambitions for the Cotton Bowl but had failed to make it. There was a bit of a storm or revolution happening with our football team at the beginning of the 1994 season. Our leadership was not strong, so leaders and captains of the football team took over motivating the team. We bonded

Stonie Clark was a creative writer as well as an outstanding football player.

together and started the season successfully with a 3–1 record heading into the Red River Rivalry game against a ranked Oklahoma team.

As a senior in high school and a freshman getting no playing time, I would lie in bed at night and dream of making a big play in the Oklahoma game. From the moment I signed with Texas, I knew the implications of winning and losing the Texas-OU game. Shea Morenz was injured, and a freshman from Beaumont named James Brown was getting his first start. James knows I love him to death, but he had not shown in practice what he showed the entire country that day in the Cotton Bowl. He was not just a sub that day.

He made plays that put us in the position to win the game. The defense stepped up, making play after play. Tony Brackens and Chris Carter were all over the field, and with two interceptions by Bryant Westbrook, we had held Oklahoma's offense to 10 points with only a couple of minutes remaining in the game. The score was 17–10. Oklahoma had driven the length of the field, and it was fourth down and goal with the ball on the 1-yard line. We weren't talking a lot in the huddle, because everyone was hot and tired.

I had talked to my dad earlier in the week, and he told me to look out for some kind of reverse. When the center snapped the ball, I was able to look between the hips of the center and guard and see the reverse handoff to OU's running back. Robert Reed turned the guy inside, and, as he dove for the end zone, I hit him and stopped him on the 1-yard line. In some of the pictures of that play you can see my feet were in the end zone when contact was made. Football is truly a game of inches.

The accomplishment that I am most proud of to this point in my life is being named team captain my senior year. The players vote on the captain, and I think that says a lot about a fellow to be named captain by his peers. I lived, worked out, ate dinner, battled in football games, and spent all of my time with my teammates. For them to name me as their leader is something that is so special to me.

276

I'm sure most people think that the stop against OU was the highlight of my playing days at UT. It's what I'm recognized for, but it's not the highlight. I was on the sideline for the highlight. We were playing Texas A&M for the final Southwest Conference championship. James Brown, who was by now a good friend of mine, was playing on a badly damaged ankle. The score was 16–6, and we needed a first down to secure the win. On third down, James dropped back and threw a bullet to Mike Adams. Mike stretched out between double coverage and made the catch. There we were, the same kids who came to campus with such big dreams and lofty goals for ourselves, realizing them.

As the captain of the 1995 team, I saw a lot of guys grow up and accept responsibility for their roles on the team and take on other roles to help us win. At times, it seemed we even had to battle our head coach, but we ended that year 10–1–1 and headed to the Nokia Sugar Bowl—an Alliance bowl, which was the beginning of the BCS bowl series we have now. During recruiting in high school, I told my mom and dad that I didn't want to go to a school that had just won the national championship. I wanted to be part of building something. Building a championship.

To be a Longhorn means being a part of the past, the present, and the future of UT and Texas football. It means the Drag and some smelly, dirty man trying to lead you to God by telling you the world is coming to an end…today. It means the Tower shining burnt orange and the fountains around campus gushing water in the spring. It means tucking my two middle fingers, covering them with my thumb and holding it as high in the air as my arm will stretch, and meaning it!

In the event of my untimely demise, open my casket and play "The Eyes of Texas." If tears don't well up in my eyes and the hair on the back of my neck doesn't stand up, you can rest assured I'm gone, off to the forty acres in the sky.

Stonie Clark was one of the stalwarts of the defensive line for the Longhorns in the mid-1990s. A team co-captain in 1995, he earned fame for a goal-line stop to preserve the Texas victory over Oklahoma in 1994.

TONY BRACKENS

DEFENSIVE END

1993–1995

COMING OUT OF FAIRFIELD, TEXAS, I wasn't a big football fan. I wasn't a guru as far as knowing the schools and what they were doing or the history behind them, because that's not what I was brought up around. From the time I can remember, it was lawn mowers and weed-eaters and pulling grass. Mine was a rancher's life.

If it was raining or if we were away from the ranch and a football game was on, we watched it. It didn't matter who it was, it was just something to watch on TV. I got wind of The University of Texas because of Winfred Tubbs, who had gone there from my high school. People would talk about, "Man, Tubbs is playing…*yada yada yada.*" The only reason I looked at a few UT games was because of Tubbs, and because the coaches in high school were trying to make a comparison. "You could get a scholarship," they'd say.

When the time came, I looked at pretty much all of the Southwest Conference schools. Rex Norris, who was the defensive line coach, recruited me for Texas, and I fell in love with him right off because of his willingness to talk and the way he communicated with others outside of the box. We clicked from a personality standpoint.

Texas was going to be far enough away from home for me that I would be missed, but not too far that I couldn't get back home. I had to be able to participate in the off-season stuff as far as the hay cutting and baling, roundups for the cows, and all the other stuff that went along with that.

Defensive end
Tony Brackens was
one of the best
pass rushers in
Texas history.

Being a rancher helped me learn self-discipline as a football player. Rancher hours are daylight to dark, pretty much. If it's not raining, there's always something to do. You don't take breaks. You make sure you get up and eat breakfast, and make sure you get lunch, and make sure you get dinner on time. Ranching hours are when the weather permits, and if something needs to be done, you get it done.

We learned at an early age that you just go out and work until the work's done. Some days we didn't eat. If something got torn up or there was a storm and we came in at 10:00 in the morning, well, we'd better get something to eat now, because we're not coming back in for lunch. Or if it was 2:00 and you had to get diesel, get a can of pork and beans and a spoon out of the store and go back to work until dark. That's what my dad instilled in us and how he worked us at an early age. It was a business from that point on. Whatever you've got to do, do it until you are finished.

John Mackovic was our head football coach, and a lot of people say this and that about him and his personality. I was brought up to where it didn't matter who it is or how they are, if I'm there to do a job, I'm going to do my job, no matter if I like you or if I don't. If I made a commitment to do a job, I'm going to do that job to the best of my ability, regardless of clashes and conflicts of personalities. That was instilled in me.

As far as I was concerned, he had a job, and he was doing it the best that he could. Who am I to say that he's doing a bad job or a good job? The way I looked at it, it's my job to make his job easier, and the way that I can do that is to do the best I can and try to help us win football games. Regardless of what he says or how he chooses to go about his business, I still have a job to do, and I can't concern myself with his personality and his conflicts with other individuals and the way that he chooses to do things.

Obviously, he thought enough of me to offer me a scholarship, and I was appreciative for that. The biggest deal for me was to go down there and do all I could instead of making excuses for the reasons why I should or shouldn't do something.

There were a couple of plays when I was at Texas that drew a lot of conversation. One was against Texas Tech. They ran a fake kick, and I hit their kicker at the sideline. I never go out to hurt anyone, but if our paths cross at a high rate of speed, that's just the nature of the beast. The Tech kicker was trying to get to a first-down marker that I didn't want him to get to. I was able to see it, and I was able to get there at the same time he did, and it was a play people remember. It was a situation where I was looking at getting off the field. If he made the first down, it meant that I had to stay out there four more downs, and I didn't really want to be out there anymore. I kind of value my free time on the sideline watching the offense. I like my rest, so anything I can do to get rest is a key factor for me.

The other play that's talked about a lot was when I ran into Coach Mackovic on the sideline at the Colorado game. People think I took a bead on him, but I didn't. I had to come a long way to get there, and I hate running to the sideline and falling down. We were chasing Kordell Stewart, and I remember him running down the sideline and weaving. I had been running for about 50 or 60 yards, and I was tired. I ran through a whole bunch of people, and I wanted to hit Kordell so bad. We had already given Rashaan Salaam the Heisman Trophy that day, so it was just a frustration deal. But Kordell went out of bounds, and I just kept going. I saw everybody was moving. I didn't pick Coach Mackovic out; I figured everybody that was watching would move, only he didn't move. I actually ran into him. He blamed everybody around him, but there was no one else around him.

I played eight years in the NFL. I reached a place where I knew I could do other things with my life. By the time I went to The University of Texas, our ranch was pretty well established. I knew how to work the land, and there was always money to be made, and I didn't have to work for anybody on a 9-to-5 basis. I could go out and do something every day, and it's not the same old routine every day. So it was a situation where I didn't really need anything. It was hard for them to hold stuff over my head because "We just won't pay you." That's fine, don't pay me. I can go home and make money. The reason I retired was that it got to a point where I couldn't justify the business side of it. I'd had nine knee surgeries, and I could make more money if I just came back home to the spot I was paying for, anyway.

When you're out here on the ranch, you never know the significance of the place that you played. When you go to the NFL, and you are around all these guys from different conferences and your school is constantly at the top, you don't have to say much. They'll come to you and say, "Aw, man, you went to UT, right?"

Being a Longhorn is tradition, it's excellence, it's all the words that you can possibly fathom to describe greatness. When I was named to the Longhorn

Hall of Honor, I didn't understand it. I couldn't fathom that I could ever be a candidate for such an honor. How did they find me out of this whole group of athletes who had come through this University? I was elated, and yet so humble to know I was even mentioned. You know, people used to talk about how ugly burnt orange was. But you find people wearing it more and more. So I guess it's not that ugly…once you start winning.

Tony Brackens was a three-time All–Southwest Conference selection and the winner of numerous team awards at Texas. He was an All-American in 1995 and helped lead Texas to the final Southwest Conference championship. He played eight years with the Jacksonville Jaguars in the NFL. He was named to the Longhorn Hall of Honor in 2006.

JAMES BROWN

QUARTERBACK

1994–1997

BEFORE I EVEN KNEW ABOUT OTHER COLLEGES, my dad suggested that I go to The University of Texas. I visited Syracuse just to take a trip out of Texas, and Gene Stallings came down to talk to me when he was at Alabama. But I guess I always knew I was going to UT after I got finished playing in high school.

When I got to The University, I didn't know what a "redshirt" was. I thought I was going to The University and at least have a chance to start. But they had Shea Morenz, and he was a pretty good quarterback, so I redshirted my freshman year. It turned out to be a good thing. I learned a lot about school and everything my first year. With Shea there, I thought it was going to be pretty much the same in my second year. I was just waiting for something to happen because Shea was the "golden boy," and he had a lot of publicity behind him.

All of that changed when he got hurt at home in the game against Colorado. I came in for one play. That was my first taste of college football. I was kind of scared, kind of nervous, kind of excited. It was just a little handoff play, and I got that out of the way.

The knee injury for Shea carried over into the next week, and that was the week of the Oklahoma game in Dallas. Everybody talks about the excitement around that game. The year before, when I was redshirting, I don't think I even got to travel to that game. But I knew it was a big game.

James Brown surprisingly predicted victory over Nebraska in the first Big 12 championship game, and he backed it up.

Shea dressed as normal, and he was on the bicycle trying to get his knee warm before the game. John Dutton and I took the pregame snaps while Shea worked with Spanky Stephens, our trainer, trying to get his knee together. There wasn't even a backup quarterback at the time, it was just Shea and the two of us. After warm-ups, we had our team meeting, and right after that, Coach John Mackovic announced that I was going to start. He didn't tell me anything, like on the side, before then. I was as surprised as anybody else. So I just said, "All right, let's go."

I played a good game, and we won 17–10. Shea and I split time from there during that year. We went to Rice and lost, and after the Rice game, I started playing more. We went on to tie for the Southwest Conference title and beat North Carolina in the Sun Bowl. After that season, Shea left to go play baseball with the Yankees.

My sophomore year, 1995, we won the last Southwest Conference championship, and I felt like I played well. I was beginning to develop a relationship with the coaches and with Donnie Little, who was working for the Longhorn Foundation. Donnie had been the first African American quarterback at Texas, and he helped me a lot along the way. The support system at Texas was the reason my father wanted me to go there. I wasn't in tune with that at the time, but I came to see what it meant.

The next season was the first year of the Big 12. We had won the South Division, but everybody was talking about the North Division champion, Nebraska. They were expected to beat us easily and possibly play for the national championship. The first-ever Big 12 championship game was to be played in the TWA Dome in St. Louis. We were 21-point underdogs.

Each week before a game, we met on Mondays with the media on the ninth floor of Bellmont Hall. The media interest was pretty high, and as the season went on, we would talk to the media all the time. The media day before the Nebraska game was really big. By the end of the day, I had been asked the same question so many times. "How does it feel going into the game where you are a 21-point underdog? How does it feel, especially knowing that you are going to lose? Are you going to put up a good fight?"

Those were the questions, over and over. Finally I said, "We have a great team, and we might beat them by 21 points." By the time I walked out, everybody on campus had heard what I said.

We went straight from there to the field for a light practice. Mackovic kind of appeared out of nowhere behind me and put his hand on my shoulder.

"James," he said deliberately, "I hope you can back up what you said."

I answered, "I think I can."

By the end of practice, Dan Neil and Chris Carter and a couple more guys came up and said, "I heard what you said, and you know what, I'm glad…because that's exactly how I feel." The team took it as a challenge. We were a confident team, and that's how we felt, and we went in, and we played that way. If the comment helped, I'm glad. It was a big booster, and if it cat-apulted us to have that great of a game, then that's a good thing, because it was a historical game.

We played very well in that game, and the only play it seems like people remember was the "fourth-and-inches" play. We were leading 30–27, but we were in our own territory, maybe about the 35-yard line. So, if we didn't make it, they only had 30 or so yards to go for a touchdown.

It was a situation in which anybody else would punt the ball. We had a TV timeout, and I guess that gave Coach Mackovic time to think. Sometime dur-ing our meetings throughout the week, he had said that if it came down to it, he would run that play. Mackovic did have that quality. He would do things in advance, and a lot of times they would come true in a game. He was always prepared, with his play sheet, more than any coach I ever played for.

We wasted a lot of the timeout. There wasn't any coaching going on. We huddled up on the sideline, and he came back and said, "Okay, we're going to run this play right here." It was part of a "rock-and-roll" goal-line pack-age. We had three running backs in the backfield. Priest Holmes was the deepest, and we had Derek Lewis, Pat Fitzgerald, and Ricky Williams. If you're the defense and you've got Priest and Ricky coming downhill into the line of scrimmage, you've got to respect that. So I just faked to them and rolled out left.

Pat Fitzgerald snuck off short, and our tight end, who was on the line on the left side, Derek Lewis, went deep to a corner route. I had my back to the defense, so I didn't know what to expect after the fake. Mackovic had said, "Come to run," so I came out, thinking, *I might have to run for this first down.* It was only a yard. Once I got into the open, I was naked. I just had time to glance up the field, and I saw Derek wide open. I gave him a nice little pass that he could catch. We had run that play so many times during my career on the goal line. It was a simple play, a play everybody had confidence in. Of course, Derek ran the ball down to the 10-yard line, and Priest scored on the next play. We won 37–27. It knocked Nebraska out of the national cham-pionship race and gave us the first Big 12 championship and a bid to the Fiesta Bowl.

The next season, we started with high hopes, but things fell apart in the UCLA game. I had sprained my ankle the week before and didn't play. They killed us 66–3. It set the tone for a disappointing year. Looking back, I wish

I had learned to be more in tune with the coach. I wish I had talked to him more and let him know what we needed as a team. We were just a young team that had some injuries to the few veterans we had. That really hurt us. People loaded up to stop Ricky, and we didn't have any experienced receivers to help. That team ended up being good in the next couple of years.

When I came to Texas, I didn't have any idea what "The Eyes of Texas" meant or how much the media followed The University. I also didn't realize the impact it would have on my life. If you ask me what it means to be a Longhorn, I'd have to say it means everything to me after the age of 18, once I got to The University. It seems like my life has been intertwined with the alumni. When I was playing in the NFL Europe in Scotland, we had a huge following of Texas fans. In fact, we have that all over Europe. In Germany, there were people with UT jerseys on. Everywhere I have been, it seems everybody either loves The University of Texas or they're intrigued by it and wish they could have been there.

The University has done a lot for me. It gave me confidence in the business world, and it has been a big part of my life. I have learned what "The Eyes of Texas" are. When I was playing, I didn't, and now I see the full scope of everything.

287

People ask me if I realize the role I may have played in the acceptance of the black quarterback at Texas. I try to stay humble and don't think about that. But I do believe that what we did against Nebraska helped the recruiting at The University, and it got athletes who were watching us to believe that they, too, could do it. I understand what that has meant, and for that, I'm proud of what we did.

James Brown led Texas to two major bowl berths. In 1995 he piloted the Longhorns to the final Southwest Conference championship with an unbeaten league record, earning an appearance in the Sugar Bowl in the Bowl Alliance. The next season, he was the principle architect of Texas's stunning Big 12 championship victory over Nebraska, which put the Longhorns in the Bowl Alliance again, this time in the Fiesta Bowl.

PHIL DAWSON

KICKER

1994–1997

As Texans, we are a proud bunch. We are a state that takes pride in our history, our music, our food, our way of life, and our football. Every time we see the Lone Star on our flag, we experience a sense of pride. We are not the "South," we are not the "Southwest," we are Texas.

My dad was a quarterback at Baylor. My mom and dad went there; my aunts, uncles, cousins—everyone went to Baylor. So I didn't grow up with the baby pictures in the Longhorns cap, and I didn't grow up with an appreciation of The University. I was on the other side of the fence. My family would get steamed up when Texas came to town and just beat Baylor up: "Here come those arrogant orange-bloods again. They're good and they know they're good." So I had a healthy respect for the school, the athletics programs and what they meant, and how intimidating they were to people in Texas who didn't go there. When I got to high school, it looked as if I might have a chance to play football at UT. I knew if God gave me the opportunity to play college football, The University of Texas would be my choice because I wanted to be part of the best.

Texas had been down for a few years, but I felt confident that they were headed in the right direction. I turned down opportunities to play at Florida State and Nebraska, and my freshman year at Texas, those two teams played in the national championship game. Both kickers had a chance to win the Orange Bowl. But I never doubted that I made the right decision. I wanted

Phil Dawson, a Longhorn team captain, went on to kick in the NFL for the Cleveland Browns.

to be a Texas Longhorn. I turned down those schools that were national pow-
erhouses to go to a rebuilding Texas program. I was still thrilled and honored
that I had the opportunity to come there. And I knew that if I came to The
University, not only would I be part of a rebuilding program, I wouldn't even
play my first year; I'd be redshirted. Scott Szeredy was going to be a senior,
and he was an All–Southwest Conference kicker his junior year. But my
respect and my admiration for The University was so great that I was willing to turn down opportunities to play immediately for national championships in order to go to a school that I wanted to be a part of. I've never
regretted it.

When I got to school, I saw guys who were so thrilled to have the opportunity to just play at Texas that they developed this mentality of, *Boy, I've
arrived, and I must be something special.* Their careers really never took off as
they should have. God had given them unbelievable talent, but they never
quite panned out. They felt that they were special because they were Longhorns. My approach when I got there was that the work was just beginning.
I was humbled by the opportunity to run out in that stadium and hear everybody singing "The Eyes of Texas," to wear that helmet, and to be part of that
history. I felt that I owed The University my best effort for giving me that
opportunity. When I got there, I didn't feel as though I'd arrived. I thought,
Oh, my goodness, I've got to get to work. I've got to earn my keep around here. Fortunately, my recruiting class seemed to have that attitude. We were a part of
turning around that program, which eventually culminated in winning the
national championship two years ago.

I would love to have played in that game. In some small way, I felt I played
a part in it, because Texas hadn't been in bowl games for several years when
I got there, hadn't won a conference championship in, I think, six years. My
recruiting class came in there—Bryant Westbrook, Tony Brackens, James
Brown, Chris Carter, guys like that—and before you knew it, we were in
the Sun Bowl the first year and everybody was thrilled. Then we won the
last SWC championship, went to the Sugar Bowl as the BCS was starting up,
and the next year, we won the first Big 12 and went to the Fiesta Bowl. That
totally changed the mindset of that program to, *Hey, this is a program that's
moving forward.* I take a great deal of pride in that.

My fondest memory may shock those familiar with Texas football history.
Many presume that the "Virginia kick" was my greatest moment [Dawson
kicked a 50-yard field goal on the final play to beat Virginia in 1995], and

indeed it is an experience I will forever hold dear to my heart. All the guys put us in a position to win that game, which started our six-game winning streak.

But at that time, the Texas Aggies had been on top for a while. They had beaten us four years in a row, and we hadn't won in College Station for 12 years. Going into that game, they had a 31-game-winning streak at Kyle Field. Remember that, if you grow up in Texas, you either go to The University or you go to the other school. There is no deciding between the two. The winner of this season-ending game would claim the final Southwest Conference championship and a berth in the inaugural Bowl Championship Series. We went over to College Station, beat the Aggies 16–6, and ended their home-game winning streak. I grew up hating the Aggies, and I got the opportunity to win the game I had dreamed about winning all of my life. We won the game as a team, and we experienced the Texas pride once again.

One of the things that to this day means the most to me was being elected team captain, because there's that whole "kicker" syndrome when you start out and you're off to the side, and everyone just wants you to go do your thing. Then you earn your stripes, you work hard, you perform, become friends with these guys, and before you know it, they're voting you team captain. Playing the position that I did, and then to be named the team captain really did mean a lot to me.

That's what's special about our university; it is a family. Good grief, just think about the people who've walked those hallways. You go in the "T" Room and see the portraits up there. I remember walking out on that Astro-Turf and thinking, *Think about the guys who have played on this field*. We'd have the barbecue the week of the A&M game and bring in all the old guys. You're watching these guys who can barely walk in there, and they look like if they yell, they might pass out. But they get to talking about the Aggies, and suddenly, they're 30 years younger. They're telling old stories, they're yelling, they're getting fired up, tears rolling down their cheeks, and you're just like...*Man, I'm a part of this. It's unbelievable.*

Playing there is so much more than being a Longhorn. We represent the whole state, and I believe everyone else in the state just wants to be like us. I guess that's why we get accused of being arrogant, and in some ways we are. But I really do feel like we represent the whole state. I have a better appreciation of that now that I'm living in Ohio. When people ask me where I went to school, I say, "Texas." They don't think of A&M, they don't think of Texas

Tech, they don't think of Baylor or SMU or TCU or Houston or Rice or any of those other schools. They know exactly what I'm talking about. I fell in love with the state of Texas when I was in school at UT. Even though I grew up in Dallas, I developed an appreciation of the people, the culture, and everything else. It was overwhelming.

You look up in the crowd and there will be just as many Texas state flags as there are UT flags. At our stadium, we fly the Six Flags over Texas. It's so in-your-face that this is our state and we are the official school of this state. Why wouldn't I want to attend the school that bears the name of the state I was so proud of? At The University, it was not simply school pride, it was Texas pride.

There are some built-in bookcases in my office, and I have some game balls and such sitting around. But there is only one helmet up on my mantel. I've played eight years as a Cleveland Brown—twice as long as I played at UT—but I'll let you take one guess which helmet is displayed on my mantel. That shows you where my heart is.

Phil Dawson's last-second, 50-yard field goal that defeated Virginia marked the first time the Longhorns had won at home on the final play of the game. He was a four-year letterman, was chosen to both the All–Southwest Conference and All–Big 12 teams, and was an All-American in 1997. He holds school records for both consecutive field goals and career field goals and has played eight years for the Cleveland Browns in the NFL.

DEREK LEWIS

TIGHT END

1995–1998

IT IS A GREAT HONOR TO BE A LONGHORN, but I didn't know it at the time I was being recruited.

When I really think about my destination and my journey to The University, I know it started much, much earlier. When I was 10 years old, Earl Campbell signed a football for me when he was playing for the New Orleans Saints. My godmother married Tony Elliott, a great defensive tackle for the Saints. I remember the wedding reception and the party afterward, and Earl was there. He signed a ball for me right on the spot. "Earl Campbell, Love and Peace." I had no idea who Earl was at the time. But I kept that ball—still have it—and I got to thinking, *Maybe this was meant to be.* It was like I was destined to be a Longhorn. When I went to The University of Texas, I bypassed LSU—I'm from New Orleans—and a host of other schools. LSU has a great tradition, but the fact remains that I wanted to go where I could be a part of something special. I could remember the year before, watching UT beat North Carolina and Coach Mack Brown in the Sun Bowl. I remember James Brown and Priest Holmes scampering around the field, and I realized, *These guys are on the verge of something special.* I wanted to share that. I wanted to be part of something that was a little bit off-the-cuff. I wanted to go where I could make a team a little bit better, not just be another guy.

When I got there, the Southwest Conference was disbanding. We won the last SWC championship that year. Then, we went back home to the Sugar

Bowl and, of course, lost to Virginia Tech, but I knew right then I'd made the right decision. At the end of the year, I came back home with some hardware on my hand, and I knew for a fact that LSU hadn't done a doggone thing that year. People asked me if I was a guru, but I told them, "No, I had just had a feeling."

The next year we came back and won the Big 12 Conference in its first year. That cemented it for me. I had a big part of that game—fourth and inches, James Brown against Nebraska—in Texas football lore. But it still felt

Derek Lewis was on the receiving end of James Brown's "fourth-and-inches" pass completion against Nebraska in the Big 12 championship game.

like, *Hey, this is something that's way, way above me, and it's way above everything I thought football would be.*

That next year, we didn't have a good season; in fact, the whole season went down the tubes with a whole bunch of freakish injuries. We just couldn't get over that hump my junior year. Ricky Williams had been tearing it up the previous three seasons but had kind of been flying under the radar because of our subpar junior year. My senior year, Coach Brown came in with a brand-new staff and a renewed vigor, and Ricky was all of a sudden up for the Heisman. Up to that point, we hadn't won a bowl game while I was there. Then we went on to win nine games and come close again to competing for the Big 12 championship but came up short against Texas Tech. Ricky won the Heisman, and we finally won a bowl game my senior year at Texas—the Cotton Bowl. And that year, Coach Brown, Coach [Tim] Brewster, and the rest of the staff sold a 6′1″–6′2″ tight end to the NFL. I played for the St. Louis Rams in the same building [the TransWorld Dome] that cemented me in college football history, and we won a Super Bowl that year.

The next year I tore my knee up, and there went my career.

I kind of ended up on the skids. I didn't get a degree, which was something I always regretted. As time went on, I ended up in some really bad situations and working some odd jobs. Finally, I was working at the bus station in New Orleans, where I saw the best of people and the worst of people. That convinced me of the fact that I needed to make a move, I needed to make a change. But I only served one year under Coach Brown, so I didn't feel comfortable asking if I could come back to school. I started going back to school on my own, took courses at the University of Phoenix, the online campus, just trying my hand at anything to get out of my rut and try to put football behind me. But my wife—my fiancée at the time—was a massage therapist at the Ritz-Carlton in New Orleans, and she bumped into the most wonderful lady—I call her my guardian angel—Frances Bennett, a tax attorney in Austin and a Longhorn. She told me to give her a call. I did, and she told me, "Okay, Derek, I'm going to do this, this, and this for you. And I'm going to call you back."

I said, "Yeah, right. Fine. Call me back."

The very next morning, she called at 8:00 AM, and she'd done everything she said she was going to do. That's what a Longhorn does. After we talked, she said, "Do you need me to call Coach Brown?" I told her, "Ms. Bennett, after all you've done, that's the least I can do." So I called Coach Brown and said, "I want to come back to school." Coach Brown, being Coach Brown, said, "Hell, Derek. What were you waiting on? You need to come see me." So I went.

Texas had just lost to Washington State. We had such fabulous teams with Roy Williams and the rest of the great players, but we hadn't really gotten over the hump and done what everybody expected us to do, which was win the national championship. I came back to The University of Texas, and Coach Brown and the rest of the staff allowed me to inject my personality and my talents into the team. I was a student assistant, earning my degree, working in the weight room with "Mad Dog" [Jeff Madden]. And going through the season, I fell back in love with football. I knew this is where I needed to be, in the same place where football had been so good to me and where we'd done so many special things. I got that euphoric feeling again, that this is what I was meant to do, and just because God took one thing away from me doesn't mean he doesn't want me to be a part of football, helping young men achieve their dreams and accomplish their goals on the field and in the classroom. I asked Cleve Bryant [associate AD for football operations] and Major Applewhite, who was my quarterback my senior year and was about to embark on his coaching career, if any one of those graduate assistants leave, I'd love to be a G.A.

We went to the Rose Bowl and won on a tipped field goal. Coach Greg Robinson got the Syracuse job and took Major and the rest of the crew with him. Cleve called me three days later and said, "Do you still want to be a graduate assistant?" I told him I did. He said, "You've got two days to get up here, take your GRE, take the job," and do all this stuff. I said, "Whoa, whoa, wait a minute. I'm in New Orleans with my family." He said, "If you want it, you need to come and claim it now. We've got a long list, and people are waiting, champing at the bit. Get up here." I hopped on the next flight, took the GRE, petitioned some colleges to get in. A great mentor of mine, Dr. Michael L. Lauderdale, suggested I go into the School of Social Work. That was some experience, going through that process. People told me, "Man, Derek. Some people take two years to prepare for the GRE." I did it in two weeks.

And my first year as a graduate assistant, we won the national championship with Vince Young and the rest of the guys, making UT history— back-to-back Rose Bowl champs.

My most memorable times were in the Longhorn dining hall with the guys, just shooting the bull and developing those relationships off the field. I have friends like Tony Brackens, Stonie Clark, James Brown, Major Applewhite, Casey Hampton, Mike Adams, Wane McGarity, Priest Holmes…the list goes on and on and on. The life expectancy of football players and coaches is short, but the relationships that you build—Coach Royal, Tommy Nobis, Kenneth Sims, Bill Little, Hall of Fame guys who are great people, great keepers of the game of football, and more importantly, great keepers of the traditions of The University of Texas—last forever. I'm fortunate to be a part of it. It's just a special, special place.

I'm grateful and thankful to the Lord, my God, that He helped me choose a place like The University of Texas. Being a Longhorn for me means perseverance, it means determination, it means never giving up on your dreams. It means family, it means commitment, and it means loyalty. I may wear a whole bunch of colors, but I bleed burnt orange. Every Longhorn has a place in my heart—I'll do pretty much anything for my family.

Derek Lewis became famous for the "fourth-and-inches" pass reception that set up the clinching touchdown in the Longhorns' 37–27 victory over Nebraska in the first-ever Big 12 championship game in 1996. He was an All–Big 12 selection in 1998 and played pro ball following completion of his college career. He served as a graduate assistant coach for Texas and in 2007 became a full-time assistant coach at the University of Minnesota.

RICKY WILLIAMS

RUNNING BACK

1995–1998

I DECIDED I WAS GOING TO BE A college football player when I was just a kid
watching a Notre Dame game on television in San Diego. Something about
college football was different from the NFL. It was the idea that you are part
of a team, you are part of a university, and you are part of a tradition that is
bigger than football.

That is something I connected with when I started looking at Texas. John
Mackovic was the head coach, and he was recruiting a lot in California.
When I got to Texas, I think there were eight or nine of us from California.
When I was looking for schools to attend, I was looking for a chance to go
to a big school that would be on television a lot but also where I would have
a chance to start somewhere as a freshman.

When it came down to it, my final choices were USC and Texas. Notre
Dame was in the mix, too. I actually took my USC trip on a weekend—it
was a Friday, Saturday, and Sunday. I flew home on Monday, unpacked,
repacked, and flew to Austin right after that trip to Los Angeles.

I had never been to Texas, so I was expecting to see tumbleweeds and
cowboy boots. I was very surprised when I got to Austin. First of all, it was
December 17, and it was 73 degrees. I thought that Austin felt and looked
very much like Southern California. The thing that sold me on the city was
when we drove out to Coach Steve Bernstein's (who had recruited me) house

Ricky Williams, UT's second Heisman winner, became the NCAA's all-time career rusher with a dramatic 60-yard run against Texas A&M in 1998.

off Bee Cave Road, toward the Texas Hill Country. I was like, "Wow, there's streams and hills and trees and forests," and it was beautiful. So Austin passed the test pretty quickly.

The next thing I experienced was being around the guys on the team. They were really like a family. I saw that if one guy had a car and another guy didn't, it was no problem to let them borrow your car. They really took care of each other, and that caught my attention.

Then, when we were walking toward the dining hall, there were these three humongous guys walking toward me, and the coaches introduced me to them. They were Octavious Bishop, Jay Humphrey, and Ben Adams, all redshirt offensive linemen who would be playing with me all four years.

Probably the most important thing was that I saw—this was before Priest Holmes hurt his knee later in spring training—that Priest was going to be the starting tailback, and there was no fullback, really, so I had a great opportunity to win a starting position. I knew Coach Mackovic had a reputation as an offensive genius, so I believed that he'd find ways to get me the ball. A lot of coaches say certain things, but with him, I could tell that he was a man of his word, and if he said that I was going to have a chance to play and get the ball, I could believe him.

So I really liked Austin, I liked the people, and it was a program that was putting itself back on the map. It had a lot of national exposure, so it seemed the perfect place for me, and I felt very grateful that I was open enough to realize that. Bucky Godbolt, my running backs coach, and I hit it off fast, and he turned out to be like a big brother and a really strong father figure for me.

One of the highlights of my time at Texas was the lifelong friend I found in John Bianco, who worked with me and the media. John was instrumental in keeping my image positive and my attitude always good when it came to the media.

I actually grew relatively close to Coach Mackovic, and everything was perfect. Texas had the academics, the program, it was a place where I could fit in, the team was young, they were coming up, and I had a chance to be a part of something big.

When I got to Austin, I went to the "T" Room and saw the pictures on the walls of all of the All-Americans. The tradition and the energy in that room were so strong that I knew it was something I wanted to be a part of. I wanted to be able to put my picture on the wall, to be able to put my name there. A lot of times, our study hall was in the "T" Room, and every time I was in there, I was inspired to be better because of the pictures and all that they represented.

My freshman year, Coach Mackovic was true to his word, and I did get a chance to play. When I first got to Texas, Texas A&M was a powerhouse. They had that "wrecking crew" defense, and they had beaten us four years in a row. To hear the guys talk about A&M that first year, especially their defense, you would think that they were superhuman. They were big, fast, strong, hard to beat, and they killed us every year.

Finally, when the end of the season came, we were playing them in College Station, one of the hardest places to play in college football, and they had the number-one defense in the country. I was a little bit intimidated. But we had had a great season, and we surprised a lot of people. The winner of the game was going to win the final Southwest Conference championship, so it was a showdown.

It was tough and loud, but in the second quarter, I broke a 22-yard touchdown, and things started clicking for us. I think I had 165 yards, and we won 16–6. In my opinion, that was when the program really started to turn around. From that point on, especially when we played Texas A&M, everyone really turned it up a notch or two. We won three out of the four times we played them and beat them pretty badly twice. It was special for me to be a part of the turning of the tables when we finally started to dominate that series.

In 1997, my junior season, there were rumors floating around that Coach Mackovic was going to be fired after the season, because we had a really tough year. I came out publicly and said that if he left, that I was also going to leave. I had led the nation in rushing and scoring, so I had the opportunity to go to the NFL. When I made that statement, I really meant it. I didn't see staying for another year—with a new coaching staff and all the changes that would come—when I didn't have to.

The last game of the season, we played A&M, and I hurt my ankle in that game and started the second half at 75 percent, and it went down from there, and we ended up losing the game 27–16. I had a good game; I wound up with three touchdowns and 185 yards, but we lost. I knew if I had been healthy the whole game, we would have beaten them. It kind of left a sour taste in my mouth. I didn't want to end my career on a game like that.

Even so, after that game, it was probably 80-20 (percentage-wise) that I would leave. When Coach Brown first came and talked to our team, he didn't win me over right away. I thought he was just a slick talker because he is so charismatic and is really good with the way he speaks. Then I knew I was leaving. It was now 90-10.

I had worn my hair in dreadlocks for years, and when I met with him for the first time, he asked me if I would think about cutting my hair. After that, I think it was like 99 percent to 1 percent to leave. I think he could tell that I was leaving, and we had another meeting. It was then that I shared with him all the things I thought were the problems on the team and the things that I thought could help us be a better team. It was a very good talk. I just laid out everything that I felt…I just put it on the table.

I saw the way he reacted. He was so very receptive, and he really listened. Right away after that meeting, he started to implement some of the suggestions that I had made. I was impressed. Over the next week or so, we had lunch, and we talked to each other a little bit more. After getting to know him better and seeing the kind of guy that he was, I was now really impressed.

302

I guess the final piece came when I went to lunch with him and a friend of mine. Coach Brown had his wife, Sally, with him at the Hyde Park Grill. Just to see him with Sally was important. I always have been a guy that judges people by their relationships. To see the two of them that way, I really had a lot of respect for him, not only as a coach but as a person. I think the next day or the day after that, we had the press conference to announce that I was staying.

I had decided that things were in place for me to remain in school, that this new coach was not going to make my life more difficult, but he was really all about trying to help the program, trying to help me, and trying to help The University take a step forward.

Coming from California, I didn't know a lot about some of Texas's legends. I didn't know much about Earl Campbell when I first came, so I got to meet with him, and I tried to tie myself to the tradition of what Texas football was all about. And when I won the Doak Walker Award after that 1997 season, I went to Orlando to the awards presentation. All of the guys from different schools were in this restaurant, and I wasn't really hanging out with them, so I just sat down at the Doak Walker table and picked up a pamphlet that described Doak. I soon realized that he was a legend, and he was very representative of what I wanted to be, the All-American person, not just a football player.

I am always very aware of how people react to me. Especially at that time, because I had dreadlocks, had my tongue pierced or something, and a couple of tattoos. When Doak finally walked in, he didn't react at all. He was a really open, very nice, very friendly guy, and we sat and talked all night. He really touched me in a very deep place. Unfortunately, after the award ceremony that year, he was paralyzed in a skiing accident. It was really sad to see such a wonderful person, who had touched so many people's lives, like that. So I really opened my heart, and I wanted to reach out and touch him and continually thank him for what he represented and what he meant to me.

That's why I asked, after he passed, if I could wear his old No. 37 when we played Oklahoma in the Cotton Bowl, because it was known as the "House That Doak Built."

That game was part of my senior season. When Coach Brown came in, we had been 4–7 the previous year, and no one expected us to do anything. When I decided to come back, there was talk about the Heisman Trophy. Even though our team record hadn't been what I wanted it to be, I'd had a great individual season my junior year, and I wasn't even invited to New York. So I knew if there was any way I was going to win the Heisman, the team was going to have to help and play, meaning the defense was going to have to do something special. We started out 1–2, losing to the No. 1 and No. 2 teams in the country in UCLA and Kansas State. After the K-State game, I had 48 yards, and we got pummeled—we got beat very badly. So I was kind of down, and I knew it was going to be tough.

But the next five or six weeks, the defense just got stingy, the offense stepped up; our quarterback, Major Applewhite, was incredible; receiver Wane McGarity played incredibly; everyone stepped up their game, and the team really came together. I say to this day that my winning the Heisman Trophy had nothing to do with me. It was just that the team really rose to the occasion, and we weren't going to accept losing at all.

It was the first time in my life—the only time in my life—that the team was put on my shoulders, and I was allowed to lead, and the team was happy to follow. I attribute that all to the way Coach Brown handled me and handled the team. It was a case of being able to turn a difficult situation into a winning season and further the Longhorns coming back on the map.

I look at my life and all my accomplishments, and the four years that I spent in Austin at The University of Texas were by far the best years of my life. I jokingly say—half serious—that I was born a Longhorn. People say that in Texas, everything is bigger, and I agree. The Longhorns, the fans, the students, the faculty, the staff, they all have bigger hearts.

What it means to be a Longhorn sounds simple, but in the deepest, most positive sense of the word, it's about pride. It's about taking pride in what you do, pride in who you are, and taking pride in how you handle yourself. It is something that I will always cherish, and something that no one can take away from me. I always feel my heart feels huge, flowing with pride—not a negative pride, thinking I'm better than anyone else—to know that you were a part of something that was bigger than yourself. It's like a family that can never be separated, never be broken up, and something that never, ever can be taken away from you.

Ricky Williams set the NCAA record for career rushing yards during his time at Texas. He won the Heisman Trophy in 1998 and earned consensus All-American and All–Big 12 honors in 1997 and 1998. He was also a two-time winner of the Doak Walker Award as the nation's top running back. He set 15 NCAA records and 38 UT records as a running back.

The
NEW
MILLENNIUM

MAJOR APPLEWHITE

QUARTERBACK

1998–2001

I REALLY WANTED TO PLAY AT ALABAMA. I didn't have much interest in Texas because I didn't know that much about it. When you live in Louisiana and you think about football, you think eastward. You don't think Southwest Conference or Pac-10. That's the way it was in Baton Rouge. If it wasn't LSU, the New Orleans Saints, or the SEC, it had no relevance. No reason to talk about it.

When it looked like Alabama wasn't going to recruit me, and John Mackovic had some interest, my dad and mom were adamant about my getting out of the state of Louisiana. Texas offered me a scholarship, and there was no comparison between the academics at Texas and some of the other schools I was considering. Plus, the city of Austin is so great; I loved it. Once we got to Austin and saw Texas, saw the folklore and the tradition—to me, it was the Alabama of the Big 12. I was excited to go to a school that had a lot of tradition.

Greg Brown, David Aaron, Cedric Mitchell, Kwame Cavil, and I all came up early, a week and a half after we walked across the stage at graduation. Lots of other kids were on senior trips, but we came up and started working summer jobs immediately. I tried to get acclimated to Austin and get used to the surroundings. That is important, so you can settle in on the school and the football side of it. I redshirted my first year, and then Coach Brown came

Major Applewhite capped his career with a record-setting performance in the 2001 Holiday Bowl.

in with Coach Greg Davis and Coach Carl Reese, and started a new program. Everything was up for grabs at every position, and Richard Walton, a senior, was the starting quarterback.

Richard started the 1998 season but ended up breaking his hand about three or four games into it. Then I became the starter. I didn't realize how well he handled things until I got far removed from it. Richard helped me because I was so very, very young and had no clue what was going on. He had waited, finally, for his turn to play, then he'd broken his hand. But he was very gracious and mature about the situation. He helped me in that starting role and helped me have a good freshman year. He had a different level of maturity than a lot of college guys. It wasn't that he wasn't a competitor, because Richard was very competitive. And it wasn't that he wasn't a good football player, because he was a damned good football player. He just understood that that was the situation he was in, and he was going to do the very best he could do in that situation. Guys like that are few and far between. He had a long-term perspective, even as a player.

Whenever Chris Simms got his opportunity, that was the situation I was in. You can do your best with it, or you can stop caring and just let the situation go awry. Richard set the mold. You're a quarterback at Texas, and this is your responsibility. Everybody's watching and waiting for someone to crack or flip out, and you just can't do it, because this game changes so much. It changes game to game, quarter to quarter, series to series, play to play—and you can only imagine how it can change in the quarterback role. You've got to be flexible, you've got to understand the team concept and give a little bit of yourself at times, sometimes more than you want to. That's what makes it enjoyable when you're successful and you have sacrificed. There were sacrifices Chris had to make, and there were sacrifices I had to make as an individual and as a player. That's just part of the game, and that's why we play it, to accomplish things as a team. There are certain things you have to do if you want to be good at a team sport. If you can't be selfless, then you just don't have a chance to be a successful team player.

Everybody's self-absorbed. That doesn't mean that they're selfish, it just means they're always wondering, *How are things going to affect me?* I was self-absorbed—*How is this going to affect me?* But at the same time, I knew there was going to be something in the end that would work out for me, and it worked out just fine.

I'm a sports historian; understanding where programs are, how they got there, who was responsible for it, and who was the coach who rebuilt an Alabama or a Texas. Those things are intriguing to me. To come to a program that wasn't achieving what it should have been—which was where Texas was—and to see what we did in '98 (we won five of our nine games in the last two or three minutes)....We broke a 47-game home winning streak in Lincoln against Nebraska and basically solidified Ricky Williams's Heisman Trophy. We beat Oklahoma State on a last-second field goal. We beat A&M on a two-minute drive at home. We beat Baylor in the last two minutes of the game. That was a great memory, because even though we didn't win a conference or national championship, that was one of the most magical Texas seasons. Because of the Heisman, because we kept coming from behind, because it was the restarting of the program with Mack Brown, and because we beat Nebraska up in Lincoln, people thought, *Maybe we're back.* I felt that that group, that '98 team, put together a foundation that Mack could build on, and he did. Mack took his skills as a recruiter and a communicator, and, man, he just threw gasoline on the fire. That's the best memory, the '98 season and how it all culminated just right to give Mack and his staff enough leverage to build on it and keep going.

As with any player, there were times I wondered, *What is that guy thinking up there in the coaches' office?* But there was never a time I wanted to quit being part of Texas football. People would ask me, "Well, Chris is starting and you're not playing. Do you want to transfer somewhere where you can play?" I would say, "And transfer where?" What a buzz-kill that would be, to leave Texas and go somewhere else. You just got through playing in front of 85,000 people, you just beat Nebraska in Lincoln as a freshman—how much fun would it be to go play anywhere else? That wasn't even a second thought for me.

I love The University. Truthfully, one of my proudest moments was the national championship game in 2006. I was interviewing for the job at Rice, and I had to get up at 4:30 the next morning to board a plane and leave Syracuse, New York. It was a Wednesday night, I was at my apartment by myself, and nobody in Syracuse was staying up to watch that game on the West Coast. They didn't care about Southern Cal or The University of Texas. Well, I was running all around my apartment, screaming, hollering, banging things around, happy, sad—devastated when I thought we were going lose there at the end. The next morning, for some reason, getting up at 4:30 in the morning had never been so easy.

That was one of the proudest days of my life. It was a "swagger" day. I got to wear my orange in the airport, and I was just happy to be a Longhorn. I was getting all these text messages with pictures of the Tower. After I took the job at Rice, my wife and I drove up to Austin the next day in a rental car. The Tower was still orange, and we didn't waste any time. We drove right up in front of the six-pack [the six buildings on the south mall] and took our picture in front of the orange Tower with the No. 1. It was so cool because it was ours. Even though those kids and those coaches actually did it, we still felt like it was a little bit ours.

I can't imagine where I would be if I had not gone to Texas. What has The University done for me? Being associated with Texas and being able to attach that onto my last name—I'm Major Applewhite from The University of Texas; that's where the credibility comes from. I'm just one of the many. I'm not only talking about the great letterman tradition, I'm talking about what you're a part of, the tradition, the network of Texas people that are out there, and how being a Longhorn enhances the quality of your life—not only job opportunities but who you know and meet. I wonder what would have happened if I had gone to another school or had not been affiliated with The University of Texas. Would I be with my wife, enjoying the quality of life I'm enjoying right now? The answer is "probably not." It's something that's hard to imagine. Being a Longhorn has affected my life, and what it's done for me cannot be measured.

Major Applewhite was the Big 12 Co-Offensive Player of the Year in 1999 and the MVP of the Longhorns' 2001 victory in the Holiday Bowl. He entered the coaching profession after his time at Texas and in 2007 became offensive coordinator at the University of Alabama.

CORY REDDING

DEFENSIVE END

1999–2002

WHEN I WAS A LITTLE KID, I was running around in the streets, playing football with my friends. One day, one of my teachers, who was a coach, saw a little talent in me and said, "Why don't you come out and play football?"

I didn't know what it meant to be dedicated to something, but all my friends were playing football, so I said, "I'll try." I noticed I had a little speed and was a little strong, but I was tall and skinny. My brother was always bigger than me, so to gain weight, I started eating more with him and hanging out with him and his friends. He played offensive line, so eating was not a problem.

Football showed me how to work to be better. I got to The University of Texas through hard work and dedication. I didn't know what it meant to have a good work ethic. I was good starting out, but I was raw. Everything was just natural, it wasn't fine-tuned. My coach kept pushing me and pushing me. I wanted to know, "Why are you on me so hard?"

"I see something in you," he said. "I see greatness. Don't be afraid of that. Always strive to do better." He stayed on me, and he showed me that I could make it.

I arrived in 1999 at The University of Texas from North Shore High School with aspirations of doing the best I could in school and making my

Cory Redding set goals for a national championship for his freshman class at Texas.

way to the NFL. Chris Simms, who came in with me, was named the outstanding high school offensive player in the country, and I was the defensive player. I remember thinking, *We are going to do well. With Chris here, we are going to win a lot of games*. I said that, and I believed with everything in my heart that we were going to get a chance to play for a national championship. With Chris, Rod Babers, Nathan Vasher, and all those guys I came in with, we had a great four years. We won 40 games, and to be part of a group that helped turn the program back around meant a lot to me. I wanted to be part of change so that when people look back and say, "This is when it turned around," they can say, "Cory Redding was a part of it."

But with all the great things that happened to us, the most memorable was the saddest. We lost a friend and teammate, Cole Pittman, in a truck wreck just before spring training of our junior year.

That next season, we dedicated the North Carolina game to him. I guess that is my most memorable moment. It wasn't the fact that I got an interception and ran it back for a touchdown—it was nothing like that. It was that I lost a dear friend, and the team came together, and we fought for this one cause. For the family—for the Longhorn family, for the Pittman family, and for Cole. I never experienced anything like that. That holds a special place in my heart, the fact that we went out and won the game the way we did.

313

Losing Cole was a hard lesson but a growing part of life. We learned at a young age that life is too short. You never know when your last breath will be. Instead of being mad at someone or holding grudges, let it go. And don't live your life through fear. Don't say, "I don't want to go skydiving because I'm scared of dying," or, "I don't ride a motorcycle because I'm scared of getting hurt." Live your life and enjoy it. You never know when it's your last day, so cherish every moment with your friends and loved ones.

We put 44 points on the board against North Carolina in the game we had dedicated to Cole and his family, and 44 was Cole's number. We missed an extra point on purpose. That is by far one of the most special moments I can remember at Texas.

In my first game as a starter, we actually lost the game. But that moment held a spot in my mind, coming out of the tunnel, hearing 85,000 fans screaming. Being in uniform, being on the field was great. I was like a kid in a candy store. I was caught up in the game and caught up in the atmosphere.

In fact, too much so. I missed assignments that led to blocked punts that cost us the game because I was trying to do too much. I learned then that you have to focus. You can't get caught up in the moment. You have to concentrate on the task at hand, which is winning and doing your job. Once everything's over, then you can look at everything around you, like the atmosphere and crowd. But once you are in the game, you have got to be tuned in.

That experience helped me to block out all distractions, regardless of whether I'm on the field or off the field. Everything I do in football I try to relate to life, and vice versa. So with my being distracted on the field, it helped me be tuned in, wired in off the field, in conversations and in listening to people. Playing now in the NFL, I have to be wired in and focused on my job. At Texas, I learned to do the little things. That has helped me in my career.

The final piece of my Texas career came in the 2003 Cotton Bowl game against LSU. Your last game is always going to be with you, and we couldn't have put a better stamp on our college careers. We won the game 35–20 and finished with an 11–2 record. That was a very good LSU team. In fact, they won the national championship the next year. We had gone into the game knowing we could win it, and we walked off the field winners. I was the MVP on defense, and Roy Williams was the MVP on offense.

We knew we had started something, and when Texas won the national championship in the Rose Bowl after the 2005 season, I was in the stands. I tried to just be a fan, but it didn't take long for people to pick me out, probably from that Longhorn tattoo I got on my arm just before our Holiday Bowl game with Washington my junior year. I felt like that was my championship, too.

That's what being a Longhorn means. Excellence. It means striving to be the best you can be at all times. A Longhorn is not going to back down. You carry that swagger, the one that says, "I don't care who you are, we are going to come right through you." You have loyalty to your comrades. I have never had a greater group of guys that I'm friends with than I did in college. In the NFL, guys have families, so when football is over, they go home to their families.

College is different. From the moment I stepped in this stadium, it was a beloved place. It is how everybody treats everyone around here. I love everything about the city of Austin. I found my wife here at The University of Texas, and when I'm done, I want to build my home here. I was born and raised in Houston, my mom still lives there, and H-Town's always going to be my city. But Mom can come see me whenever she wants, because this is where I want to call home.

I came back to school in the spring of 2007 to finish my degree. People ask me, why, with all the success I've had in the NFL, would I do that? The answer is, I do a lot of motivational speaking everywhere I go. I can't go to these schools and tell kids, "Education is important and you need to get your degree," if I don't have mine. I'm not going to talk the talk; I'm going to walk the walk, too. I want to be an example in everything I do. I have to get my degree. I must get my degree. It means something to me to get my degree and to have it there on the wall next to my wife's so I can preach education to my children, so they'll say, "Mom and Dad got theirs, so we have to get ours." Then I'll get my "T" ring and show them in one more way what it means to be a Longhorn.

We came in, that class of 1999, and set a standard, with Mack Brown telling us what we needed to do and how we were going to get there. We set a standard, and we took it and ran with it. Everybody who was recruited then knew that this was no laughing matter. We were all about business and trying to get to the national championship. So when they win, I feel like I win, because I'm still a part of the program. I walk with my chest out and my head high because my boys did it, and we, the 1999 crew, were the mixture. We mixed the stuff, and it was tough and it was grimy, but once that year was over, we laid the foundation and it got hardened. They built on top of it, and it feels special.

315

Cory Redding was the nation's top high school defensive player when he came to Texas in 1999, and he went on to help the Longhorns move into the 21st century as a national power. A co-captain of the 2002 team, he was a two-time All–Big 12 and All-American selection and has followed his Texas career with an outstanding professional career in the NFL with the Detroit Lions.

CHRIS SIMMS

QUARTERBACK

1999–2002

M Y STORY OF GETTING TO TEXAS BEGINS, really, in North Carolina. From the start, Coach Mack Brown was recruiting me at North Carolina when I was a junior in high school in New Jersey. Then, my senior year, he went to Texas.

He didn't recruit me at first. I think there was a part of him that wondered whether a guy from New Jersey would go all the way down to Texas. Nonetheless, he started calling me, and I went for a visit to Austin. I absolutely loved the school, the city—I loved everything about it—and of course, the football program. But the situation wasn't quite exactly what I would have liked it to be, because Major Applewhite was there at quarterback, and he was a redshirt freshman. I knew if I went to Tennessee, I'd redshirt my first year, and I pretty much knew that I would be the starter after that.

So I committed to Tennessee. But every time I would tell my friends in high school, or anybody, about my visits, I found myself talking about Texas. I was always thinking about Texas and that I'd like to be there. Finally, I said, "If I'm always thinking about Texas, why am I going to Tennessee?" So I called Coach Brown and told him I was thinking about changing my mind. He said, "Let me know when you definitely know for sure." I called him up the next night and said, "Coach, I definitely want to come to Texas." He said, "All right, let's do it."

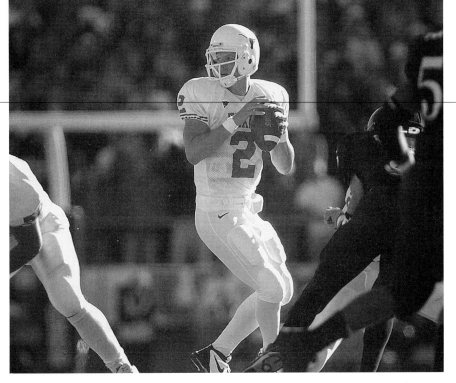

Chris Simms quarterbacked the Longhorns to 26 wins as a starter, threw for 7,097 yards, and later became the quarterback for the Tampa Bay Buccaneers.

    We were the number-one recruiting class in the country, and to me, the greatest thing about going there was that we had a chance to make a difference. Texas football had been somewhat down for a few years before Coach Brown got there, and I remember talking to Cory Redding and the other guys in my class about how awesome an opportunity it was that we were going to be able to go to The University of Texas and bring them back to that national level they deserved. That was definitely one of the key components of my wanting to go to school there and play football.

    There were so many great moments while I was at Texas, but two that were particularly significant for me were the last two games of my senior year. We played our last game at home against Texas A&M, and we beat them

50–20. I remember that game maybe more than anything. I felt like I was floating when I ran around the field and slapped hands with thousands of fans. But there was a sadness, too—coming off the field at the end of the game, knowing that it was the last time I would play in that awesome rivalry and in that stadium. I'll never forget that.

From there, we went to the Cotton Bowl and played a good LSU team. That, too, was a special moment in my life. The Cotton Bowl stadium was a place where I'd never won as a starting quarterback, and we hadn't won there as a team in a few years, since I was a just a freshman. We beat LSU, and we fought through a little adversity in that game. That was kind of the signature of our class. We hung in there and came back to win and beat a good LSU team pretty well.

After the game, I remember how happy I was that we'd won. What a great feeling it was to end my career at The University of Texas with a win. At the same time, I had something of an empty feeling because there was this question mark: "What's my life going to be like now? I don't have football at The University of Texas anymore." I was definitely happy, but there was a part of me that was a little sad, too.

There are so many things you learn in college, and getting to know people and make friends is the best. That was why, before our senior year, a trip some of us took back to New Jersey was so important to me. I invited three of my closest friends—my receivers, Roy Williams, B.J. Johnson, and Sloan Thomas—to visit my home in New Jersey so we could work out together. I had become such good friends with so many people down there in Texas, and they are relationships that I will have the rest of my life. So to bring them up to New Jersey—there were so many great things about it.

The first thing I loved about it was that—okay, I'm kind of from rich, white suburbia. People in Texas have their thoughts about people up in the Northeast, and everybody in the Northeast has their thoughts about how people in Texas are different. So it was great to have Roy, B.J., and Sloan come up here and let these people up here see that things really aren't that different—how great these kids are. Of course, those guys were extremely helpful in introducing me to the ways of Texas, as well. There are so many things I learned in college outside of the classroom, as far as cultural experiences, that I definitely don't take for granted.

When Cole Pittman, one of our teammates, was killed in a truck wreck, it was the first time I had experienced death like that. It changed us all. On the football field, there was the issue of who would start at quarterback, Major Applewhite or me? It was not the easiest thing to go through, but when I look back at it now…six, seven years removed from that whole scenario, it was something that definitely made me better and stronger. Was it fun to go through? No. But we all have our journeys, and that was just my particular path to take. I can't tell you how much I learned from it and how it made me a stronger person.

It taught me a lot about life, and it taught me how to be a professional athlete, as well. When you are the quarterback at a major university like The University of Texas and you're a quarterback in the pros, you are going to go through ups and downs. People are going to criticize you, and it is not always going to be the smoothest road. But it made me more focused, and it taught me how to block the outside influences out of my mind and really focus on what is important, and that was football and working hard and trying to be a good teammate.

When I consider what it means to be a Longhorn, I am thankful that I was part of such a rich tradition—to be a part of that, and to realize that I played a significant role. But there are people who came before me and who will come after me who have played and will play significant roles. I'm just glad that I was a part of it. I got to experience being at one of the greatest universities in the whole world, and to play football at maybe the best football school in the country. I know I'm truly grateful for the experience and everything that went along with it.

Chris Simms set the Longhorn record for passing in a regular-season game when he threw for 419 yards in a victory over Nebraska in 2002. When he finished his Texas career, he ranked second in total victories as a Longhorn quarterback with 26 (trailing only Bobby Layne). He was selected as a captain and was voted the MVP of the 2002 team. He entered the 2007 season, his fifth in the NFL, as the starting quarterback of the Tampa Bay Buccaneers.

MICHAEL HUFF

DEFENSIVE BACK

2001–2005

THERE WERE FOUR MINUTES LEFT in the Rose Bowl game for the national championship, and we knew that it came down to us. Vince Young had just scored, and we were trailing 38–33 to Southern California.

The game had been going back and forth, and Vince and our offense were playing well. We knew as a defense we had to step up and get one last stop.

When we, the recruiting class of 2001, had come to Texas, we believed we would one day be playing in this game. That's one of the reasons we came to Texas, to play in big games and win big games and win national championships. We came because we wanted to play with the best and against the best.

Our goal had been to win the national championship for our school and for the state of Texas—for all the high school coaches and high school players in the state. They deserved this.

I was just a skinny kid growing up in Irving, Texas, and was more of a track guy than a football player when Hardee McCrary stopped by my high school my junior year. That was really the first time I thought I had a chance to play college football. A lot of little schools had come by, but that was it. We sat down and had a little talk, but after that, the thought kind of died down.

My senior year, I had a pretty good year, and I got a call from Coach Brown to come down and visit the week of the football banquet. I came to Austin and fell in love with everything. That was the first time I had met

Michael Huff, UT's first Jim Thorpe Award winner, was the outstanding defensive player in the BCS National Championship game in 2005.

Coach Brown in person, and he was kind of a father figure, which I felt I needed, leaving the Dallas area and coming to Austin. That was a big step for me. I was overwhelmed.

When I got to Texas in the fall of 2001, I met Coach Duane Akina. It was my first year, and it was his first year at Texas. I had heard all the great things he had done as a defensive backs coach and coordinator at Arizona, and he immediately played a huge role for me. I needed someone who would mentor me, and he did that.

All of that seemed a long time ago that night in Pasadena. All season long, people had talked about us and Southern Cal. It was the biggest game of my career. Everything's relative when you are growing up, but you could add all of the years of high school, Little League, Pop Warner, and college, and the next four minutes of that Rose Bowl game were about to be the most memorable part of any game I'd ever been in.

I'm not really a vocal person, but that was the last college game I ever played in, so that was the first time I ever spoke up and tried to get everybody together. The starting safety, Michael Griffin, was hurt, and so was one of our corners, Tarell Brown. We had a lot of young guys in there, so we just had to keep everybody's head straight.

Rod Wright, Aaron Harris, and I were the leaders of the defense, and it was our job to make it happen. If we didn't stop them, we weren't going to win. We got everybody in the huddle, and said, "It's up to us to win the game."

The downs flew by. It was first down, second down, third down, and now, it's fourth-and-two at our 45-yard line with just a little over two minutes left in the game. Earlier in the game, LenDale White had gotten me. He made a good run. He broke my tackle, so this time I just had to get him back. We knew Reggie Bush was on the sideline, and they had big personnel in there, so they lined up to run the ball right at us. It was our destiny to stop them.

I was supposed to cover the tight end or something, but I just played on instinct and kind of knifed by their pulling guard. Everybody was in their gaps, where they were supposed to be. Brian Robison threw one guy out of the way, and Rod Wright had good penetration. I got past the guard and got to White to fence him and make sure he didn't lean forward.

When the play was over, everybody got up, and we were looking at the yard marker, and we knew he hadn't made it. And we knew, at that moment, that we were going to win the game. It was the most incredible feeling I have ever had in my life. We got spoiled most games at Texas. Most games weren't that close. But to be in a game like that, and for it to be for a national championship, is special. Nobody said anything after the play, just, "Find Vince." We wanted to find him because we wanted to challenge him. That's something the defense and offense had done to each other since our voluntary workouts began after the first Rose Bowl win. We knew he'd lead us to victory, but we wanted to get to him and challenge him like he did us the series before. We told him, "Now what are you gonna do?" And he showed us.

I was honored to be named the Defensive Player of the Game, but you could have given it to a lot of our guys. When we won, 41–38, scoring on the drive after that stop, Vince and the offense got and deserved a lot of credit, but I'm proud of what we did when we had to do it.

When I came to Texas, Coach Brown preached family atmosphere, and we won that game as a family. He said to think of all the players as your brothers, and all the coaches and their wives as parents. It is just one big family, so if you ever need anything, you know where to go. You know you are going to get scolded by Coach Brown, like a father figure, but when we're young kids and leaving home for the first time, what you need is a father figure.

I was fortunate to win the Jim Thorpe Award as the nation's best defensive back that season, and when John Bianco called me and told me they wanted me to come back to the awards ceremony in 2006 as a former winner, I asked John about an idea I had. Aaron Ross had won the award, and that meant that Coach Akina had coached two straight winners.

My rookie season at Oakland had gone well for me, and so I asked John if he would check with the Thorpe committee to see if I could buy a replica of the trophy and give it to Coach Akina. They agreed. When we walked into the ballroom that night, Coach saw three trophies and asked what that was about.

"There must have been a tie," I said.

But when I got up to present it to him and looked into the glisten in his eyes, I understood that we had done something good. It goes back to family. I wouldn't have won the award without him.

What does it mean to be a Longhorn?

It made me who I am. Those five years changed my life. They molded me into the man I am today, and it is something that is going to be with me for the rest of my life.

Michael Huff became the Longhorns' first Jim Thorpe Award winner as the nation's best defensive back in 2005. An All-American selection, he was named the Defensive Most Valuable Player in the 2006 BCS national championship game. Michael is now starting in the secondary for the Oakland Raiders.

DAVID THOMAS
TIGHT END
2002–2005

I's hard to look at my career at Texas without going straight to the 2006 national championship game in the Rose Bowl. That whole week leading up to the game is still as fresh today as it was then. It was a moment for which I had been waiting a long time.

I grew up a lifelong Texas fan. There are pictures of me when I was a little kid, wearing a Texas helmet and a Texas jersey. I've still got the first Texas jersey I ever owned hanging in my closet. The first thing I ever remember about watching Texas was Tony Brackens annihilating that Texas Tech kicker near the sideline. The guy couldn't even walk off the field.

I started wearing a shirt that said, "Texas," on it under my pads. I wore it in seventh grade, eighth grade, and all through high school. I was just waiting on Coach Brown to send me a letter saying they had a scholarship for me. And when it came, it was pretty much a done deal. It was a dream come true to go to a school like Texas.

Being from Lubbock, everybody wanted to see me be a Red Raider, and I have a lot of respect for Texas Tech and for the coaches there. But that didn't sway me from my childhood roots and all my memories as a Texas fan.

But, back to the championship game. I remember how excited we were to be playing in that game. Everybody thought we were the underdogs, and that gave us a little chip on our shoulder. We felt like we were one of the best teams in the country. All we had to do was go out and prove it. I remember

David Thomas
caught 10 passes
in the BCS National
Championship win
over USC.

how hard we worked in practice and how much fun we had after practice, just being with each other. All of the things that the bowl does for a team were good—Disneyland, Lawry's. The tight ends—Neale Tweedie, Steve Hogan, Peter Ullman, Jermichael Finley, and I enjoyed hanging out together, whether it was just around the hotel or in our meetings. We had fun in meetings the whole year, but that week—that was the best part about the week, spending time with all my teammates.

Going into the game, I knew the way the coaches had set up the game plan that I had a chance to catch some balls, and I knew I might have a big game. In my mind, that meant four or five catches. Six passes would be awesome.

I think I had that many in the first half. It seemed like every time I caught a ball, it was another catch, another memory. Just to be part of something that big, and to have a big role in a game that big, was something I'll never forget. I never counted the passes. I knew I had a lot in the first half, and then it continued in the second half. But I had no idea I had 10. I had no clue I was in double digits.

At some point in our time at Texas, Vince and I formed a bond. We came together. We were from such different backgrounds, but we worked so hard to develop our timing. It was great to catch those balls from him and for all that stuff to finally show itself on such a big stage. We had a good year going in, but for it to come out like that on that big of a stage was pretty special for us personally. He was from Houston and had had a rough childhood, and I was from West Texas. We learned a lot from each other and had a lot of respect for each other. We both worked so hard to get to Texas and to get where we were while we were at Texas. When we came in, we were so different, but we developed a relationship with a lot of respect and love for each other.

All of that came out on the final drive against USC. Brian Carter had a couple of catches early in the drive that really got it going. And then, I'll never forget the last play. When Vince scored, I was on the far side of the field, but I knew he was going to step in—I'm getting chills just talking about it now—I jumped up in the air and extended my arms. He had about five yards to go, but I knew he was going to score and that we were going to be national champions.

On the final drive, it was very businesslike. Nobody said anything dramatic. It was like, *This drive is for the championship. Let's go get it.* You could see it in everybody's eyes. There wasn't any doubt, and there wasn't any fear. It was just a matter of us doing it. You looked in the eyes of the linemen and receivers and running backs and Vince, and you could see it. It was that confidence we had in each other and in the team that we were going to get it done. That's what I remember most—how confident we were. We were excited, but nobody was amped out of their minds. It was simply, *Let's go win the national championship.*

After the game, Coach Brown told us to let this be a great moment in our lives but don't let it be the greatest. To have that kind of perspective from him, in such a big moment, says a lot about him and his character and who he is. That was a great moment, but for him to remind us that this shouldn't be the greatest thing that ever happened to us—that we were just on a hill, on the way up, and that we've all got bigger and better things in store—was pretty telling of him and his character.

I remember how excited everybody was. We were all taking pictures together. We had our hats and T-shirts on, just celebrating. We were running around on the field like crazy, but when we all got to the locker room, what we had just done sank in. It seems like it went by so fast. Everything leading up to the game flew by, and then the game flew by, as did all the celebrating. The thing that made it really sink in to me was coming back to Austin for the big celebration in the stadium, and for the first time, seeing the Tower lit up orange with the No. 1 on it. I had seen it lit for baseball and for women's track, but I never went up close to it because I wanted the first time I ever saw it like that to be for my national championship—for our team's national championship. And I remember going up there and just sitting and looking at it, and that's when it hit me. We really had won the national championship, and it was ours forever to keep.

The White House was a fun trip because every time we got together it brought up all the memories. We had all the stories to tell all over again, and I'm sure it will be like that the rest of our lives. Every time the guys get together, it'll go back to that game. It was a big honor for President Bush to call us on stage, and he talked about the things we had done besides football.

Being a Longhorn is the pride and tradition that you carry with you when you have been here at this school, and you've got that burnt orange in your heart. It's the pride that you carry, knowing you were a Texas Longhorn, a pride that you can carry throughout this state. You know people see you, and they know that you played for Texas. It's the way you can carry yourself when others know you were a Texas Longhorn, and that is something that they respect.

327

You can't forget all the memories that you have, and nobody can take them from you. It is all the people you've met, the camaraderie that you have with all your coaches and teammates. It's the people that make being a Longhorn so great—the people who were before us and the people who will come after us, who will carry the tradition, that pride on their shoulders, and keep it going. That's what makes it great to be a Longhorn.

David Thomas was one of the major reasons the Longhorns won the national championship in 2005. A steady, reliable go-to guy for Vince Young, he caught 10 passes in the national championship game in the 2006 Rose Bowl. He was an All–Big 12 selection and holds Texas records for tight-end receptions in a game, season, and career. He is currently playing in the NFL for the New England Patriots.

VINCE YOUNG

QUARTERBACK

2003–2005

WE WERE ALMOST HALFWAY THROUGH the 2004 football season. We had just lost to Oklahoma, and we had beaten Missouri, where we didn't play well but won.

I felt like we weren't getting respect as a team. We kept hearing that we were soft. I felt that if someone disrespects your family, you have to do something about it. So I told the guys that we needed to change this rumor that was going around that we weren't tough.

The next week we played Texas Tech, and I played the game with a lot of—I wouldn't say "hate," but—determination. People were talking about my teammates and The University of Texas, and they were also talking about me—I can't throw…I can't do this…I'm not a quarterback…I should be playing wide receiver—things like that.

It angered me, and I wanted to go out and show the world that I could play quarterback, and that we were for real. We were real talent, and we were good-hearted people. So I told the guys in the locker room, "They respect us, but they don't respect us like they are supposed to." The guys accepted the challenge, and we just went from there. For the next 20 games, through the 2005 national championship, we never lost again.

The recruiting process for me had been crazy. I didn't know that Texas had interest in me, and I didn't think that I would get an offer to go to The

Vince Young scores the game-winning touchdown against USC in the BCS National Championship game of 2005.

University of Texas. I'd had my mind set on other schools until I started getting more letters from Texas my senior year.

I was raised up with black and Hispanic kids, and I was looking for a school where I could learn about different cultures. I felt like The University of Texas had that. I was concerned about my education, and I had always heard about The University of Texas as a great academic school. Knowing that the academic part was pretty cool, I wanted to know about the team—how they were as a family. Then I saw the respect the team had for Coach Brown and the coaches. Mrs. Brown and the wives were into it. They did things like show you certain forks to use when you ate and things like that. I thought that was pretty cool.

When I got here on a visit, B.J. Johnson and Richard Hightower (we called him "Peanut") were my hosts. They showed me a lot of love and explained a lot of stuff to me. That's when I thought, *Hey, this is the place I need to be.* It was two hours away from home, and my family could drive back and forth. I feel like that was one of the great choices I made in my life.

After we won the 2005 Rose Bowl against Michigan, we got back home, and it was time to get started back up, working out and getting prepared for spring. I just checked the guys' heart. I felt like we had the team. But at our first meeting, guys came in with hats on, leaning back in their chairs, relaxed because we had won the Rose Bowl. I felt like we weren't finished yet, and it was time for us to get back to work.

So I asked them, "Are y'all ready to take this challenge of going all the way? And beating Ohio State [our second game of the 2005 season]?"

That summer I told them, "This is what we need y'all to do. We need you to be up early in the morning, working out. We need skill guys, linebackers, we need y'all out for seven-on-seven practice, and we need everybody there."

We didn't need half the team, as it had been in the previous years. The coaches cannot work out with us in the summers, and it is up to the players to motivate themselves. People asked me about what I wrote on the locker room board when we returned for the summer in June. I wrote, "Anyone who wants to beat Ohio State, be at the field at 7:00 PM tonight," to let everyone know it was time for us to get together and run our own preseason practices. The note was the easy part, but the fact that all of the guys stepped up and accepted the challenge was the most important part. Not just the quarterbacks, receivers, and defensive backs like in the past, but the whole team. We said, "We're not satisfied with winning the first Rose Bowl, we're going to the championship."

We needed a lot of guys participating in the workout, going to summer school, going to class, taking care of business—and when it was time to go to work, work as a team, with guys showing love to each other. We dedicated ourselves during that summer to finishing the season and "taking dead aim" on everything we did, like Coach Brown had said.

Having been to the Rose Bowl helped us the next year, and beating Ohio State gave us more confidence. We had worked hard to get where we were, and now, nobody was calling us "soft" anymore.

As we stood on the sideline in the final minutes of the national championship game against Southern Cal, we knew what we had to do to get what we had come for. I had a lot of faith in my teammates, as well as a lot of faith in myself. Before we got to the championship game, our guys had come together many times, believing that when the defense was on the field, they would get us the ball, even though we were down. It was the same in this game.

That's what I was preaching in my mind. *If the defense gives us the ball back on this last drive, we have to score.* We all had such a belief that we were going to win. They gave us the ball back, and now, we had to go out there and score a touchdown.

That's basically what I told the offensive linemen and the guys in the huddle. "Man, y'all guys stay relaxed. We've been here before." We had a bunch of inside jokes that only the guys knew about, so I told a couple of jokes and got the guys laughing. With the game on the line, the message to them was, "Come on—we're in this situation, and I'm cracking jokes." They saw in my eyes that I was still relaxed and calm, and it kept them the same. The jokes got the guys laughing, and we just went down and took over the game.

It was pretty basic. Just go out there and do what you've been doing all week, and what you've been playing for all season. Don't try to do differently. Just stay in your assignment and take care of business, and we'll win the game. Just stay relaxed. And we drove the ball down and finished it off.

On the last play, I was looking to throw the ball to David Thomas for the first down, and Coach called time out, and we changed the play. The USC defensive guys did a great job of reacting. They played David well and dropped back and took out Brian Carter, who was running a little option we had. I got to my third check down, and I saw a lane that Justin Blalock had made a good block in, so I just reacted. The next thing I knew, I was in the end zone.

That gave us a one-point lead with 19 seconds left, and when we went for two, we wanted to drive the ball right up the middle for the score. That made it 41–38.

Now, one more time, we had to be a team, and the defense held and was on the field on the final play.

There is a picture of me with the confetti falling all around, looking up with the lights behind me. People have asked me what I was thinking when that picture was taken.

I thought about being a young black male, coming from the neighborhood I was from. I thought of all the people that doubted me, and all the stuff that I went through in my life—for me to make a choice to do good in life. It got me to a great college and it got me to a point of meeting great guys like my teammates and my coaches. White, black, we all came together as a team, and we weren't thinking about race. We came together as Texas Longhorns, as coaches, as fans—the whole University of Texas—we went to the championship and won the game.

I was looking at the fans, looking at my teammates running around, looking at the coaches. I could see my girlfriend, my mom and family, our alumni guys like Bo Scaife, who came down, and Steve McNair, who had been a good friend—and he was excited. I could just see all the love that we hadn't seen in a long time—since Coach Royal and those guys won the national championship.

Finally, for me, to accept the challenge with what was going in my life as a kid, it shows that God is really out there. He really works, and so does prayer. If you do right and take care of your business, He'll grant you a life like the one he put me in. And in that moment, you just see all that.

So what does it mean to be a Longhorn? To me, it's love. It's the love that everybody has for each other; not just for football but for all of our sports. It's the love that the alumni and fans and the teachers have for the kids. They want us to be successful, particularly the teachers, who wake up every day trying to do something for somebody. You feel that love. The University of Texas is like a big family, and it always shows love.

Vince Young became a Longhorn legend in a dramatic run that started midway through 2004 and climaxed with the national championship in 2005. During that time, he guided the Longhorns to 20 straight victories. He was the MVP of the Longhorn Rose Bowl victories over Michigan and USC. He was a consensus All-American, runner up for the Heisman Trophy, and winner of the Davey O'Brien Award, the Manning Award, and the Maxwell Award.

RD TERRY · NOBLE DOSS · ROOSTER ANDREWS · KEIFER MARS

O WOMACK · WALTER FONDREN · BOBBY LACKEY · BOBBY GURW

T · DUKE CARLISLE · DAVID MCWILLIAMS · TOMMY NOBIS · BILL

KOY · HAPPY FELLER · EDDIE PHILLIPS · JERRY SISEMORE · JULIUS

H MORELAND · EARL CAMPBELL · ALFRED JACKSON · BRAD SHEA

NIE JOHNSON · JOHNNY "LAM" JONES · MIKE BAAB · DONNIE LIT

· ROBERT BREWER · JERRY GRAY · TONY DEGRATE · TODD DOD

ERE · STONIE CLARK · TONY BRACKENS · JAMES BROWN · PHIL DA

· CHRIS SIMMS · MICHAEL HUFF · DAVID THOMAS · VINCE YOU

· BILL SANSING · JAMES CARROLL "T" JONES · TOM STOLHANI

ITZ · JACK COLLINS · MIKE COTTEN · BOBBY MOSES · JAMES SAXTO

BRADLEY · CHRIS GILBERT · BOB MCKAY · TOM CAMPBELL · JAMI

WHITTIER · JAY ARNOLD · PAT KELLY · DOUG ENGLISH · ROOSEV

R · RANDY MCEACHERN · GLENN BLACKWOOD · DWIGHT JEFF

TTLE · KENNETH SIMS · WILLIAM GRAHAM · MIKE HATCHETT · B

E · JOHN HAGY · ERIC METCALF · OSCAR GILES · CHRIS SAMUELS

ON · DEREK LEWIS · RICKY WILLIAMS · MAJOR APPLEWHITE · CO

G · HOWARD TERRY · NOBLE DOSS · ROOSTER ANDREWS · KEI

SKE · DELANO WOMACK · WALTER FONDREN · BOBBY LACKEY · B